IN THEIR OWN RIGHT:

WOMEN AND HIGHER EDUCATION IN NEW ZEALAND BEFORE 1945

Kay Morris Matthews

ௐௐௐ

NZCER PRESS

Wellington 2008

NZCER PRESS

New Zealand Council for Educational Research
PO Box 3237
Wellington
New Zealand

© NZCER, 2008

ISBN 978-1-877398-36-0

Designed by Cluster Creative
Printed by Lithoprint

Distributed by NZCER Distribution Services
PO Box 3237
Wellington
New Zealand
www.nzcer.org.nz

This book is dedicated to
Daphne Morris and Jock Morris,
whose belief in the value of education
has underpinned their own teaching careers
and the nurturing of two daughters

Kay Morris Matthews makes known so many amazing women from our past: revealing their aspirations and struggles to get educated and be educators. These aunts, mothers, and grandmothers trailblazed our institutions of higher education, co-opting its forms, reforming its pedagogy, and getting a first rung on the ladder that a later generation of nieces and daughters, like Kay Morris Matthews herself, were able to fully climb.

For Kay Morris Matthews, *In Their Own Right* is the culmination of a career as a scholarly detective determined that the presence of girls and women will not be sidelined or forgotten in our remembered and recorded history of education in New Zealand.

Helen May, Professor of Education
Dean, University of Otago College of Education

In Their Own Right reminds us that history is not just made by politicians, or generals, or revolutionaries, but also by remarkable women whose individual acts of determination have collectively changed the world. It is important that we hear these stories. They remind us of the debt we owe to those women who had the courage to be pioneers—and they inspire us to know that, just because some professions are still dominated by men, women today can change that.

Shenagh Gleisner
Chief Executive, Ministry of Women's Affairs

Kay Morris Matthews provides a rich and engaging survey of the aspirations and achievements of many able, determined women, giving due credit to the families, mentors, and institutions that supported them—sometimes gently subverting patriarchal officialdom to do so. An essential reference, and excellent reading.

Barbara Mabbett
New Zealand Federation of Graduate Women

Contents

Acknowledgements

This book has been many years in the making and its evolution reflects the steps in my career as an academic researcher. Sincere thanks are due: to Professor Ian McLaren, Professor Sue Middleton, and Professor Jane Ritchie, my academic mentors from postgraduate days at the University of Waikato; to Professor Kuni Jenkins from Te Whare Wānanga o Awanuiārangi, co-researcher and writer on our many projects over ten years related to Māori girls' education; to Dr Judith Simon and former colleagues in Education at the University of Auckland; to Professor Pat Thane, now at the University of London but formerly of Sussex University where I also worked with Professor Carol Dyhouse, both of whom stimulated my interest in women graduates abroad; to Professor Joyce Goodman of the University of Winchester for her ongoing enthusiasm for this project over many years and her generous sharing of ideas and resources; to Professor Geoffrey Sherington of the University of Sydney and Professor Tom O'Donoghue of the University of Western Australia who kept reminding me to finish this book; to Professor Gary McCulloch of the University of London whom I succeeded as historian of education at the University of Auckland, and who since that time has remained very supportive of my scholarship; to Professor

Helen May, now of the University of Otago, with whom I have worked over twenty years in different settings, for her interest and real passion for research in New Zealand's educational past; to Susan Kaiser, College of Education, Victoria University of Wellington; to colleagues in the School of Education Studies at Victoria University of Wellington who sustained me on a daily basis; to the postgraduate students I have taught and supervised for their warm reception of new ideas and theories I have put in front of them; and to new colleagues at EIT-Hawke's Bay for support during the final phases of this book.

At the level of researcher there are always many who made suggestions or went that extra step to contribute information, and here I want to particularly thank the library staff of the New Zealand and Pacific Collections at both the University of Waikato and the University of Auckland; the staff at the Auckland War Memorial Museum Library; the archivists at Auckland Girls' Grammar School, Diocesan School for Girls, Auckland, Waitaki Girls' High School, and Southland Girls' High School; the staff at both the W. J. Scott Library and the Beaglehole Room, Victoria University of Wellington Library; staff at the Alexander Turnbull Library; the National Library and National Archives; the MacMillan Brown Library, University of Canterbury; the Canterbury Museum Library; the Hocken Library at the University of Otago; University of Winchester Library; and the Girton College Library, University of Cambridge. Sincere thanks to the schools and universities for permission to use photographs, and to research assistants Michael Harcourt and Katie Lock who helped to collect and collate these. Particular acknowledgement is due to the mainly women researchers and authors of the school jubilee and centennial publications. Without their attention to detail, such as listings of staff and pupils and inclusion of named photographs, the educational past of many women would have been lost. Further, those schools that maintain their own archives or have placed them within regional or national collections are to be congratulated.

To Bev Webber of the New Zealand Council for Educational Research, thank you for continuing to value historical scholarship in education; thanks to Rob McAlister and Joanna Morton for the book design and production; and to Anne Else, thank you for the superb editing of the manuscript.

As always, warmest thanks to my family for their interest in this project, and to Richard for his support and care throughout.

CHAPTER 1

Introduction

Maypole dance, Napier Girls' High School, 1934. NAPIER GIRLS' HIGH SCHOOL

Over the last 150 years, education has profoundly changed the patterns of women's lives in New Zealand. *In Their Own Right* traces and analyses the development of secondary and university education for girls and women in New Zealand from the 1850s to 1945, the end of World War Two. It aims to make visible, for the first time, a variety of perspectives on New Zealand's educated daughters.

This is a history of generations of women: those who lobbied for access to secondary schooling and higher education; those who took it for granted; those who overcame financial hardship in order to participate; those who attended state, church, or privately owned girls' schools, including the Māori denominational schools, district high schools, and technical high schools; those who graduated from the University of New Zealand in its first fifty years; those who went teaching; and those who were taught and became the next generations of educated women.

The story told here centres on three interwoven themes: access to institutions; beliefs about what young women should and should not learn; and the impact of education upon women's life choices. The unpacking of each of these themes highlights the ways in which social, political, cultural, and economic conditions have, at different times and in different ways, both enabled and constrained the education of New Zealand girls and women.

As an educationalist, I have long been fascinated by the connections between education and young women's future choices, compared with those of young men. As an educational historian, I wanted to understand why the number of New Zealand women university graduates often matched, and at times even outnumbered, that of their male counterparts in the nineteenth century; why such a high proportion of these women achieved master's degrees; and why leading social commentators of the day became so anxious about the educational success of women in relation to men.

Origins of girls' and women's higher education

Historically, girls' and women's participation in senior schooling and higher education has been inextricably bound up with wider social and economic factors. In nineteenth and early twentieth century New Zealand, these included the concern of the Anglican and Catholic churches with the education of Māori girls, so that they would in turn become the 'carriers' of 'Christian civilisation' to their people. The secondary schooling of Māori girls is explored in Chapter 2. They also included the expectations of settler parents for their daughters; the decline in fertility rates; and the opening up of a range of employment opportunities within the infrastructure of a new colony. All contributed to extending new pathways for young women, which in turn enabled them to move in alternative directions, rather than having to confine themselves to the traditionally expected roles.

In doing so, however, young women, rather than young men, attracted the full attention of those opposed to the higher education of women and their resulting entry into the professions. These opponents found it difficult to accept that educated women were modelling a way of life that gave them an identity in their own right, rather than one defined through their fathers and husbands. Although, from the 1870s on, increasing numbers of girls and women attended secondary schools and universities, and there was growing acceptance of this trend, the anxiety remained and perennially resurfaced.

The opposition faced by girls and women seeking higher education has been constantly resisted by women, individually and through organisations, and by liberal thinking men. As women overcame each obstacle put in their way and emerged as 'the new professionals' in their respective fields, it became clear that their education was advantageous to the small colonial society closely tied to the British Empire. Increasingly, secondary schooling especially became seen as the mechanism through which girls could be appropriately prepared for their future roles as wives and mothers; but for girls to become educated, suitably educated women teachers were required.

The push for all avenues of access to education to be open to women came initially from a constituency of voting parents which, from 1893, included women themselves. Many settler parents had little formal schooling, and wanted something better for their children growing up in New Zealand. Many realised, too, that without the support of extended family, both boys and girls would need the knowledge and skills to be financially independent if their parents died. Others believed that schooling might enhance a daughter's

Class in progress, Napier Girls' High School, 1900. NAPIER GIRLS' HIGH SCHOOL

chance of marrying well. However, it should be emphasised that the majority of early secondary school pupils were the children of middle-class parents who could afford to pay school fees and boarding fees, and were more likely to support their daughters for three or four years of university study. They valued education for its own sake, as well as for its more practical outcomes; indeed, some of them went further, advocating the liberal ideals of philosophers John Stuart Mill and Mary Wollstonecraft, and upholding equal rights and opportunities not only for their own middle-class children, regardless of gender, but for all children.

Whether in the all-female environments that at first prevailed, or at the coeducational district high schools and technical schools that developed later, secondary schooling became the vehicle for girls' intellectual stimulation and growth. Those schools that did it well made it possible for subsequent generations of young women to take themselves seriously and consider other educational pathways after they had left school. In New Zealand it was possible to enhance one's own social standing through education, since this gave access to the professions. However, the first generation of educated women in New Zealand came mainly from privileged home backgrounds, although there were some notable exceptions, who succeeded thanks to scholarships.

Teaching was both the most obvious and the most likely profession for an educated woman. Nearly three-quarters of the women who graduated from the University of New Zealand between 1878 and 1920 went teaching, the majority in secondary schools. It was this group of highly qualified women who modelled for the first time a nonconforming and very public professional role to the girls in their schools. They took education seriously, practised it with due diligence, and pioneered a range of educational and recreational opportunities for girls. These women valued their education for a range of reasons: love of knowledge; employment and career opportunities, enabling them to support not only themselves but, in some cases, dependent relatives; and the ability to forge their own identity as independent professional women.

However, the competing demands of self, family, and profession have placed stress on generations of educated women. Early women graduates had to face up to the expectations that others held for them and they held for themselves: that is, how best to use a hard-won education, while coping with familial and social expectations that they would become wives and mothers 'at home'. One widely held perception is that these women largely remained single, and they have been traditionally stereotyped as 'spinsters'. In fact, large numbers of educated women did marry before World War One, often after several years of teaching. From 1900 on, however, it became clear that university-educated women had quite different choices from those available to their less-educated counterparts. They could elect not to marry and be financially independent of men; they could marry and control their own fertility by having fewer children; or, if widowed, they could return to teaching to support their own family.

What actually occurred in New Zealand was a mixture of all three, as subsequent chapters show. Four chapters explore the education and subsequent lives, work, and career paths of early women graduates from Otago (Chapter 3), Canterbury (Chapter 4), Auckland (Chapter 5), and Wellington (Chapter 6). A final chapter looks at the activities and influence of these women as citizens of the world, particularly through the Federation of University Women.

The development of secondary schooling in New Zealand

Chapters 2–6 discuss in detail the developing patterns of secondary education for Māori girls and for girls in Otago, Canterbury, Auckland, and Wellington. The Māori denominational boarding schools, including girls' schools such as St Anne's (1855), St Joseph's (1867), and Hukarere (1875), were among the earliest schools in New Zealand offering some form of higher education (see Chapter 2). The church founders believed that by being trained in Christianity and European ways of living as well as by being given a basic education, young Māori, especially girls, would pave the way for the assimilation of their people into Pākehā society. Other early sponsors of secondary schools included the

New Zealand Company, the Otago Provincial Council, and Governor Grey. Most of the schools they helped to found were for boys only. The only specific provincial council provision for European girls' secondary education before 1877 was in Otago, where Otago Girls' High School (1871) had been founded eight years after Otago Boys' High School (1863). In 1877, the government report on secondary education listed six colleges and high schools, four for boys (Auckland College and Grammar School; Nelson College; Christ's College; and Otago Boys') and two for girls (Otago Girls' and Canterbury Girls' High School, later to become Christchurch Girls' High School).[1]

While, by the 1870s, some professional, merchant, landed gentry, and business families valued a new kind of education for their daughters, a majority of colonial parents did not view secondary education as an option for their daughters. Very few parents could afford to send their children to secondary school, especially from rural communities, and many families depended on family labour for survival. The predominant Victorian work ethic meant that parents could not accept that able-bodied youngsters should continue at school when they could be involved in 'real' work. It was common for children who reached school-leaving age, initially set at thirteen years, to be withdrawn from their studies and begin to contribute to the family economy. Female labour was vital to production, and girls were expected to contribute to the family economy as soon as they were able. Accordingly, they learnt quickly that the good of the family came before the gratification of individual desires; any personal ambition a girl might harbour had to be subjugated to her parents' wishes, and to meeting the daily needs of other members of the family. In rural areas it was usual for girls to be employed without pay on the family farm. In towns, while boys had a wide choice of paid employment, it was common for girls to help at home or work for low wages in domestic service and factories, and later in offices and shops.

Young women from families with limited resources who did wish to continue at school could attain further education in two ways: by becoming a pupil-teacher, or by winning an entry scholarship to an endowed secondary school. When primary education was made free and compulsory in 1877, and thousands of children flocked into their local schools, teachers were desperately needed.

Waitaki Girls' High School, Oamaru.

REPORT for Term ending May 5th *1899*

Girl's Name Maggie Marwick's middle *Class.*

SUBJECT	No. Present in Class at Examination	Place in Class by Examination	Percentage in Class by Examination	Written Work	REMARKS
ENGLISH — Literature	18	10	57		
— Grammar and Composition	15	10 eq	58		
HISTORY	12	6 eq	43		Very good. work is being done
GEOGRAPHY					
FRENCH	9	2	95		
LATIN	13	6	92		
ARITHMETIC	8	5	60		
ALGEBRA	16	5	85		
EUCLID	13	8	74		
SCIENCE	16	10	69		
SCRIPTURE	18	9	75		
WRITING	Good				
DRAWING	20	15 eq	65		
ATTENDANCE	Excellent				
CONDUCT	Excellent				

Signed Catherine _____ M.A. *Lady Principal.*

The pupil-teacher apprenticeship system was known and understood by the inaugural inspectors of schools, some of whom had had first-hand experience of it as pupil-teachers in England. It was these inspectors who oversaw recruitment. During school examination visits, they would identify the more able Standard 5 and 6 pupils, who would then be offered contracts of up to four years' duration, with an initial payment of approximately £20 per annum.[2] This attracted parents and daughters alike; a young woman could continue her studies while training for an occupation which would improve her social standing and enhance her marriage prospects, and at the same time augmenting the family income. As certificated teachers at the end of the four years, many continued teaching in local primary schools. The pupil-teacher system began to be gradually phased out

WAITAKI GIRLS' HIGH SCHOOL, OAMARU

15

from 1906, and was finally abandoned in 1926. By then there were four teacher training colleges in operation, which admitted students who had passed the Matriculation Examination to be paid to train as primary school teachers.

Inspectors might alternatively recommend that parents struggling to make ends meet allow their clever daughters to seek one of the limited number of secondary school free places available from 1908, or a scholarship.[3] Most scholarships guaranteed one or two years' tuition for children under fifteen years of age. However, as Ruth Fry points out in her history of the curriculum for girls in New Zealand:

> … girls required determination and encouragement from their teachers if they were to continue their schooling. Parents, who were more likely to spend money on their sons, needed to be convinced of its value if they were to budget or make sacrifices for the education of their daughters.[4]

But what was this value? There was no national secondary school syllabus. Some parents, such as those who sent their daughters to Nelson Girls' College in the 1880s, believed that an academic curriculum leading to matriculation was the purpose of a secondary education. Others, such as the parents of girls at Wellington Girls' High School in the same era, were happy to pay fees to have their girls also taught music, drama, singing, and domestic science. Most, however, including the male-dominated boards of governors, were content to be guided by what the school principal thought appropriate.

Access to secondary education

The debates that led to the passing of the Education Act 1877, bringing in free, secular, and compulsory primary education for all New Zealand children until they turned thirteen, had as much to do with maintaining the existing social structure as with providing state-funded education. The 1877 Bill's sponsor, Charles Bowen, made it clear that the government did not intend 'to encourage children whose vocation is that of honest labour, to waste in the higher schools time which might be devoted to learning a trade'.[5] It was then generally believed that working-class children would not and should not go on to secondary education. A few years of primary schooling was deemed sufficient preparation for their destined roles—for boys, in agriculture and trade; for girls, in domestic work, whether paid or unpaid. Access to the fee-charging (but publicly endowed) secondary schools was generally viewed as a middle-class prerogative.

However, two clauses of the Education Act did offer minimal provision for secondary education: education boards could establish secondary 'tops' (provision for secondary schooling of usually no more than two years in a separate class at the primary school site) in district high schools, and could award scholarships to help senior primary pupils pay the fees of the

Assembly, Otago Girls' High School, 1911.
OTAGO GIRLS' HIGH SCHOOL

incorporated or endowed secondary schools. Moreover, the Education Reserves Act 1877 set aside large blocks of land for the endowment of secondary schools. In 1890, the government reported more boys (1293) than girls (767) attending the twenty-one separate single-sex secondary schools for which it had oversight.[6] These schools included fourteen for boys and seven for girls (attendance in brackets), at Auckland (92), Wellington (126), Nelson (73), Christchurch (136), Napier (47), Oamaru (37), and Dunedin (159). In addition, girls could attend high schools established in some towns where they were taught in separate classes from the boys, as at Thames (22), New Plymouth (26), Rangiora (13), Akaroa (2), Ashburton (17), Timaru (29), and Invercargill (25).

Like the English grammar and public schools on which they were modelled, the endowed schools in the larger towns offered both girls and boys a classical curriculum, built on a narrow academic base of Latin, French, English, Euclid, and algebra. These were the subjects which teachers and parents alike considered appropriate for secondary scholars, and which were also required for teacher training and university study. In 1888, the University of New Zealand formalised its endorsement of this curriculum by making classical subjects the basis of the Matriculation Examination giving entry to university.

By 1890, as well as the 2060 children attending secondary schools, there were 964 children above Standard 6 attending state schools.[7] While the government expected parents to pay fees for older children attending the senior classes and the district high schools, many schools did not in fact levy rural families.

It soon became evident that the university graduates appointed to teach in the district high schools, who also coached senior pupils in the classical subjects for the Matriculation Examination, were being rewarded with success. The much-publicised district high school pass marks impressed parents and increasingly led them to support their local schools, rather than send their children away to board at the endowed secondary schools.[8]

From 1889, all pupils seeking a secondary education were required to complete their primary schooling by passing the examination for the Certificate of Proficiency, but this gatekeeping measure did little to stem the flow of pupils into district high schools. With an election pending, the government was forced to reconsider its two-track system. Unless the endowed secondary schools agreed to set aside numbers of free places, their rolls would suffer as rural parents continued to send children to the district high schools.

As a result of regulation changes in 1901 and 1902, many endowed schools accepted free-place pupils, subsidised by the state at £6 per head, or provided scholarships of their own to the value of one-fifth their annual endowment income. A few schools would not agree to the conditions attached to the state grants, fearing loss of prestige if access was opened up to working-

Hukarere pupils, early 1900s.
HUKARERE GIRLS' COLLEGE

class pupils. In the main, these were schools with large land endowments, such as Wanganui Collegiate and Christ's College, which elected to provide secondary schooling on a private fee-paying basis. Three boys' schools (Auckland Grammar, Wellington Boys', and Christchurch Boys') and two girls' schools (Wellington Girls' and Wanganui Girls') chose to provide their own scholarships, and resisted taking free-place pupils until the state made it compulsory.[9]

In 1903 the Secondary Schools Act allowed any pupil who had passed Proficiency to apply for a free place in most New Zealand secondary schools. By 1907, 70 percent of the 2800 pupils in the twenty-six endowed secondary schools were holders of free places. The district high schools and the newly established technical high schools had 2452 pupils.[10]

The Education Act 1914 made free places available in all publicly funded secondary schools. Even so, secondary education was a luxury many families could not afford. By 1917, only 37 percent of primary school leavers went on to secondary school.[11] Even by 1937, the year after Proficiency was abolished, only 65 percent of primary school leavers went on to receive further education.[12]

'Drafting boys and girls'

The battle over what should be taught to which pupils at secondary school, and who had the power to decide, is central to the story told here. One major battleground was over educating children for differing destinies, according to their class and 'race'. When George Hogben succeeded W. J. Habens as Inspector-General of Education in 1899, he launched a two-pronged campaign to bring the Māori denominational schools and the district high schools into line with his view that for Māori and lower-class Pākehā children, secondary schooling should prepare them to stay in their own communities, not compete with middle-class Pākehā on the labour market. Once back in their local districts, educated Māori girls and boys would, as the Inspector of Native Schools put it, 'bring an uninitiated but intelligent and high-spirited people into line with civilisation'.[13] The response of the Māori denominational schools is outlined in Chapter 2.

The district high schools received a similar message, but in 1899, Hogben's senior inspector of schools noted parents' resistance:

In our view, the curricula of the District High School is [*sic*] far too academic for most pupils. However, it seems to be supported by the majority of rural parents who are mainly interested in the provision of inexpensive ways in which their children can qualify for public examinations.[14]

Given the strong parental (voter) support for the kind of curriculum that met examination requirements, the state needed to find a way of promoting what it considered to be a more practical and appropriate curriculum. The solution was found in the Manual and Technical Instruction Acts of 1900 and 1902. This legislation paved the way for new technical schools, and offered funding to all schools that introduced subjects such as woodwork, cookery, elementary science, and agriculture.

Isolated rural primary schools, which already offered some tuition in practical subjects, leapt at the chance to collect more government revenue. Those schools in or near towns sent their senior pupils to the newly established manual training centres. Secondary schools, however, remained aloof. The smaller district high schools and Māori denominational schools generally

Ensuring a healthy nation

Physical education was given a boost by the Physical Drill in Public and Native Schools Act 1901. Girls' secondary schools were now required to arrange for the teaching of physical drill to all pupils. Part of the push for physical education was linked to sustaining good health and wellbeing, as advocated by eugenicist thinkers such as Dr Lindo Ferguson; in 1899, he stated that: 'Whether New Zealanders are to figure as a strong, healthy nation, or as a weedy, neurotic, decadent one, depends very largely on the stamina of the mothers of the future.'[15] In some girls' secondary schools, callisthenics, swimming, drill, and games were already commonplace, but the 1901 legislation resulted in an upsurge of class time spent on regimented exercise. For example, at Woodford House, a private school for girls, principal Mabel Hodge had for some time recruited teachers from England who had been trained at the Hampstead Physical Training College in London.

The reason was that its founder was the renowned Martina Bergman Osterberg of Sweden's Central Gymnastic Institute. Although other New Zealand women principals would later visit both institutions and be persuaded to introduce this particular style of rhythmical exercises to their schools, Mabel Hodge had acted early and popularised 'Swedish drill' through public displays, which involved the girls dressed in white 'gym tunics', arranged in straight lines, waving large sticks and swinging clubs in rhythmical movement. By 1911, Mabel Hodge reported in her prospectus a particular triumph when she advised parents that 'physical culture and dancing would be taught by a student of Madame Bergman Osterberg … qualified to counteract any physical deficiency or weakness by remedial drill or massage'.[16]

Similarly, organised games were viewed as an essential part of a girl's education by many

believed that a technical education would detract from the amount of time they could devote to the academic subjects required for examination purposes, while the endowed schools thought the introduction of practical subjects would downgrade the academic image of their institutions.

The fact that the district high schools refused to implement state education policy particularly irritated George Hogben, and in 1902 he cautioned them about the inappropriateness of their curricula: 'There is too much tendency at present in the district high schools to give the secondary pupil a little Latin or French and a little elementary algebra or Euclid and to avoid science and manual and commercial training.'[17]

In the end, the state got its way: under the Secondary Schools Act 1903, those schools that accepted free-place pupils, or agreed to provide scholarships of their own, traded government funding for certain conditions. Among these was an opening up of schools to Department of Education inspection and examination and, by implication, state influence over curriculum content. Over time, the Minister of Education acquired the power to make grants for school

principals, who advocated the teamwork, discipline, fitness, and health benefits of games such as tennis, cricket, and hockey. For years, many principals had regularly grumbled about the lack of school fields or tennis courts for girls, compared with the acres of grounds provided for boys' schools, but the upsurge of interest in producing healthy, fit young bodies resulted in many boards of governors acquiring adjacent or nearby land to add to existing girls' school grounds. This was the case at Woodford House in 1914, where Mabel Hodge reported that 'the new playing field had caused a greater interest to be taken in games'. However, alluding to the fact that not all girls viewed sport with enthusiasm, she added, 'that the time devoted to "games" should be utilised to try and excel, instead of to loaf and if possible to evade'.[18]

Woodford House Swedish drill, 1904. WOODFORD HOUSE

Teaching domestic skills at Hukarere, late nineteenth century. HUKARERE GIRLS' COLLEGE

buildings, equipment, and maintenance, thus ensuring that even the most reluctant of schools bowed to the pressure of financial inducement and introduced the teaching of technical subjects.

The introduction of technical high schools finally ensured that a range of practical subjects was taught to a new secondary school population. This is what Hogben had wanted for some time. In 1907, he told a conference of school inspectors that a weakness of the secondary schools was 'that we let in some who will not get so much benefit from attendance at the secondary schools as if they went to work and attended the ... technical schools. That is the proper place for a good many of them.'[19] Some politicians, such as J. A. Hanan, MP for Invercargill, went further. In 1910 he told the House of Representatives that:

> I think there should be some system for drafting boys and girls into the technical
> or high schools according to their capabilities and natural bent ... The high school
> is the place for those boys who are endowed with superior mental capabilities or
> gifts, such as are required for the professions.[20]

Indeed, a form of 'drafting' had already occurred. The immediate success of the technical schools was due to the fact that pupils did not require a pass in the Proficiency Examination in order to gain admittance. All they needed was a new Certificate of Competency, introduced in 1903 for those senior primary pupils who had shown they had completed a satisfactory programme of work, but had not secured a pass in the Proficiency Examination.

In this way, the state was able to achieve its aim of stratifying secondary schooling. Because of their less stringent entry requirements and emphasis on vocational skills, the technical high schools came to be regarded as the poor relations to the other providers of secondary education. However, the calibre of the teaching staff at these schools belied their inferior image. Many highly qualified university graduates seeking positions in larger centres were employed to teach general subjects in the technical high schools, such as Seddon Memorial Technical College and Auckland Technical School, Napier Technical School, Wellington Technical School, Hutt Valley Technical High School, Petone Technical High School, Westport Technical School, and Christchurch Technical School. One unexpected result was that many students passed the Matriculation Examination. Instead of entering trades, the state had to accept that some students from the technical schools actually entered the professions.

The power of the principal to determine what was taught was a source of consternation for government officials. Inspectors of schools were required to report on individual secondary schools, but had no power to convince them to change what they were doing. It was only when the government became involved in funding the schools to open up increased free places from the early 1900s that it could insist upon accountability in exchange for continued state support.

A proper female education

The sequence of moves outlined above also enabled the government to take control of girls' education and ensure that, beyond the primary level, it became linked to a domestic role. Studying women's involvement in technical education, Barbara Day concluded that:

> … in New Zealand, it was argued that a man well cared for by his domestically trained wife would be more content, more likely to stay with his family, more economically productive and hence, more likely to maintain the supremacy of the English race and the British Empire.[21]

Such beliefs had their origins in Social Darwinism, with its fear 'of a moral degeneration of the English race' if citizens were 'not properly trained' for their roles within society.[22] In New Zealand, other ideologies were also involved. The first cast girls and women as permanently inferior to boys and men, both physically and mentally. This meant that girls and women could never catch up with their male counterparts, and attempts to do so via higher learning would prove dangerous. Instead, the aim of education should be to equip women better for their preordained roles as wives and mothers. In particular, the middle-class

Nelson Girls' College staff. Principal Margaret Lorimer (MA Canterbury) is seated second from right.
NELSON GIRLS' COLLEGE

women whose main function was 'the raising of a healthy and vigorous race' should be educated to ensure 'national fitness and national greatness'.[23]

This view was linked to an international eugenicist movement which stressed the importance of racial fitness and purity. Eugenics was considered to be a scientific theory that drew upon contemporary research in genetics, human biology, anthropology, and demography. In New Zealand, its champions included medical figures, politicians, bureaucrats, and educationists. For example, Dr Truby King, Dr Frederick Batchelor, and Dr Lindo Ferguson, all part-time lecturers at the Otago Medical School, presented learned papers and spoke at public meetings against allowing young women to indulge in higher academic study. New Zealand historians Ruth Fry, Erik Olssen, and Margaret Tennant[24] have each outlined the arguments advanced by King and his colleagues. For girls, domestic science, physiology, and hygiene should take preference over French, algebra, Euclid, and Latin, because the stress of undertaking such unsuitable academic work, at school or at university, would damage them physically and mentally, making them unfit for motherhood.[25]

In New Zealand, the eugenicist view was aimed clearly at Pākehā women, particularly Pākehā married women who were obviously practising contraception. The birth rate for the average Pākehā family had fallen from 6.5 children in 1878 to 3.4 by 1911.[26] There was also a fear that immigrants such

An Advanced Female.

IMAGINE a lovely woman taking to a flatulent diet and study ; losing her hair, and depending on sheep dip ; trusting to a dentist to make her mouth presentable, so that each gasping sentence can be finished with wide expansive mouth and strange unnatural guffaw. This is a purely imaginative picture of what may happen to any girl who fills herself up with scientific small talk, statistics, blue book, leagues, women's rights, &c., and then swaggers round full to the collar-stud with her own supremacy and independence of that poor failure man. The result—an inflated female, beyond control, strained up to bursting point with intense conceit. Has anyone a pin? We shall have strings of old maids strolling, school like, on the Parade, exchanging vows and comparing patterns of tweeds with which they propose to encase themselves when woman shall burst the bonds and stand revealed in all her glory in a badly-fitting suit of dittos A manly tread, calculated to silence the elephantine stump of a twenty-stone policeman, will be adopted. Her glorious hair will be shorn, and in the place of the tricky little bonnet, which we love so well, and are only too pleased to pay for, a dowdy straw hat will be plugged down on the closely-cropped nut. Such a future is awful to contemplate. Soft ! the Muse ! Bring hither the guitar and eccentric tin whistle.

Away with all your dreams of something lovable and sweet :
Here's a female with a strange guffaw that would clear a busy street ;
She knows the latest scandal, and she loves to get a stare,
And she's longing for a J.P.-ship, or else to be the Mayor.

Selah.

This sketch was aimed at Katherine Browning, Girton College graduate, while she was teaching at Napier Girls' High School in the 1880s. NAPIER GIRLS' HIGH SCHOOL

as the Chinese, who had flocked to the New Zealand goldfields and stayed to establish market gardens and retail businesses, would produce large numbers of 'non-White' children with the potential to dominate the population base.

It was not coincidental that education for domestic duties and motherhood was being so strongly promoted at a time when women were entering higher education and the paid workforce in larger numbers than ever before.[27] Those who promoted the acquisition of domestic skills were predominantly from the middle classes, and were beginning to find it difficult to attract women to work as domestic servants. Educating young women for their 'natural role' was seen as the answer to many of the young colony's problems.

The campaign by King and others to educate women for the domestic sphere was reasonably successful. The most important change came in 1917. Although girls could study the same subjects in secondary school as those studied by boys, a pass grade in a compulsory course in domestic science became required of all matriculating girls.[28] The message was clear: even scholastically able young women destined for university or teacher training had to learn the rudiments of good household management, cooking, and sewing, for the inevitable time when, it was assumed, they would take up their 'proper' role in adult life. By 1919, girls taking home science for matriculation could present arithmetic instead of full mathematics.[29] These curriculum concessions were at the expense of pure mathematics and science. They contributed to the growth of the attitude that girls were intellectually less able than boys and, in any case, would have

Cookery class, Napier Girls' High School, 1906. NAPIER GIRLS' HIGH SCHOOL

Speaking out against home science

By 1917, a new generation of women principals had mixed reactions to the drive to enforce domestic education for girls. One of the strongest statements of objection came from Esther Baber (MA Canterbury 1898), the principal and owner of Wellington's Fitzherbert Terrace School (later Samuel Marsden Collegiate School). In the local newspaper, she made clear her views on the compulsory requirement that all girls learn home science:

> In the primary school, for example, consider the absurdity of a clever pupil spending one day out of five learning cooking, which her mother could teach her in half an hour! In the higher walks of education the university is blindly following the foolish lead and proposing to add to a girl's trials in matriculation, a test in home science. This is again handicapping the serious minded student.[30]

Esther Baber (MA Canterbury 1898) was principal and owner of Wellington's Fitzherbert Terrace School from 1907 until 1931, when the school was sold to the Anglican Church and became Samuel Marsden Collegiate School.
ALEXANDER TURNBULL LIBRARY, WELLINGTON, NZ. DOMINION POST COLL EP-NZ OBITS-BA-01

Saving her trump card for last, Esther Baber predicted that in the future, 'wifehood and motherhood—will be for the few ... nursing, the medical profession, teaching and other work of all kinds, gardening and farming, all offer scope for women'.[31]

Fitzherbert Terrace School, Wellington, 1904. SAMUEL MARSDEN COLLEGIATE SCHOOL

27

less use for such subjects. As early as 1911, the School of Home Science was opened at the University of Otago. (Chapter 3 examines this development in depth.) The result was that until relatively recent times, the scholastically able young women who entered university were more likely to study home science than other sciences.

A vicious circle was thus established. Because many women graduates, the teachers and role models of the next generation, taught mainly arts and languages, their pupils followed in their footsteps. In 1923, for example, of all women university students in New Zealand, 67 percent were taking arts and languages courses; 7 percent were studying medicine; and only 5 percent were taking science courses. That year, there was only one woman among the twenty-eight science graduates.[32]

Finding early women graduates

Part of the research project on which this book is based was a tracing of the educational and career profiles of the first women who attended and graduated from the University of New Zealand. From the early 1870s, women as well as men could attend each of the four university colleges, Otago (1869), Canterbury (1873), Auckland (1883), and Victoria University of Wellington (1899). All were foundation constituent colleges of the federal University of New Zealand. They were responsible for teaching students, but it was the University of New Zealand which granted the degrees.[33] In addition, until 1884, a number of secondary schools were affiliated to the University of New Zealand. Up until 1926, senior secondary school pupils could apply for Junior University Scholarships and be admitted to degree classes taught at selected secondary schools, such as Auckland Girls' Grammar and Nelson Girls' College.[34]

In order to identify the women graduates who took up teaching as a career, I used a variety of search tools, including the *New Zealand Gazette*, which listed all registered teachers in primary and district high schools; the lists of teachers in state schools that appeared in the annual reports of the Department of Education; individual school histories; community histories; church histories; and the respective university college histories. Of the latter, James Hight's and Alice Candy's 1927 *A Short History of the Canterbury University College* was valuable, featuring as it did many women graduates and their achievements. Alice Candy (MA Canterbury 1911), the first woman academic historian appointed to a New Zealand university, was also one of the few women academics at Canterbury in the 1920s. Her coauthor, James Hight (MA Canterbury), had been a pupil-teacher before starting his first degree part time while at training college. The book reflects their interest in local networks of scholars and is mentioned here because it includes the accomplishments of women graduates, a rare feature among published university histories.

Canterbury graduates and their counterparts from Otago were highlighted in W. Gardner's 1979 book, *Colonial Cap and Gown*. His study indicated that many of the women with Bachelor and Master of Arts degrees from these two institutions went on to become teachers. A cross-checking of the graduate lists with those names included in school jubilee and centennial publications confirmed this, as well as providing detailed biographical information on those who became principals. Some of these women featured in the 1991 publication, *The Book of New Zealand Women*, and progressively in the first three volumes of *The Dictionary of New Zealand Biography*.

The *Alphabetical Roll of Graduates of the University*, compiled by the University of New Zealand (1948), reputedly lists all students who graduated with University of New Zealand qualifications between 1877 and 1949, with details of the college each attended, scholarships awarded, master's subjects studied, and degrees attained. Women students are easily identified by their full name but, if married, are listed by that later name in the first instance. However, my cross-checking of the data for women graduate teachers revealed that many of these women did not appear in this supposedly comprehensive list. The earlier they graduated, the more likely they were to have been lost.

At first, I thought the additional names might be those of overseas women graduates; but in the main their degrees were categorised and were obviously different from those of their New Zealand sisters. Checking Auckland University College records against the final listing, year by year, I found that over sixty names were missing. These lists were initially recorded line by line in handwriting in college registers, and later typed up for the purposes of the annual calendar. It was clear that errors had occurred in the first transfer of names, and then again in the 1948 collation for the 'full listing'. The practice of listing women by their later married names was partly responsible for such errors. I have since worked with the university college registers and calendars, and added over 100 names to make up the final list of 767 women who graduated in New Zealand up to 1920.

Such challenges are not new to those who research and write about the lives of those not traditionally recorded in histories of New Zealand's past. It is difficult enough to locate historical evidence on any group other than those who have occupied high-status positions in public life, because in the main they remain invisible and 'off the record'. This is perhaps why educated women in New Zealand have mainly featured in school histories as recorded by their peers. It has only been since the 1980s that 'gender' has become a recognised field of study within academic disciplines, enabling individual women and groups of women to be written back into historical accounts, and their lives to be analysed in relation to those of men, as well as to the social, political, and economic contexts of the time.

Graduate women: patterns of connection

Female education clearly fostered patterns of friendship, solidarity, and identity among women as they pursued their studies. For those young women who went on after secondary school to study at university or, later, at a teachers' training college, a combination of study programmes and staff and peer influences were to prove pivotal in what they did after completing their degrees.

Strong friendships and networks are often forged during life as a student. In a colonial society with a small population, there existed from a very early point a strong educated-women's network. Those who had studied together remained in contact via old girls' associations, professional associations, and women's organisations. As identifiable groups of women emerged in each generation of teachers, their members often moved together or followed each other to teaching positions in the same school. Making the decision to move away from the known university setting into an unknown new town, because they sought new opportunities for themselves, no doubt seemed more secure when they were joining like-minded friends.

As they did so, the first generations of graduate women teachers were presenting redefinitions of what young women might aspire to. Critical thinking is central to a higher education, and women who attain such an education have been able to imagine possibilities for themselves and take the necessary steps to achieve them. That so many educated women did this from the 1880s through securing high-status positions in New Zealand schools modelled possibilities for their colleagues and their students. Many educated women cite other educated women as influencing their future life choices through words and deeds.

As women entered teaching they were frequently reminded by politicians, newspaper editors, and school inspectors that their special attributes suited them well for this role. After all, they were told, the feminine mind and nature uniquely equipped them to guide young people into piety, purity, and knowledge. This was especially true of those who taught in girls' schools. The ideology rested comfortably with male employing authorities, as it required little stretching of popular notions of 'the female'. Women, as teachers, were merely making visible their unique role as the guardians of the young. As a group, they were perceived as being less concerned with selfish considerations of personal gain, personal comfort, or financial reward. It was generally thought that women would be grateful to be able to perform this vital work, which provided companionship and financial independence until such time as they would marry.

This normalising of the professional woman teacher to traditional female character traits had consequences for generations of women teachers to come. There was no national system of salary scale for secondary teachers until the introduction of the 1920 Dominion Scheme, and even then, the differentiation between women's and men's salaries remained. All women, even those with the best degrees, recognised as exceptional in terms of their academic achievements, were paid less than their male counterparts. The long fight for equal pay was not to be won until the Government Service Equal Pay Act in 1960. Women primary school teachers, who in the main were not university graduates, could at best aspire to lead an infant department in a town school.

For secondary school teachers, the fact that they did hold university degrees meant they could elect to apply for teaching positions across the schooling sector

Staff, Wellington Girls' College, 1902.
Standing: May C. Morrah (MA Canterbury 1891); Margaret N. Gellatly (MA Otago 1885).
Sitting: Wihelmina S. Fraser (BA Canterbury 1899); Alithea Batham (BA Canterbury 1901), later senior mistress at Wellington Girls' College and then principal of Wellington East Girls' College (1925–1937); Mary J. McLean CBE (MA Canterbury 1890), principal (1900–1926), also principal of Timaru Girls' High School (1898–1900); Isabel Ecclesfield (MA Auckland 1892); Elizabeth A. Newman (MA Canterbury 1901), at Wellington Girls' 1902–1927. WELLINGTON GIRLS' COLLEGE

and if strategic, earn higher salaries through winning more senior positions by moving from school to school. Many did so quickly and early in their careers, and this group in particular challenged prevailing notions about the role of women as teacher professionals. Armed with comparative analyses from other schools and regions, they were not prepared to accept lesser standards of working conditions, and lobbied for improvements both for themselves and for the girls they taught. If these were not forthcoming, they looked to other schools which were better provided for, and moved on. Far from being docile and content with their lot as teachers until the perfect man appeared, many of the first women graduates in New Zealand were politically minded and ambitious.

They were also predominantly women with strong Christian values, and members of local church congregations. Through these connections, they were attracted to join the Women's Christian Temperance Union (WCTU), established in New Zealand in 1885.[35] University-educated women, including many teachers, were among those who met regularly under the WCTU banner. While gaining the vote for women became a major focus from the late 1800s until it was won in 1893, WCTU supporters were also heavily involved in other battles being waged for women, notably for equal pay and equal access to education. Some of the most prominent, such as New Zealand's first woman graduate, Kate Edger, and Christina Henderson, the founder of the Women Teachers' Association, are discussed in later chapters.

Both movements, education and suffrage, were harassed by the kinds of pseudoscientific predictions of failure and doom outlined above. Those women who were involved in both were in the front line for public scrutiny. In certain quarters, access for women to both higher education and the suffrage were seen as being destructive of the 'good woman', whose delicate moral sensitivities could only be weakened by forcing knowledge and public activity upon her. Despite these dire prophecies, women continued to attend secondary school, gain higher qualifications, and enter the professions. They proved they could leave home, attend universities, and go on to earn a livelihood without suffering physical, mental, or moral collapse. In so doing, they not only laid the foundations for the type of gender equality now taken for granted by most New Zealand women and men, but also constructed for themselves lives of remarkable freedom and achievement.

Notes

1   *AJHR*, 1878, H-1.
2   Morris Matthews, 1988.
3   Cumming & Cumming, 1978.
4   Fry, 1985, p. 29.
5   *NZPD*, 1877, p. 37.
6   *AJHR*, 1891, E-1.
7   *AJHR*, 1891, E-1 B, pp. 1–37.
8   McKenzie, 1987.
9   Murdoch, 1943.
10 *AJHR*, 1908, E-1, p. xxvii.
11 *AJHR*, 1918, E-1, p. 48.
12 *AJHR*, 1938, E-1, p. 31.
13 *AJHR*, 1900, E-2, p. 16.
14 *AJHR*, 1890, E-2.

15 Varnham, 1994, p. 26.
16 Varnham, 1994, p. 27.
17 *AJHR*, 1902, E-1, p. xvi.
18 Varnham, 1994, p. 27.
19 *AJHR*, 1907, E-1, pp. 4, 6.
20 Openshaw, Lee, & Lee, 1993a, p. 106.
21 Day, 1992, p. 71.
22 *Ibid.*
23 King, 1925, p. 149; Olssen, 1980, p. 167.
24 Fry, 1985; Olssen, 1980; Tennant, 1977.
25 *White Ribbon*, 21 May 1909.
26 Pool, Dharmalingham, & Sceats, 2007, pp. 77–78.
27 Olssen, 1980; Tennant, 1977.
28 Fry, 1985, pp. 86–87.
29 Fry, 1985, pp. 46, 51.
30 *The Dominion*, 12 December 1917.
31 *Ibid.*
32 New Zealand Council for Educational Research, 1943, pp. 33–43.
33 Parton, 1979.
34 *Ibid.*
35 The WCTU had traditionally attracted women concerned about the effects of liquor on the general population; the plight of deserted wives and children; those who through financial circumstances were forced into prostitution; the double standard in testing prostitutes for contagious diseases and not their male clients; and the lack of women police and prison officers. It is best known for the role it played in the successful campaign to enfranchise women; but for many members of the WCTU, eligibility to vote in the general elections became an issue only in the late 1880s when they experienced at first hand the indifference of members of parliament to their temperance-aligned concerns (Grimshaw, 1987).

CHAPTER 2

Prioritising schooling for Māori girls*

(1850s–1945)

One of the oldest photographs of Hukarere Native School for Girls, late 1870s. HUKARERE GIRLS' COLLEGE

---

* 'Prioritising schooling for Māori girls' draws upon ten years of research conducted with Kuni Jenkins, and she is therefore acknowledged as coauthor of this chapter.

Ngā pūtake—key background events

It was Māori girls who were first identified by the Anglican and Roman Catholic missionaries as being worthy of special schooling attention. It was believed that through education, Māori girls would conform to a model of ideal womanhood and become the future guardians of morality and agents of Christianity through their roles as wives and mothers. The Pākehā middle-class concept of woman as 'angel of the house' was as closely tied to the transformation of young Māori women as 'saving' their souls was. As Tanya Fitzgerald's work with missionary diaries and letters has revealed, missionaries commonly regarded Māori girls and women as promiscuous. Early Anglican missionary families knew only too well that their own missionary men, such as Thomas Kendall and William Colenso, had been 'defrocked' for illicit liaisons with Māori women.[36] Thus, as Helene Connor points out, Māori girls as a group were singled out ahead of Pākehā girls for formalised schooling, in a bid to teach them that the model of femininity was the Virgin Mary. 'She stood for piety, subservience and goodness, whereas Eve and also Mary Magdalene represented the fallen woman—fallen from innocence, corrupt and corrupting.'[37]

The philosophy upon which Māori girls' schooling was based was twofold. The missionaries aimed to convert Māori girls to Christianity, while the state, which from 1867 established a publicly funded 'native school' system and subsidised the Māori denominational schools, aimed to 'civilise' the Māori through assimilation. Education policies for Māori were to reflect settler views about what non-European populations should be taught, in order to bring them more into line with accepted European societal norms.

This was not a new concept for the British colonial government. Earlier expansion in Africa, India, and Australia had already brought the British into contact with indigenous populations, and this, in turn, resulted in views about the social significance of race.[38] Links were made from the differences between the indigenous Māori and the Pākehā settlers to social differences on a hierarchical scale, giving rise to the concepts of 'Christianising' and 'civilising' a native population.

According to J. A. Mangan, 'imperial education was very much about establishing the presence and absence of confidence in those controlling and those controlled'.[39] This goal was reflected as early as 1844, when the state made clear what schooling for Māori was to be all about in the Native Trust Ordinance. Schools were to 'assimilate as speedily as possible the habits and usages of the native to those of the European population'.[40] Central to the assimilative process was the requirement that schools were required to teach in English in order to obtain state subsidies. There was an increasing belief by the settlers that Māori should not only learn English, but should also stop learning Māori. Assimilation could be more quickly realised through actively discouraging Māori language, belief systems, and culture, and actively promoting their British replacements. As Māori academic Ranginui Walker argues, 'this represented "cultural surrender", or at the very least, the suppression of Māori identity'.[41]

The emphasis on 'Europeanising' not only their pupils, but also the Māori communities in which they lived, was made clear to native school teachers in the 1880 Native Schools Code:

> Besides giving due attention to the school instruction of the children, teachers will be expected to exercise a beneficial influence on the natives, old and young; to show by their own conduct that it is possible to live a useful and blameless

Māori girls' school, Tauranga, 1862. AUCKLAND WAR MEMORIAL MUSEUM ALBUM 90 C31466

life, and in smaller matters, by their dress, in their house, and by their manner and habits at home and abroad, to set the Maoris an example that they may advantageously imitate.[42]

The native school system ran parallel to the public primary school system until 1969; Māori pupils could attend either.[43] However, once Māori pupils reached Standard 6, there was no state-funded Māori secondary schooling available. Until the establishment of the Māori District High Schools in 1941, the only avenue open to young Māori wanting to extend their studies was to attend a district high school, where Māori pupils were rare, or gain entry to a Māori denominational boarding school via a Department of Education scholarship, or have parents pay the necessary fees. The New Zealand government did not replace the word 'native' with the word 'Māori' until 1947.

Ngā kura mō ngā kōtiro Māori—schools for Māori girls

A small number of Māori denominational boarding schools had been established prior to 1880. Among them were the Anglican Māori girls' schools: Queen Victoria (1844, 1903) at Parnell, Auckland; the Bishop's School at Tauranga (1860s); the original Hukarere at Waerenga-a-hika inland from Gisborne (1865–1867); and Hukarere on Bluff Hill in Napier (1875). The Catholic Church established St Anne's in Ponsonby, Auckland (1855–1863) and St Joseph's Providence (1867) on Bluff Hill in Napier. Schools for Māori boys included St Stephen's (1845) and Te Aute (1854). Later, the Presbyterian Church established Turakina Māori Girls' College (1905) near Marton, and Te Wai Pounamu was set up for Māori girls in Christchurch by the Anglican Church in 1909.

The church founders were keen to remove intellectually able young Māori from their homes and place them in a European environment. The intention of the Church was that on leaving school, this group of elite Māori youth would take their newly found lifestyle back to the kāinga (home). It was hoped that with the teaching of new ideas, worshipping God, and practising Pākehā ways, the kāinga would be more quickly transformed, paving the way for assimilation of Māori into Pākehā society.

For Māori girls, this meant that once they arrived at boarding school from their homes, many of which were in remote areas, they were to be educated along the lines of an English middle-class Victorian girl's schooling. They were to dress, behave, and speak as befitted a Victorian middle-class woman. However, unlike their English counterparts, Māori girls were also expected to assist with every aspect of the daily running of the school. This meant that after making their beds and cleaning their dormitories and bathrooms, they assisted with meal preparation and serving, laundry work, general housekeeping, and gardening. The training in these tasks was also part of the mission of the school. Girls were to be 'domesticated' as part of the 'civilising' process.

This training illustrates the political socialisation of young Māori women. Gender and race were underpinned by a supposed 'natural relation'; that is, the belief that educated Māori women would be responsible for ensuring the physical and moral health of future generations in their role as bearers and rearers of children. This meant that for Māori girls, 'valued knowledge' was defined as 'useful' domestic knowledge, the kind needed to run Pākehā-style homes, while their Māori men, defined as the breadwinners, would be employed in full-time paid work of a kind which would reflect their lower position in the class structure. The Māori girls would be brown-skinned English middle-class

Hukarere pupils 'taking tea' in the dining room, late nineteenth century. HUKARERE GIRLS' COLLEGE

women who would teach their children that to all intents and purposes they were 'like Pākehā'; they exemplified a model Māori citizen, whose place it was to work and live off the land and be content to remain there. This shaping of collective awareness through the stereotypic image of what constituted 'ideal' Māori citizenship is an example of the use of curriculum to perpetuate social control. The curriculum became the means of demonstrating 'political authority'.[44]

Within official education reports, girls attending the Māori denominational schools were described as being the guardians not only of the next generation, but also of their husbands. Much time and money was invested in making sure that what these girls were taught would adequately prepare them for the task ahead. Such strategies to target Māori were, however, selective. The targeting of Māori girls within the elite denominational schools was crucial in segregating and differentiating one section of Māori from another. It was a screening process allied with class, religion, and national identity. It classified and stratified Māori

Queen Victoria School for Maori Girls, 1903. SPECIAL COLLECTIONS, AUCKLAND CITY LIBRARIES (NZ) 7-A12340

according to a Pākehā hierarchy, where a Māori ruling class would represent civilisation and adherence to Pākehā norms. Below them in the hierarchy were those who were savage and wild, yet to be civilised, yet to be assimilated. This is consistent with the stereotype predominant in the nineteenth century, when Māori were conceptualised as a noble but barbaric race.

In New Zealand, political intervention via educational reform set about reconstructing Māori as New Zealand citizens. Shortly after his appointment in 1901, the Director General of Education, George Hogben, visited the Māori denominational boarding schools. His report indicates that he recommended these schools strengthen the instruction in English and introduce manual and technical instruction, such as carpentry, metalwork, cooking, sewing, hygiene, and drill. At the same time, Hogben wanted the Māori secondary schools to abandon studies in Latin and Euclid, because English and manual training were:

> … more important than bookish forms of instruction which might tend to unfit Maori boys and girls for the simple life of the pa and give them no training that would enable them to perform willingly and intelligently the work that had to be done in connection with their homes.[45]

While girls did receive a compulsory training in domestic skills, they were also, at least initially, given access to a comprehensive curriculum, based on the English grammar school model. For example, at Hukarere, an Anglican Native School for Girls subsidised by the state, principal Maria Williams believed that the most suitable academic programme for the girls in her care was a classical curriculum consisting of English, Latin, algebra, physiology, drawing, history, drill, singing, and dressmaking. That she chose to emphasise an academic programme was perhaps the motivation behind a letter she received on 9 August 1898. It was written by Mr J. B. Fielder, who, as a member of the school board of governors, wanted to see a more practical education for Māori girls. He wrote asking Miss Williams for the following details:

> Whether the pupils of the school under your charge are receiving any technical instruction in the following subjects: (1) Plain cooking and general household management; (2) cutting out and making up garments for personal wear; (3) music, and voice culture for either elocution or singing; (4) any other subject in art or science: and if so, what is and has been the result of such education; and whether the girls

Pupils of Turakina Maori Girls' College,
1910. ALEXANDER TURNBULL LIBRARY, WELLINGTON, NZ. PACOLL-5736

after leaving the school have taken service in families or employment in the many branches of work open to their sisters of the European race, or if married, do they generally live in the native or European style? [46]

The letter went on to ask Maria Williams to comment on the merits of technical education and whether or not she had suitable domestic appliances for practical instruction. The letter concluded with the promise that if she so desired, 'any suggestion made by you as to improvements will receive the earnest consideration of the trustees. An early reply will oblige.'[47]

Maria Williams did not take up the hint to plead a case for new equipment, nor did she rush her response. Some seven weeks later, she set out the nature of technical instruction to the board, yet at the same time carefully avoided giving details of her classical curriculum, which she knew full well was documented in the annual reports of the 'native schools' inspector:

(1) That the pupils are taught to do the ordinary work of the house, and the older ones are taught plain cooking. This year they have had a course of six lessons in cookery from Miss Millington, who was much pleased with the results.

(Anna) Maria Williams b.1839 d.1929

(Anna) Maria Williams
—founding principal,
Hukarere, Napier.

ALEXANDER TURNBULL LIBRARY, WELLINGTON, NZ. WILLIAMS COLLECTION F-029572-1/2

By the late 1850s, (Anna) Maria Williams was teaching at the Waerenga-a-hika Anglican Mission School inland from Gisborne. She was born at the Waimate mission station near Pahia in 1839, the daughter of Jane Williams and her husband William Williams, Church Missionary Society missionaries. Raised in Māori communities, Maria was bilingual with an excellent knowledge of Māori tikanga. In 1867, William Williams, then bishop of Waiapu, moved his family to Napier and took a keen interest in Te Aute College for Māori boys in central Hawke's Bay. Encouraged by his wife Jane and his daughter Maria, the bishop was persuaded that a sister school for Māori girls should be established, along similar lines to the one the Williams women had run at Waerenga-a-hika from 1865.[48] According to Ruth Flashoff, 'Maria's considerable organising ability, her knowledge of Māori language and her

(2) They are taught needlework and mending and when sufficiently advanced they
   learn to cut out and make up garments for personal wear. Sewing machines are in
   constant use.

(3) They receive instruction in singing, and a few learn instrumental music. They also
   learn to knit socks, vests, shawls and other useful articles.[49]

On the broader matters, Maria Williams indicated that some girls went into domestic service and others went home. She pointed to the increasing trend for girls to take up professional nursing training. Perhaps sensing an audit on the value for money spent on Māori girls' education, she added that 'in the majority of cases the instruction received is not by any means thrown away'.[50]

Maria Williams demonstrated her commitment to a professional pathway for Māori women when she recommended former pupil Agnes Down as her sucessor at Hukarere.

The advocacy of a more practical curriculum was to prepare Māori for staying in their own communities, rather than to equip them with professional skills whereby they could compete with Pākehā for white-collar jobs in the expanding bureaucratic, commercial, and professional sectors in large towns. The Secretary of Education and his department officials promoted the dignity of manual labour so that Māori youth would want to return to their local district upon finishing school.

Such views had been resisted by Māori elders for some time. Scholars such as Apirana Ngata and Peter Buck, for example, spoke for parents with children

strong spiritual faith encouraged him to found in 1875 what was known as the Bishop's School and later as Hukarere Native Girls' School'[51] on a site adjacent to the Williams' family home on Bluff Hill in Napier. Known as 'Miss Maria' and superintendent of Hukarere, Maria Williams ran the school and taught the scriptures and English. Her two sisters, Lydia Catherine ('Miss Kate') and Marianne ('Miss Mary Anne') also taught at the school, and with Maria were known by their pupils as the 'Hukarere Aunts'. Maria was principal of Hukarere until 1899, when she retired.

However, she continued to teach scriptures and her association with the school continued until her death in 1929.

Maria Williams earlier identified one of her pupils as her successor. Over a number of years, she mentored and prepared Agnes Down as a pupil and then a teacher at Hukarere. It was in this way that the first Māori woman principal of a girls' secondary school was appointed in 1891.

Agnes Down (m.Hope) b.c.1860 d.1951

Agnes Down was one of the first pupils enrolled at Hukarere in July 1875. She was the eleventh of fifteen children of Mere Riripeti and George Down of Wairoa.[52] It is likely that she was brought to Napier by the school's founder, Maria Williams, as part of the Church Missionary Society bid to recruit young Māori girls from the hinterland of the Waiapu Diocese. As Maria travelled with her father, Bishop William Williams, they were able to convince parents of the value of a Hukarere education for their daughters.[53] Maria chose well. Five years later, Agnes took up a position as assistant teacher at Hukarere. By the time her younger sister Laura was enrolled at Hukarere in 1887, Agnes was a senior teacher. When the ageing 'lady superintendent' Maria Williams contemplated retirement in 1891, she wrote to Inspector Pope advising him of her intention to appoint Agnes Down as her successor. Within two days, Pope replied, agreeing that Miss Down 'has enough energy and ability' to take on the role.[54] In this way, Agnes became the first Māori woman to head a Māori denominational school. The photograph taken of her at this time depicts a confident woman attired in a dark Victorian costume complete with jewellery. Next to her on a table is an English china tea set. The image leaves no doubt that Agnes is a thoroughly 'Europeanised' Māori who, as Maria Williams' protégé, is more than competent to lead a school and its sixty young Māori students. Inspector Pope certainly thought so. Three months into her stewardship of Hukarere, he reported that 'the form of the school has never seemed to me better than it has been today, and I have complete confidence in Miss Down's ability to manage the school and to teach the children to the department's satisfaction'.[55] The inspector remained impressed with Agnes' management of Hukarere.

By 1893, she had two new colleagues, both Māori women who had been educated at Hukarere—her

Agnes Down (m.Hope), first Māori secondary school principal, Hukarere, 1891–1898.
HUKARERE GIRLS' COLLEGE

sister Laura Down, and Matire Ngapua, who had come from Kaikohe in 1888.[56] Together, they represented the first all-Māori women teaching staff in a denominational boarding school, a record held to this day.

It was under this new regime that students flourished at Hukarere, as Māori parents came to recognise the uniqueness and quality of education offered there. This was reflected in the inspection reports, which consistently praised principal Agnes Down for 'good discipline and good tone'[57] and in 1896 said that 'the school gives the impression that it is pervaded by great earnestness and that the teachers are thoroughly devoted to their work'.[58] Agnes Down received the ultimate accolade from Inspector Pope the following year: 'Miss Down's work needs no comment; she is very competent.'[59] Agnes remained head teacher of Hukarere until 1898, when, after twenty-four years as a live-in pupil, teacher, and principal, she left Hukarere, having married local clerk John Hope. Together they combined the raising of three sons with teaching in three different native schools until 1917. At that time, they retired from teaching to go farming at Matawai, where Agnes died in 1951.[60]

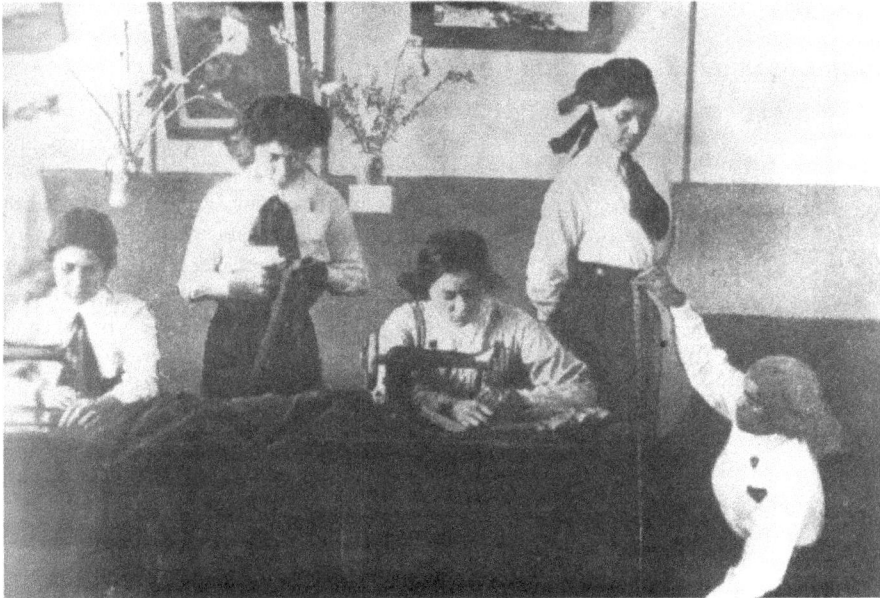

Hukarere pupils receiving technical instruction. These photographs featured in the Department of Education's 1913 annual report. ALEXANDER TURNBULL LIBRARY, WELLINGTON, NZ. BK-821-8A

enrolled in the Māori denominational schools. They could themselves, they said, teach practical skills to their children. What they wanted in return for paying substantial school fees was the kind of knowledge to better equip Māori youth for professional education.[61] The government was not deterred. In 1900 and 1902 it introduced the Manual and Technical Instruction Acts, offering schools money in exchange for the establishment of more practical subjects in their schools.

When recalcitrant Māori denominational schools did not take up such offers and conform to state policy, they were sought out and publicly admonished. For example, in 1903 Nina Greensill, principal of Queen Victoria School for Maori Girls, offered a curriculum of English, Latin, Euclid, arithmetic, geography, physiology, drawing, singing, scripture, gym, and domestic science.[62] However, it was made clear by the Inspector of Native Schools that because of the high Māori infant mortality rate, and because educated Māori women were destined to teach and positively model Pākehā household management systems, instruction in the various elements of domestic science should predominate for Māori girls. The principal of Queen Victoria School had different ideas about the future role of her students, saying that 'it was leaders I especially looked

Nina Agatha Rosamond Greensill (m.Barrer) (MA Canterbury 1902)

Queen Victoria School for Maori Girls, 1903. Founding principal Nina Greensill (MA Canterbury 1902) with (sitting left) Miss Mirams, teacher, and (sitting right) Mrs Mirams, matron. SPECIAL COLLECTIONS, AUCKLAND CITY LIBRARIES (NZ) 7-A12538

Nina Greensill (MA Canterbury 1902) was the first university graduate to lead a Māori girls' school. She was appointed principal of Queen Victoria School for Maori Girls, in Parnell, in 1903. Nina Greensill was born in Picton and attended private primary schools there. Her father, a local merchant, mayor of Picton, and an Anglican lay reader, sent her to Wellington Girls' High School in 1894 and then to Canterbury College, where she studied science, graduating with a BA in 1901, and an MA with first class honours in natural science in 1902. She taught for one year at Hukarere in Napier before being appointed to Queen Victoria School, where she was principal for two years until her marriage. As Nina Barrer, she spent the rest of her life in the Wairarapa, where she and her farmer husband raised a family of four children. She was very active in a range of organisations, including the Workers' Educational Association, League of Nations, Red

for and hoped to train'.[63] Her own views on the academic success of Māori women were clearly at odds with official expectations. When she insisted on continuing to offer a traditional academic programme, the inspector's rebuke included the statement 'that it is a great mistake to attempt to teach Latin and Euclid in such a school',[64] while other critics accused her of 'aiming too high'.[65] What was wanted by the inspector was more 'cooking, laundry work and other branches of domestic instruction … I should also like to see cottage gardening added'.[66] But Nina Greensill mobilised her school's parents' association, and its 1908 report 'emphasised that the school was there to benefit the Māori race, not to benefit Europeans in need of servants'.[67]

Such opposition to state policy resulted in the Commission of Inquiry into Te Aute College in 1906, when the Department of Education set out to deter principal John Thornton from coaching promising Māori male scholars for the entry examination for the University of New Zealand.[68] Academic studies were to be discouraged and replaced with agriculture and horticulture instead. When Thornton and his church-based board refused to implement a technical curriculum, the state retaliated by withdrawing government scholarships.

Cross, New Zealand Women Teachers' Association, Pan Pacific Women's Association, United Nations Association of New Zealand, and Council of Adult Education. In Masterton, she helped establish the Wairarapa High School and in 1931 chaired the Wairarapa Secondary Education Board, being one of the first women to hold such a position. Nina Barrer was also president of the Masterton Women's Division of the New Zealand Federated Farmers' Union (1927–1930), edited its magazine *New Zealand Countrywoman* from 1933 to 1935, and was a member of the co-ordinating committee for the Women's Division and for the Dominion Federation of Country Women's Institutes from 1937. Not surprisingly, her combined knowledge and organisational skills led to her becoming a prominent member of the New Zealand National Party in the 1940s. She was awarded an MBE for her services to education in 1959.[69]

Queen Victoria pupils practising maypole dancing, 1900s. AUCKLAND WAR MEMORIAL MUSEUM DU 436.1277B36

Essentially, Thornton was being too successful. The first Māori graduates had emerged from New Zealand universities in the 1880s and had played a prominent role as ministers of the Crown, lawyers, and doctors. This new educated Māori elite had been quick to seize those aspects of a Pākehā education that would secure qualifications, higher education, and the commensurate rewards. However, many spoke out publicly against state policies that served to disadvantage Māori, providing what Yuval Davis describes as 'boundary management'. As a collective, they played 'crucial roles in the continuous (re) construction of collectivities and collective identities and the management/ control of their boundaries'.[70] Such actions highlight the complexities and inner contradictions associated with analysis of Māori education, which has traditionally painted a picture of a 'grateful' indigenous elite receiving a quality Pākehā-styled education, and returning to rural settlements to work the land. To counter the resistance to the implementation of a more technical curriculum in the Māori denominational schools, financial inducements were increasingly offered to help change the professional curriculum to one that emphasised agriculture, carpentry, domestic science, and hygiene. By 1913, the native schools inspectors were confident that the state was making more progress:

> In none of the secondary Māori schools at the present time is there any attempt or desire to give what is usually understood by a "college" education. Generally speaking, the girls' schools afford further training in English subjects and in various branches of domestic duties—cooking, sewing and dressmaking, housewifery, nursing and hygiene; the boys' schools in English and manual training—woodwork, elementary practical agriculture and kindred subjects and that is all.[71]

The inspector was in fact reflecting the ideal rather than the actual outcome; Māori students were then excelling in higher school examinations. Many young women went on to take up nursing and teaching studies, and while few then attended university, a large number of their boarding school brothers were allowed and encouraged to seek tertiary education. This trend had more to do with attitudes about women's future role than the intellectual ability of Māori girls. Despite credible school qualifications, Pākehā writers have perpetuated the myth that 'a less academic standard was set' at the Māori girls' schools because 'the girls were encouraged to realise the influential part they could play as Christian wives and mothers in their home communities'.[72]

This view from the outside popularises the myth that the goals of assimilation were successful, and relegates Māori girls to a stereotype of being low academic achievers, but able to be trained in domestic skills. What Pākehā writers of the past found difficult to accept was that Māori girls in the denominational schools were taught by highly qualified staff (both Māori and Pākehā), so that their examination results were comparable with those of the Māori boys' schools, and they might seek entry, as indeed they did, to tertiary institutions and a range of professions.

Through the secondary school curriculum specifically designed for Māori girls' boarding schools, young Māori women were constructed as having limited rights in the labour market, and were used by the state to foster links between the concepts of idealised motherhood and nationhood. It was a mechanism for reconstructing Māori women and through them paving the way for the transformation of Māori society. While Māori women, more than Māori men, were charged with this responsibility, they were also to be educated in order to develop a collective awareness of 'knowing their place'. In the first instance, they had to accept that Māori women were to blame for producing large numbers of babies, and for the high infant mortality rate. Secondly, they had to be educated appropriately, for the best of care depended on a compassionate nurturing mother who had primary responsibility for child welfare.

This narrow definition of caring failed to recognise the communality of child rearing practised by Māori, so that the care of children is shared between members of an extended family. For example, it is common for the grandmother to raise the eldest grandchild and for the care of a child to be taken over by a close relative for years at a time. Further, the Victorian concept of motherhood did not take into account the impact of other factors. After the land wars of the 1860s, many Māori families had their land confiscated by the state. In many cases they lost their source of income, lived in inadequate housing—often with no electricity—and struggled to feed their children. A broader definition would have required the state to fund social services for the many, rather than an educational campaign for the few.

Makereti Papakura (m.Staples-Brown) b.1873 d.1930
Rangitiaria Ratema (m.Dennan) b.1897 d.1970

Makereti Papakura (Margaret Thom) arrived at Hukarere from Rotorua in 1886. Famous as Whakarewarewa's Guide Maggie, Makereti (m.Staples-Brown) was also an Oxford scholar in anthropology. She died weeks before presenting her BSc honours thesis. HUKARERE GIRLS' COLLEGE

Guide Rangi of Whakarewarewa. Rangitiaria Ratema (m.Dennan) said of her schooling at Hukarere from 1910–1914 that 'it played a greater part in my life than any other single agency'. HUKARERE GIRLS' COLLEGE

Māori girls understood the purpose of the secondary education they received. Makereti Papakura, better known as Guide Maggie of Whakarewarewa, but also an Oxford University scholar and author of The Old Time Maori, recalled that she was sent to Hukarere in 1882 at ten years old. She wrote, 'You are taught everything in that school and must know about keeping house, cooking, washing, sewing and cleaning, as well as lessons.'[73] Her cousin, Rangitiaria Dennan (Ratema), later the famous Guide Rangi, went to Hukarere in 1910. In her autobiography, she wrote of the importance of Hukarere girls putting their secondary education

> to good use … we needed examples from our own people—a steady stream of examples to convince the masses that the Māori could do it, given the chance. The foundations were already down, led by Sir Apirana Ngata, Sir Peter Buck, Bishop Frederick Bennett, Maggie Papakura … We wanted Māori nurses, Māori doctors, Māori lawyers, Māori bankers—not one of each, but many.[74]

By 1930, up to three generations of Māori women had passed through the Māori denominational schools where, unlike their state counterparts, school principals determined the curriculum with greater degrees of autonomy. However, in 1931 the Director of Education, T. B. Strong, made clear the official view that a 'knowledge of the Māori language is unnecessary to natives who know only English. The Māori language has no literature and consequently in this direction too, the natural abandonment of the native tongue inflicts no loss on the Māori.'[75] The Māori principal of Hukarere, Mere Hall, must have challenged the official view because, as students under her tutelage attest, they were taught Māori language, albeit at an introductory level. Four years later, the state introduced a new policy for Māori: assimilation was to be changed to adaptation. It was now thought appropriate for the school curriculum to reflect aspects of Māori culture. However, 'in the case of girls', it was written, 'a practical knowledge of housecraft, including plain sewing, cooking, washing and care of clothes, house cleaning and beautifying, mending and nursing [must] be considered essential'.[76]

Those responsible for the education of Māori girls did not necessarily share this philosophy. The writings of Mere Hall, for example, indicated that she wanted more for her pupils than being good homemakers.

Throughout her stewardship, Mere Hall's annual reports indicate her philosophy in leading what had now become a large Māori girls' secondary school. She resisted the state's emphasis on a domestic curriculum, although she acknowledged its importance. Perhaps more than other Māori women of her generation, she realised that such goals were restricting. Mentored by the Williams and Bulstrode sisters, she had become a teacher and lived her life as an independent single woman. As principal of Hukarere, she enjoyed considerable status with the Anglican Church, the Department of Education inspectors, and the wider community. Described by her pupils as 'human and warm hearted', she also mentored them towards careers in teaching and nursing. She stressed the importance of examination success at the senior level in order to access professional training. However, she also knew that rural Māori parents could not afford the fees charged to keep their daughters at school for the additional examination year. Mere Hall was quick to point out to the Department of

Education that while Māori boys had benefited from Industrial Scholarships for more than thirty years, the state's only similar contribution to Māori girls' education over this time had been to allow two Hukarere girls a year to be selected for a one-year nursing training course at Napier Hospital. She added that even then, Hukarere had provided a home for them during their training. She also thought it most unfair that when the nursing course was extended to two years, with full registration upon completion, Māori female graduates were required to return to work in their home communities.[77]

It is clear that her effective lobbying assisted in the Department of Education establishing, in 1939, Continuation Scholarships for Māori girls to train as teachers. In 1944 she reflected that, 'In 1939, our first girls entered the Training College and up to the present we have had twenty-three. The government inspectors keep in touch with them and report very favourably upon their progress.'[78] Not all of these girls were state funded. Mere Hall convinced the Hukarere Old Girls' Association to raise money to provide scholarships of their own for deserving students. In this way, Mere Hall did more than promote her girls into the professions. She set in place what was to become a flood of Hukarere pupils into nursing and teaching, thus establishing new career pathways for Māori women. Their combined influence upon the communities and institutions in which they lived and worked was to be unprecedented.[79]

Mere Haana Hall b.1880 d.1966

HUKARERE GIRLS' COLLEGE

Mere Haana Hall was a pupil at Hukarere from 1893. She became a teacher and was principal from 1927–1944. She lived at Hukarere for fifty-one years.

When Agnes Down was teaching at Hukarere in 1893, a priest rode up to the school, passed over to Maria Williams a shy young girl, and left without providing any information as to the identity of the child. It was in this way that Mere Haana Hall, later to be the longest serving Māori principal, arrived at Hukarere. She became part of the family of the Williams sisters and in turn, of English women Jane and Emily Bulstrode, who followed Agnes Down as head teachers in 1899 and 1917 respectively.[80]

Until recently it was thought that the reason Mere Hall remained at Hukarere for fifty-one years without contact from her family was because she had been orphaned. However, it now seems more likely that she, and later her sister, had simply been 'handed over' by her parents to the Church. Mere came to know her origins in later life, and her family researchers have now recorded her tribal links to Ngāti Rangiwewehi of the Rotorua region. Her father, the Englishman John Hall, was clerk of the Residents' Magistrates Court at Ohinemutu.

Behind the scenes, Mere Hall was also changing attitudes towards the preservation of Māori culture and language. When she had been a pupil in the 1890s, Māori language was not allowed to be taught, but the Williams sisters had conducted Hukarere Chapel services in Māori, and clearly did not discourage girls from speaking their own language outside the classroom.[81] For many years, Mere Hall, as teacher and principal, resisted official discouragement of teaching the Māori language and took introductory lessons with the girls.

Many girls who went to Hukarere did not go home for the whole time they were at school, and often this was for many years. Mere Hall, therefore, like the headmistresses who had cared for her, assumed the mantle of both principal and parent. Described as 'a very strict person but very fair',[82] she administered discipline that would be remembered for a lifetime. But this legendary woman was also loved and respected, and fostered a family-like community. She ensured that her girls enjoyed a range of experiences outside school, supporting them in sporting activities, taking them swimming, to the Royal Show, and on trips to various other places. She was also responsible for appointing a number of outstanding teachers, both Māori and European, who worked with her for many years. Together, they crafted a unique school culture for Māori girls, while the Māori girls themselves formed a strong sense of sisterhood that would help sustain Hukarere for future generations of Māori women.

Her mother was Rangimakehu Ainsley, who had an English father and whose mother, Haana Ngaki Te Kapapiwaho, was a grandchild of Ngāti Rangiwewehi chief, Te Kapaiwaho.[83]

Writing in 1944, Mere Hall recalled her arrival and the possible reason for it. She explained 'that there were about fifty girls under the control of Miss Maria Williams, the Bishop's daughter, with Mrs Hope [Agnes Down], an Old Girl, as head teacher. Any parent who could pay did so, but most of the girls were free pupils; no girl was refused because she could not pay her fees.'[84] Mere never forgot the goodwill of the Church in ensuring that she was raised, cared for, and educated at Hukarere. She became head prefect, a pupil-teacher, and a Hukarere teacher for twenty years, and then from 1927 to 1944 was principal. She won the appointment in open competition with European applicants. Had she married, she would have been expected to relinquish the position; but because she did not, she remained principal until her retirement.

When Mere Hall left Hukarere in 1944, she ended an association of fifty-one years with the school. Her services to education and the Māori community were recognised in 1952 when she received an MBE. Former pupils and colleagues have written and spoken about Mere Hall, not only as an educational leader, but also as a leader in life.

Whilst teaching opened up employment opportunities for Māori women, including leadership positions in and across the Māori denominational schools, there were fewer Māori women religious (nuns) within the Catholic secondary school system. At St Joseph's at Greenmeadows, for example, Māori women religious were appointed as teachers from the 1950s, when former pupil Theresa Mariu returned to teach at the school as Sister Mary Katarina. Four contemporaries quickly followed her, but it was not until 1985 that former pupil and university graduate Georgina Kingi took the helm as principal, the first Māori woman graduate to be so appointed.[85] There was a range of reasons for this, including the gap highlighted by Mere Hall's advocacy for Continuation Scholarships to enable senior girls to sit the Matriculation Examination, the entry requirement for university as well as for teaching. For many families,

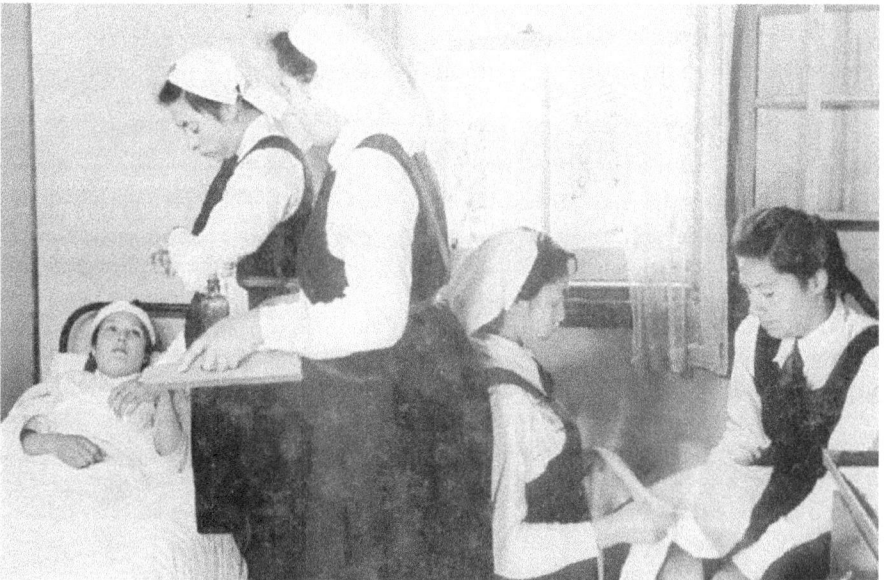

Home nursing practice at Hukarere. HUKARERE GIRLS' COLLEGE

54

the fact that teacher trainees were paid as they studied made this particular path preferable to university. There was also another reason. Without mentors, role models, or Māori peers, university could be a very lonely place, even if the funding were available. Mira Petricevich (m.Szaszy) was one of the first Māori women to graduate from university. She attended Queen Victoria School in the late 1930s, before studying arts at Auckland University College. She graduated with a BA in 1946.[86]

Māori girls at state secondary schools

While some parents continued to send their daughters and sons to the Māori denominational schools, the fees charged by those schools remained beyond the reach of the majority of Māori. Those who had passed the Proficiency Examination in their final year of primary school, and gained access to a secondary education, therefore had limited options. The majority of the Māori population was rurally based, and the only secondary education available in smaller towns was the district high schools, but Māori pupils were a minority

Biology class, Hukarere. HUKARERE GIRLS' COLLEGE

there, and Māori girls were often streamed into homecraft courses. Ruth Fry summed up the situation:

> This meant that there was some segregation according to sex and race: a homecraft class could be largely Māori girls and a technical class entirely Māori boys. While there was an undoubted gain in confidence and camaraderie from such togetherness, these were off-set by the feeling among the Māori pupils themselves that they were "no-hopers".[87]

Even after the Proficiency Examination was abolished in 1937, Māori attendance at secondary school was low. For example, in 1940 the Inspector of Native Schools reported that of 778 Māori pupils who left public and native schools at the end of Form 2, only seventy-eight continued to secondary school.[88] The government intervened by establishing Māori District High Schools, but it was made clear by the Inspector of Native Schools that Māori pupils would be prepared for their future role in New Zealand society as the state envisaged it:

> The Māori is not sufficiently removed from his past to be suited for commerce … the core of the curriculum is home-making, home-making in the widest sense, including building construction … furniture making, metal work and home management.

English lesson with Miss Pedersen, Hukarere, 1940s. HUKARERE GIRLS' COLLEGE

The aim is to teach the skills and develop the tastes that make the house not merely a place of habitation but a home in the best sense of the word.[89]

In the new, specially provided state secondary schools, Māori girls, like Māori boys, were to continue to be trained to 'know their place'.

From the 1940s, large numbers of Māori moved from the rural areas into the cities in search of work. In 1945, 19 percent of Māori lived in cities; by 1971, this had reached 68 percent. The arrival of Māori children in local secondary schools produced a crisis for many schools and the teachers within them. While the Māori district high schools worked hard at employing Māori teachers, there were simply not enough Māori teachers, and even fewer Māori graduate teachers, to go around. For many young urban Māori, secondary school was an alien environment, and one to escape from as soon as the leaving age was reached. This meant that large numbers of unqualified Māori left school to take up largely semiskilled or unskilled jobs in the workforce.

Such uncomfortable truths about educational, social, and economic outcomes for Māori were raised by Māori women members from groups such as the Māori Women's Institutes from 1929; Te Rōpū o te Ora, the Women's Health League, from 1937; and the Māori Women's Welfare League from 1951.[90] Many of the members of these groups were educated women from the denominational schools. Their vision for Māori education would not begin to be realised until land, language, and Treaty issues erupted in Māori political action in the 1970s, leading to Māori educational initiatives such as Te Kōhanga Reo from 1982, Kura Kaupapa Māori from 1985, and the increasing numbers of Māori graduates and graduate teachers from the 1990s.

Notes

36 Fitzgerald, 2001, 2003.
37 Connor, 2006, p. 15.
38 Goldberg, 1993.
39 Mangan, 1990, p. 6.
40 *The Native Trust Ordinance*, 1844, p. 140.
41 Walker, 1991, p. 5.
42 *AJHR*, 1880, H-I F, pp. 1–7.
43 Simon, 1998.
44 Musgrove, 1978, p. 100.
45 Bird, 1930, p. 17.

46 Jenkins & Morris Matthews, 1995.
47 *Ibid.*
48 *Hukarere Girls' College MS Collection.*
49 *Ibid.*
50 *Ibid.*
51 Flashoff, 1993.
52 *Prentice Papers, Down Whakapapa,* Hawke's Bay Museum Library.
53 Jenkins & Morris Matthews, 1995.
54 *Hukarere Native School Records,* NA BAAA 1001 938c.
55 *Ibid.*
56 Jenkins & Morris Matthews, 1995, p. 163.
57 *Hukarere Native School Records,* NA BAAA 10011 939a.
58 *Hukarere Native School Records,* NA BAAA 939a 56g.
59 *Hukarere Native School Records,* NA BAAA 939a.
60 *AJHR,* 1903–1906, 1910; *Gisborne Herald,* 21 August 1964; Hukarere Girls' College MS
    Collection, 1940.
61 Buck, 1899; Ngata, 1897.
62 Taua, 1983.
63 Barrer, 1966, p. 184.
64 *AJHR,* 1904, E-Report, Inspector of Native Schools.
65 Taua, 1983.
66 *AJHR,* 1904, E-Report, Inspector of Native Schools.
67 Taua, 1983.
68 *AJHR,* 1906, G-5.
69 Barrer, 1966; Van der Kroght, 1998; *Wairarapa Times-Age,* 18 September 1965.
70 Yuval Davis, 1997, p. 67.
71 *AJHR,* 1913, E-3, pp. 7–10.
72 Woods, 1981, p. 253.
73 Writings from Makareti Papakura's scrapbook held in the Pitt Rivers Museum
    Archive, United Kingdom. Courtesy of Dr Ngahuia Te Awekotuku, cited in Jenkins &
    Morris Matthews, 1995, p. 47.
74 Dennan & Annabel, 1968, p. 61.
75 Strong, 1931, p. 193.
76 *AJHR,* 1931, Vol 2 E-3, p. 4.
77 Bird, 1930; *Hukarere Annual Report,* 1944, p. 2.
78 *Hukarere Annual Report,* 1944, p. 2.
79 Jenkins & Morris Matthews, 1995.
80 *Hukarere Annual Report,* 1944, p. 1.
81 *Hukarere Girls' College MS Collection,* Eve Magee MS, 1975.
82 Jenkins & Morris Matthews, 1995, p. 64.
83 Hall & Leibowitz, 1998.
84 *Hukarere Annual Report,* 1944, p. 1.
85 van der Linden, 1990.
86 Taua, 1983.
87 Fry, 1985, pp. 171–172.
88 *AJHR,* 1941, E-3, p. 2.
89 *AJHR,* 1941, E-3, p. 3.
90 Else, 1993.

CHAPTER 3

Daring to be different at Otago
(1869–1945)

University of Otago, Dunedin. HOCKEN COLLECTIONS, UARE TAOKA O HAKENA, UNIVERSITY OF OTAGO S07-096A

The South Island province of Otago provided the first publicly funded schooling for girls in New Zealand. Scottish settlers brought to Otago a democratic model of public education based on open access to schooling for all children. Central to the terms of land purchase in 1842 was that one-eighth of the proceeds of the sale of lands in Otago was to be set aside for religious and educational purposes, under the control of the Presbyterian Church of Otago. In 1852, the Otago Provincial Council set the guidelines for educational policy:

> ... with a view to making more permanent provision for Education, the Government should purchase or make reserves of land in each Educational District ... within the Province ... for the benefit and advancement of education and for the endowment of a High School and College in Dunedin.[91]

In 1856, the Otago Education Ordinance was more direct: it set out the plan to open a public high school to both boys and girls. This very good beginning signalled what was to follow: Otago modelled to other New Zealand provinces ways of providing education for young people, including systems of public secondary and university education. However, shortly after the establishment

Learmonth Dalrymple 1827–1906

OTAGO SETTLERS MUSEUM

Learmonth Dalrymple—champion for girls' and women's higher education.

Learmonth Dalrymple and her sister Isabella had attended a boarding school at St Andrew's in Scotland. Learmonth then spent time in Europe, where she learnt to speak French fluently. In 1853, her merchant father emigrated to Otago with his three daughters and two sons. They settled at 'Craigilea' at Kaihiku, west of Balclutha, and it was from there that Learmonth spearheaded the bid for higher education of women in her new homeland. Her reasons for doing so included her dissatisfaction with her own schooling, especially not being allowed to study mathematics because her father disapproved of such a subject being taught to girls. Her 'hopeless yearnings for mental culture' are made clear in an article published in the *Otago Daily Times* in 1866, which summed up her arguments for a high school for girls:

> Those among us who have given even a little serious thought to the question of a girls' education, cannot but have arrived at the conclusion, that we ought to be far from satisfied with the ordinary systems followed at most girls' schools at Home. ... When a young lady leaves school, she can generally read and write nicely—knows so much history, geography, arithmetic, and various sorts of fancy work—can dance, sing, play and speak a little French; and, moreover, has picked up from the many catechisms professing to show short roads to learning, certain stray scientific facts; and thus equipped, sallies forth into the world, under the impression, for the time

of Otago Boys' High School in 1863, when there was no sign of a similar institution for girls, a number of local citizens began what was to be a seven-year campaign for the opening of a girls' high school. Leading the charge was Learmonth Dalrymple.

The legacy of Learmonth Dalrymple

One of Dalrymple's staunchest allies was her friend and neighbour, Major (later Sir) John Richardson, Member for Clutha and Speaker of the Otago Provincial Council. While he totally agreed with her and thought 'that something should be done for a superior education of girls',[92] he did not think there was any hope of getting a high school for girls at that time. What was needed in the first instance, he suggested, was a petition. If she obtained the signatures, he would present it to the provincial council. Although the petition was presented in December 1865, went before the Select Committee for Education, and was commended, nothing came of it. Undeterred, Learmonth Dalrymple continued to put the matter before the provincial council, writing between 700 and 800 letters to

being, that she is well educated. But this, we all know, is not education.

Fortunately for this young colony, we have not time honoured systems to uproot and overturn; our privilege, and a high privilege it is: is to found, to establish … . Why is it that men, rather than women, generally speaking, have firmer characters, are better reasoners, express themselves with greater exactness, and have a truer sense of the meaning and significance of words? These, no doubt, are the results of the thorough mental training they undergo whilst they are boys at school: and this consists of years spent in classical study—exacting the closest attention to the choice of words, much dictionary work and great exercise of the memory … this "training to think" is deliberately dispensed with as part of the education of a woman; for this defect it must be our endeavour to find a remedy.

Under this conviction, then, it is for us to consider what best can be done to effect a change, and promote a better culture. And the first step, it appears to the writer, towards this end should be, to make the curriculum of studies the most comprehensive and liberal that can be possibly offered. Hitherto it has been commonly considered that these higher branches of study belong to boys, and their rewards in pleasure and satisfaction were theirs by a sort of Divine right; but happily, this assumption has already begun to wane, and it is frankly owned by one of our best and wisest men, that "there is no sort of right knowledge—no form of honest intellectual culture which is essentially unfeminine. Intellect is of no sex; and science, history, religion, poetry, truth, address themselves to the human being as such, whether man or woman."[93]

people throughout New Zealand and in Great Britain. Her personal lobbying within Dunedin was made easier by her moving to Port Chalmers. Throughout, she was supported by the editors of the *Otago Daily Times* and the *Otago Witness* with editorials and lead articles. Major Richardson provided public support by delivering public addresses on the merits of higher education for girls. When the superintendent of the province, Mr MacAndrew, proved harder to convince, Learmonth Dalrymple lobbied Mrs MacAndrew instead, resulting in her arranging a meeting with her husband. This strategy worked.

Initially, the provincial council considered coeducation a possible option; perhaps, in the interest of economy, girls could be taught alongside the boys at the already established high school. This suggestion prompted public debate, lively letters to the newspapers and another petition, with the result that the provincial council accepted many of Dalrymple's resolutions and proposals, as set out in her letter accompanying the final petition.[94] Otago Girls' High School was opened in 1871, as the first provincial girls' high school in New Zealand. In 1960, the school named its specialist teaching building the Dalrymple Block, and a portrait of Learmonth Dalrymple is prominently displayed. As Sir Julius Vogel put it, she was the 'parent of this institution, the lady through whose immense energy it absolutely sprang into existence'.[95]

Otago Girls' High School and the University of Otago

Otago Girls' High School was opened to girls over nine years of age, with an annual fee of £8. Boarders were to be received at £50 per annum. The curriculum covered all branches of instruction, but it was made clear that if parents wanted daughters to be taught languages other than French, or given tuition in music, these 'extras' would be charged for separately. Both the rector of the Boys' High School and the lady principal of the Girls' High School were to be provided with furnished residences; but the first lady principal, Margaret Burn, was to receive £250 per year, compared with the rector's annual salary of £550.[96]

Other publicly provided forms of girls' secondary education in Otago and Southland followed. Like Otago Girls', all began operating classes for girls in parallel with classes for boys, on adjacent sites and/or with shared facilities, until such time as resources and numbers dictated the establishment of separate buildings on separate sites. In this way, secondary schooling for girls commenced at Invercargill (in 1879), becoming Southland Girls' High School; at Timaru (1880), becoming Timaru Girls' High School; and in Oamaru (1887), becoming Waitaki Girls' High School. These schools served not only their local towns; the boarding accommodation associated with each meant that rural parents had a choice of types of secondary schooling for their daughters, and for many, the advantages of a town girls' school won out over a local district high school or technical school.

Meanwhile, a range of Church and private schools offered parents other choices for their daughters. These opened and closed depending on the initiative, resources, and health of owners, as well as the demand. The most longstanding included the Presbyterian Columba College in Dunedin (established in 1914), later incorporating the earlier schools Braemar House and Girton College (1886). There was also the Anglican St Hilda's Collegiate, Dunedin (1896), and Invercargill's St John's (1918). Those of shorter duration included Archerfield Girls' School in Dunedin (1913–1932) and Melrose College in Invercargill (1918–1922).

Although girls' secondary schooling got off to a flying start in Otago, obtaining university qualifications took a little longer. While the Scottish settlers achieved the establishment of New Zealand's first university at Otago in 1869, the question of women being admitted on the same terms as men had not been considered by the founding fathers. However, it had been considered by Learmonth Dalrymple and her supporters. On 8 August 1871, she presented to the university council a petition signed by 149 women, setting out why 'women should be admitted to all lectures, degrees and scholarships'.[97] What the university council agreed to, however, was 'that women be admitted to all classes, and allowed to compete for all certificates,

Otago Girls' High School, Dunedin, 1871—first public girls' school in New Zealand. OTAGO GIRLS' HIGH SCHOOL

Caroline Freeman (BA 1885), first woman graduate of the University of Otago, 1885. She completed her degree part time whilst teaching. She was the owner/founder of Girton College for Girls, Dunedin (1886–1914) and Girton College for Girls, Christchurch (1897–1911).
OTAGO SETTLERS MUSEUM

equivalent to degrees, conferred by the University of Otago'.[98] This was clearly not equality; it meant that, as in the Oxbridge university model, women had to be satisfied with certificates of competency in the subjects they passed, but would not be awarded degrees.[99] Such discriminatory practice exercised by their own university incensed many locals, who wrote letters to the newspapers and petitioned the university council, but to no effect. It was only when the University of Otago affiliated to the University of New Zealand in 1874, and surrendered its power to grant its own degrees, becoming subject to University of New Zealand regulations, that women were eligible to be awarded degrees on the same conditions as men.

However, the first University of Otago matriculated woman student did not enrol for a degree course until four years later. A major factor in this delay was said to be the professor of classics, G. S. Sale, whose intimidating teaching manner alarmed both men and women students. To women students in particular, Professor Sale was 'a veritable ogre'.[100] It took a strong and able woman to measure up to his standards. Caroline Freeman, a local headmistress and part-time student, did so, and became Otago's first woman graduate in 1885.[101] Two other Otago women later became the first in New Zealand to graduate in their specialist areas: Emily Siedeberg, in medicine, in 1896,[102] and Ethel Benjamin, in law, in 1897.[103] By 1920, 241 women had graduated from Otago, comprising one-third of all New Zealand women graduates. Further, many were not content with a first degree: ninety-eight—40 percent—had also added master's degrees by 1920.[104]

Despite the later entry of women to degree programmes at Otago, Otago Girls' High School's achievements were impressive. Between 1885 and 1920, it educated at least 102 (42 percent) of the women graduating from the University of Otago.[105] These results, however, were often achieved at considerable personal cost. Some women had won University of New Zealand Scholarships, which entitled them to £40 per year for three years; but for most, there was no such assistance.[106] For example, at the University of Otago between 1878 and 1911, only forty-three (27 percent) of the women graduates had been scholarship winners.[107] With examination fees of approximately £18 per year, a scholarship enabled a woman to make ends meet if she had free board and lodging supplied by her family or friends. Women without scholarships, particularly those from country areas, were even more dependent on the goodwill of their families, in an era when it was less acceptable for middle-class women to work in part-time paid employment.

Combining university study with teaching

University costs could be significantly reduced if a student attended training college, went to university part time, and completed a degree while teaching. Nearly half of the women enrolled at the University of Otago in 1898 came into this category. The author of the women's notes in the *Otago University Review*

Emily Hancock Siedeberg (m.McKinnon), first woman doctor, 1896. Dr Siedeberg also completed a BSc in 1901 as well as postgraduate qualifications at Dublin, Berlin, and Edinburgh. She practised medicine in Dunedin for over 30 years.
OTAGO SETTLERS MUSEUM

in May of that year wrote: 'The attempt to combine *university* with a *Normal School* or *pupil-teacher's* course [original italics] … is simply madness.'[108] Caroline Freeman would no doubt have agreed. It took her seven years to complete her degree, combining it as she did with teaching at Otago Girls' High School, including a period as first assistant. Between 1873 and 1877, she had to study for the matriculation examinations while teaching full time as infant mistress at Caversham Primary School. Completing one degree part time was clearly difficult; but Janet Paterson, a teacher at the George Street School in Dunedin, appears to have completed her BA in 1894 and then her MA in 1895. She then launched herself into secondary teaching, at Waitaki Girls' (1901–1902); Southbridge District High School (1902–1905), where she was graded B2 and earning £136 per year; Lawrence District High School (1906–1911), where she was promoted to B1 and earning £138 per year; and finally Balclutha District High School (1912–1925), where, as senior mistress, she earnt £155. She married a

Mr Hewat at some point.[109] Coila Stevenson (BA 1916) started her degree on campus, but completed her final units while teaching at Ashburton High School.[110]

It was even harder to be a teacher in a remote country school and enrolled as an 'exempt' student—that is, not having to attend lectures, but eligible to sit for examinations. The pattern here was to have gained as many university units as possible at training college on a part-time basis, by attending university lectures in addition to a full-time course at the college. In this way, a trained teacher embarking on her career might obtain four or five of the nine units required for degree completion. The more tenacious would then complete a unit a year over four or five years while teaching, in order to graduate. They did so with minimal assistance from the university, other than a recommended text and past examination papers to serve as curriculum guides.

However, at least the partially completed degree students had some face-to-face experience and prior knowledge of the university system and academic expectations. Almost incredibly, there were a few students, including five women primary teachers from Southland, who studied for their entire degrees as 'exempt' students. According to Otago-based historian Dorothy Page, 'the numbers who

Waitaki Girls' High School and pupils, 1904. WAITAKI GIRLS' HIGH SCHOOL

took advantage of the system were never great',[111] but Jane Jamieson, the first dux of Southland Girls' High School, was one who did so. Painstaking research by Page reveals that, having finished her secondary education with distinction (becoming dux in both 1884 *and* 1885),[112] Jane returned to her home farming district of Wild Bush in Southland, where her parents ran a small farm to support their thirteen children. It was thought that as the community was struggling to find a teacher, Jane would be well suited to be the sole-charge teacher of the Wild Bush School; her pupils included five of her brothers and sisters.[113] It is not clear just when Jane began her university studies extramurally, but even if it was in her first year of teaching in 1886, she did remarkably well to complete all nine units in six years, graduating as she did in 1893, while still based at Wild Bush.[114]

By 1894 there were as many women as men graduating from the University of Otago. Back row:
J. Pringle (BA); A. H. Adams (BA); Elizabeth J. Anderson (m.Morrison) (BA); G. H. Fenton (BA).
Middle row: Rose M. Davey (m.Matthews) (BA); Janet Paterson (m.Hewat) (BA); J. Collie (BA);
Edith H. Pearce (m.Bear) (MA); Margaret N. Gellatly (BA).
Front row: C. B. Snow (BA); Katherine MacGregor (m.Paterson) (BA); A. R. Falconer (BA).
Edith Pearce and Margaret Gellatly had both been dux of Otago Girls' and were scholarship holders.
Rose Davey, Janet Paterson, and Margaret Gellatly graduated MA the following year. All went teaching.
Rose Davey was later a missionary in India. HOCKEN COLLECTIONS, UARE TAOKA O HAKENA, UNIVERSITY OF OTAGO S05-049D

For those who studied on campus in Dunedin, the university buildings were not particularly welcoming places, for women or for men. Lecture halls were draughty and ill-lit; convention required that women sit at the front. There was little organised social activity, and the attitudes of some of the male students left much to be desired. In later years, Janet Barr (MA 1903) recalled a science class at Otago: 'I always tried to be in my seat before men arrived in great numbers. This was to avoid having to walk in to the accompaniment of stamping and whistling.'[115]

Although a few women qualified as doctors and lawyers, the majority of Otago graduates took up teaching, with 157 (65 percent) doing so by 1920.[116] Otago provided a high proportion of female secondary principals for over fifty years throughout New Zealand, particularly for private girls' schools. The first woman-graduate principal of Otago Girls' High School was Maria Marchant (MA 1894), a former dux of, and later teacher at, Wellington Girls' High School (1890–1895). She was only twenty-six years old when she was appointed to Otago Girls' in 1895.[117] The combination of her youth and the fact that she was a woman succeeding bachelor Alexander Wilson (MA) were used to justify her starting salary being £100 lower. As the Dunedin correspondent for *The New Zealand Schoolmaster* 'analysed' the situation:

> Quite a bit of indignant correspondence appeared in our dailies at the proposal to engage a woman for the position at a lower salary than that paid to Mr Wilson. Why should there be a difference in the pay of a woman for identically the same work performed by a man?—ask some. Can a woman do the same work as a man? Are they not physically unfit for the strain of continued teaching, and its attendant troubles and worries? Besides, consider the expense of a man. His clothing costs more, his hand is ever in his pocket for things that are unheard of in the economy of women, and last but not least, in nearly every case has he not to provide for his family? The main object of most women is to marry, and then they enter into the practical consideration of their husband's salary, and rarely have to provide at any time for more than themselves.[118]

Maria Marchant's successors, both University of Otago graduates, were Flora Allan (MA 1880), who had been dux of Otago Girls' High School and then taught there for thirty-two years,[119] and Mary McGowan King (MA 1906), who had attended Waitaki Girls' High School, had already been principal of Southland Girls' High School, and was to remain as principal of Otago Girls' for twenty-two years.[120]

Mary Harriet McGowan King (MA 1906)

OTAGO GIRLS' HIGH SCHOOL

Mary King—principal with flair, c.1935.

Mary King was an outstanding scholar, teacher, and principal of two girls' high schools in turn. Her command of the English language could be described as Churchillian and her English classes as magical. She was also a radical and a political activist.

It was clear that from a young age, Mary King, the daughter of an Oamaru storeman, was going places. By fourteen she was the senior dux of Waitaki Girls' High School and topped the Junior Scholarship list for the whole of New Zealand. At the University of Otago, she won two Senior Scholarships; this financial support no doubt enabled her to complete a BA, followed by an MA in 1906, with first class honours in English and French. At the age of twenty-three she joined the staff of Southland Girls' High School. By 1909 she was first assistant and by 1919 she was principal.

When Mary King was appointed principal of Otago Girls' High School in 1922, some in Dunedin were not at all sure about her suitability. It was all very well that she had already been a principal of a girls' high school, 'but was she a lady?'[121] The unorthodox Miss King dyed her bobbed hair, wore light-coloured stockings, played tennis with a partner in braces, rode a bicycle, and had the audacity to carry strawberries uncovered through the streets of Dunedin. Her style was so untraditional that some remained as shocked about her appearance and behaviour as they did that she was not a former 'old girl'. To make matters worse in the eyes of some parents, from 1930 she and her sister Helen were major shareholders in a local taxi business. Later they turned to hiring out cars. Mary King, a theosophist, was drawn to the concepts of social credit because of the notion of individual freedom. In 1931, she presented a public lecture on these ideas and was quickly reprimanded by her school's board of governors. Although she was more careful from that point, after her retirement she was a foundation member of the New Zealand Social Credit Political League when it formed in 1953, and was for a time national vice-president.

As a teacher and then principal for twenty-two years, Mary King was the opposite of the traditional, aloof, and very proper 'lady principal'. The school history records that 'the inescapable thing about the new order was its vitality', which 'flowed over into every aspect of school life'.[122] She did insist on the maintenance of high academic standards, but she also kept reading from the Apocrypha in assembly, and all the while displayed her personal flair and liking for brightly coloured, richly textured clothes. She was followed everywhere by a series of golden retrievers—all called 'Rufus'. They were favourites on the sports field. Her love of English literature, drama, dancing, and music was reflected in the dances, concerts, and dramatic and musical productions she organised throughout her career. For example, at Otago Girls' High School, she wrote and produced *The Ballad of Light and Beauty*, which was talked about for years afterwards. Her view of a school course, she said, was 'not an aggregation of subjects to be learned but a field of experience, an environment presenting opportunities for the acquisition of knowledge and the exercise of faculties, suited to the age of the pupil'.[123]

Otago Girls' High School on parade, 1906. OTAGO GIRLS' HIGH SCHOOL

Women graduates (1885–1920) from the University of Otago who became secondary school principals

Caroline Freeman	BA 1885	Girton College, Dunedin	1886–1911
Catherine Ferguson	MA 1892	Waitaki Girls' High School, Oamaru	1893–1920
Isabel Fraser	MA 1889	Wanganui Girls' High School	1894–1910
Rachel McKerrow	MA 1896	Prince Albert College for Girls, Auckland	1896
Frances Ross	MA 1900	Girton College, Christchurch Columba College, Dunedin	1897–1911 1914–1930
Emma Rainforth	MA 1893	Prince Albert College for Girls	1897
Mabel Salmond	BA 1896	Prince Albert College for Girls	1898–1900
Barbara Watt	MA 1900	Timaru Girls' High School	1900–1924
Marion Thomson (m.Thompson)	MA 1899	Prince Albert College for Girls Solway College, Masterton	1901–1906 1916–1942
Margaret Smyth	MA 1897	St Andrew's College, Dunedin	1903–1919
Lena Hampton	BA 1902	St Matthew's Collegiate, Masterton	1903–1913
Christina Cruickshank	MA 1896 MSc 1906	Southland Girls' High School Wanganui Girls' High School	1907–1911 1911–1932
Violet Greig	MA 1900 BSc 1905	Napier Girls' High School Wellington Girls' College	1910–1926 1926–1938
Fanny Shand	BA 1908	Craighead, Timaru	1913–1926
Flora Hodges	MA 1901	New Plymouth Girls' High School	1915–1916
Janet Barr	MA 1908	New Plymouth Girls' High School Iona Girls' College, Havelock North Timaru Girls' High School	1916–1921 1921–1924 1924–1938
Gloriana Gibson	MA 1903	Melrose College, Invercargill	1918–1922
Mary Harriet McGowan King	MA 1906	Southland Girls' High School Otago Girls' High School	1919–1921 1922–1944
Jessie Wilson	MA 1918	Waitaki Girls' High School	1920–1949
Alice Budd	MA 1904	Queen Margaret's College, Wellington	1920–1921
Patricia Clark	MA 1915	Christchurch Girls' High School	1925–1940
Margaret Samuel	MSc 1914	Southland Girls' High School Avonside Girls' High School Christchurch Girls' High School	1926–1931 1932–1941 1941–1948
Agnes Loudon	MA 1913	Epsom Girls' Grammar	1930–1947
Jenny Stewart	BA 1910 MA (Dublin) 1924	Nelson Girls' College Christchurch Girls' High School	1932–1946 1948–1954

Women graduates and marriage

Although University of Otago staff member Dr Truby King had earlier accused university-educated women of turning their backs on marriage in favour of a career, 100 (41 percent) of Otago women graduates up to 1920 did in fact marry. Page's analysis of the first twenty-eight married women graduates to 1900 reveals that they mostly had smaller-than-average families of two or three children.[124] While some graduates married immediately, others did so after a period of paid employment in other parts of New Zealand. Some outstanding Otago scholars to do so included Jessie Polson (BSc 1896, MA 1896). Jessie's father, a farm manager in North Otago, had sent Jessie to Waitaki Girls' High School in Oamaru, where she was the first dux in 1888.[125] She was also the first winner of the Otago Women's Scholarship, and the first woman to gain degrees in both arts and science.[126] Jessie taught for eighteen months before marrying a Mr Kelly, a Hawke's Bay farmer. The couple had five children.[127]

While Edith Pearce (MA 1894) taught for longer, she too ended her career in Hawke's Bay. Considered by Professor Gilray (English language and literature) to be 'the best student he had ever taught at Otago',[128] Edith was the daughter of the Caversham Town Clerk. She had been dux of Otago Girls' High School in 1888, a Junior Scholarship holder, and, in the senior scholarship examination, winner of the prestigious John Tinline Prize in English.[129] Perhaps because there were no teaching positions available in Dunedin, she left Dunedin in 1895 to take up a position as secondary teaching assistant at Ashburton High School. After two years there she moved to Nelson Girls' College where, in 1897, five of the staff were graduates, including Barbara Watt, also from Otago. The principal, Beatrice Gibson (MA 1888 Canterbury), reflected in later years that these Otago graduates added 'some of the grit of the Southern University ... to Nelson's school'.[130] Edith remained at Nelson Girls' for five years.[131] Although she is not documented in the Napier Girls' High School history, official records list Edith as a teacher there in 1902. Her career ended shortly after when, at the age of thirty-one, she married Bruce Bear, manager of the Napier Gas Company, and did not teach again. The couple had one daughter who died in infancy, but no other children.[132]

Like Edith Pearce, many women graduates married later in life, a trend identified both in Dorothy Page's research on the women graduates at Otago to 1900, and in Barbara Solomon's research on American women graduates. For example, Mabel Salmond (BA 1896) began her eighteen-year teaching career at Prince Albert College in Auckland the year after she graduated. In 1900, she returned to Dunedin, where she taught at Otago Girls' High School for nine years before moving to Wellington Girls' High School, remaining there until 1915.[133] According to Page, she was '43 when she took on the family of widower William Kidston'.[134] Jessie Banks (MA 1918) married only when she retired in 1949, after a twenty-nine-year career at Waitaki Girls' High School.[135] Emily Siedeberg (MB ChB 1896, BSc 1901) was even older, marrying at the age of fifty-five.[136]

While marriage officially ended a woman's career, there were a few exceptions among the Otago graduates. For example, it was deemed appropriate to employ married women during periods of war, when male teachers were serving overseas; or in a case of economic hardship caused by the ill health or death of a husband. Married Otago graduates who taught during World War One, for example, included Kate Webber (m.Buckland) (BA 1897) and Isabella McKellar (m.Hercus) (BA 1899).[137] Their contemporary, Charlotte MacGregor (MA 1899), later Mrs Wood, the wife of a local clergyman, taught at Wellington Girls' College between 1918 and 1926. Her salary of £354 per year was no doubt a welcome relief.[138] Earlier in her career she had taught at

The Farnie family

Lawyer Thomas Cheyne Farnie (MA) graduated in law from the University of Otago in 1882. He believed in the value of a university education for his daughters. All three of his daughters attended Timaru Girls' High School, went to the University of Otago, and gained master's degrees before taking up teaching. The first was Violet Cheyne Farnie (MA 1912); having graduated, she taught at Akaroa District High School until 1922, but then resigned, presumably to marry a Mr Stevenson.[139] Her sister, Dorothy Cheyne Farnie (MA 1915), returned to her old school in Timaru to teach for a year in 1915 before moving to Geraldine District High School in 1916, then marrying a Mr Slater. Winifred Cheyne Farnie was dux of Timaru Girls' and won a University Entrance Scholarship. She graduated MA in zoology in 1917, having also won the Bowen Prize for outstanding scholarship in that subject. She taught for three years at Geraldine District High School before taking up a teaching position at Waitaki Girls' High School, where she remained from 1925 to 1943.[140]

Nelson Girls' (1901–1903), Ashburton High School (1903–1905), and Hampden District High School (1906). This level of experience had no doubt impressed principal Mary McLean (MA 1890), who employed two other married women around the same time. One was another Otago graduate, Annie Cox (Otago Girls' High dux 1901, MA 1906), a teacher of even longer standing. Annie had served Palmerston North Girls' High School as a teacher for eleven years before coming to Wellington Girls' to teach as Mrs Chrisp between 1917 and 1919.[141]

First women lawyers and doctors

While women graduate teachers came to be generally accepted as essential, especially after the opening up of free secondary places, they were not in competition with men teachers for jobs, because virtually all secondary positions were specified as for either a man or a woman. The same was not true of the women who graduated in law and medicine from the University of Otago between 1885 and 1920. Only three women graduated in law during this period: Ethel Benjamin (LLB 1897), Annie Rees (LLB 1911, MA 1902), and Esther Ongley

Ethel Benjamin (m.De Costa) (LLB 1897)

Ethel Rebecca Benjamin (m.De Costa) (LLB 1897), first woman lawyer, 1897. Ethel practised law in Dunedin for a number of years before moving to London.

The daughter of a Jewish businessman, Ethel Benjamin attended Otago Girls' High School and went on to study law at the University of Otago. At her graduation in 1897, she was accorded the honour of being the first woman to make an official speech at the university. She took the opportunity to warn those assembled that although she was the first woman law graduate, the bid by women for equal rights in all fields was 'growing keener and keener day by day and year by year'. The Female Law Practitioners Act 1896 enabled her to establish and run her own practice in Dunedin, but it is likely that her lack of local legal contacts was what forced her to advertise her legal services. She may not have realised that this was actually against the law. This unfortunate start served only to fuel the wrath of the District Law Society, and as Page puts it, 'her exclusion from the Bar Dinner was symbolic of the District Law Society's attitude to her'. Ethel ran her practice for several years, married a stockbroker, Mr De Costa, in 1907, at the age of thirty-two, and some time after moved to England. Apart from the fact that the marriage was childless, little more is known of Ethel's career. She died in a bombing raid on London in 1943.[142]

(LLB 1919, BA Victoria 1916).[143] More is known about Ethel Benjamin than the other two, although it is likely that Annie Rees taught at private school/s in the years between gaining her master's and law degrees. It is also not clear just why Esther Ongley, a former pupil of Waitaki Girls' High School,[144] chose to change universities and study for her law degree at Otago, given that she had been a successful arts student at Victoria University College, and that institution had already produced its first woman law graduate in 1913.

Of the first women medical graduates of the University of Otago a lot more is known. By 1900 there were six, and by 1920 this had increased to twenty-five. Emily Siedeberg and Margaret Cruickshank were the first, graduating in 1896 and 1897 respectively. The four women doctors who graduated together in 1900 (out of a graduating class of eleven)[145] included Constance Frost. She had attended Auckland Grammar, and completed a BA at Otago in 1892. She is listed as a teacher with the Otago Education Board in 1891, and may well have taught locally for a time while studying to be a doctor.[146] Dr Frost worked firstly in Adelaide and then at Auckland Hospital as a bacteriologist. It was there she contracted influenza and died in 1920.[147] Her contemporary, Jane Kinder, a farmer's daughter from South Otago, attended Otago Girls' High School and, like Constance Frost, did some teaching during her medical studies. In 1897 she taught at the Stony Creek School, north-east of Balclutha.[148] Dr Kinder died only two years after graduating MB ChB in 1900, as a result of treating Torrens Islanders with plague.[149] The other two women doctors of the same class combined family life with lifelong careers, and both were also active in community work. Daisy Platts (m.Platts-Mills), the daughter of a clergyman and former Otago Girls' High School student, was for six years the house physician in the children's ward of Wellington Hospital. She worked tirelessly for the YWCA, League of Mothers, Society for the Protection of Women and Children, and as a member of the Wellington Hospital Board.[150] Alice Woodward (m.Horsley) ran a large medical practice in Auckland until she was nearly eighty years of age, and was also honorary anaesthetist at Auckland Hospital. She was awarded an OBE in 1939 for providing free medical care at the Dock Street Mission during the Depression. Less well known is her untiring work to educate about and promote the use of contraception, long before it became legal or common practice.

Margaret Cruickshank (MB ChB 1903)
Christina Cruickshank (MA 1896, MSc 1906)

Dr Margaret Cruickshank (MB ChB 1903), 1897.

Christina Cruickshank (MA 1896, MSc 1906), c. 1930. Principal Southland Girls' High School 1907–1910; principal Wanganui Girls' High School 1911–1932.

Two early outstanding scholars were the Cruickshank twins from Outram in Central Otago. Their father was an engineer who was responsible for road and bridge construction in Waiheno County. Their mother died when they were young and the twins and their younger siblings were raised by an older sister.

Their father obviously believed in his daughters' education, and Christina and Margaret were sent to Otago Girls' High School. They were joint duxes of the school in 1891, and both won University Entrance Scholarships in the same year, gaining exactly the same marks. They studied at Otago University, boarding with Mr and Mrs Neill, the local stationmaster and his wife, and cooking meals for harvesters at Cherry Farm to earn money during the holidays. Christina became the founding principal of Southland Girls' High School, and later was principal of Wanganui Girls' High School. Margaret became a doctor and took up general practice in Waimate; after she died treating patients in the influenza epidemic of 1918, the residents erected a large statue in her honour, one of very few public monuments to a New Zealand woman.

Dr Cruickshank had been Waimate's doctor for over twenty years when she died while treating her patients in the 1918 influenza epidemic. The nine-foot statue, believed to be the first dedicated to a New Zealand woman, was unveiled in 1923 by her twin, Christina Cruickshank, then principal of Wanganui Girls' High School.

Dr Daisy Platts (m.Platts-Mills)
(MB ChB 1900), house physician,
Wellington Hospital and later
Wellington Hospital Board member.
ALEXANDER TURNBULL LIBRARY, WELLINGTON, NZ. SP ANDREW COLL
G-14569-1/1

Helen Baird (BA 1898, MB ChB 1903)
set out for the University of Glasgow
with her sister Agnes in 1898 and both
graduated in medicine. As Dr Cowie
she ran a lifelong general practice in
Masterton alongside her husband.
ALEXANDER TURNBULL LIBRARY, WELLINGTON, NZ. COWIE FAMILY COLL
F-190383-1/2

Completing a medical degree at Otago was one thing, but travelling to the other side of the world to undertake postgraduate study was something else again. The first to do so was Helen Baird, later Dr Cowie. Helen Baird, the daughter of a clergyman, attended Southland Girls' High School, where she was dux in 1892.[151] Interestingly, her first degree was not in medicine but in arts (BA 1898). Nevertheless, she and her sister Agnes set off to study medicine at the University of Glasgow. Both sisters qualified. Helen married Dr Cowie and together they ran a lifelong medical practice in Masterton, where they were later joined by their son.

Doctors Platts-Mills, Woodward, and Cowie practised medicine all their working lives. That they did so as married women established new precedents. Fifteen (60 percent) of Otago's female medical graduates in the period 1896–1920 did marry.[152]

Introducing domestic science as a university subject

Otago was early to establish both medicine and domestic science, but for very different reasons. Central to the lobbying for domestic science as a university subject were two of the medical school lecturers, Dr Frederick Batchelor and Dr Truby King.

Initially, both men were opposed to all forms of higher education for girls and women, as Chapter 1 outlined; but as more and more women graduated from the University of Otago, they adapted their views to focus on what university subjects would be appropriate for women to study. It was clear that neither believed medicine was one of these. For example, in a 1909 public address in Dunedin on 'The Effect of Advanced Education of Women on the Vitality of the Race', Batchelor commented that:

> ... Our present educational system encourages and invites young women to enter a course of study for which Nature never intended them ... The average male (medical) student and sometimes the student below the average usually turns out a fairly useful and successful practitioner: the brilliant female student at best only attains mediocrity.

Taking up this theme, his colleague Truby King's speech added:

> As to the education of women for the professions, I agree with Dr Batchelor that it is an absolutely indefensible thing ... It is impossible for me to convey how strongly I feel that the common education of men and women upon similar lines was one of the most preposterous farces ever perpetrated.

Emily Siedeberg (MB ChB 1896), New Zealand's first woman doctor, who attended Otago Girls' High School, studied at the University of Otago, and practised in Dunedin, spoke out against such statements by Batchelor and King:

> Speaking for myself, I can only say that the result [of gaining a medical degree] has been increased good health and increased happiness. I can also think of nine lady medicals who have passed under Dr Batchelor's own hands and who have never broken down and are at this moment in excellent health, four or five of whom are now married, with healthy families. I should like Dr Batchelor to point to one case of a lady doctor who has permanently broken down during a course of study .... I do not agree with Dr King that it is a heavy mental tax and nervous strain upon them [women medical students] .... As a doctor I find it is the girls

who are kept at home with no mental interests who develop neurasthenia in the most marked degree, especially of the morbid or melancholy type, and that their sisters who take up some occupation to keep their minds engaged are the most healthy-minded ones, taking a broader and happier view of life altogether.[153]

Dr Agnes Bennett, the Superintendent of St Helen's Hospital in Wellington challenged Batchelor and King in *The Dominion*:

Who will arrogate to themselves the right to say what Nature did intend for women or men? … Man may develop every latent faculty in his brain. … Is woman to stifle the inborn yearnings of her intellect that she may be no more than a healthy animal to minister to and apparently compensate for the impaired vitality of the man? Can true progress possibly consist of a man of highly cultured intellect pacing side by side with a woman who is no more than an intelligent vegetable?

That women in the medical profession only reach mediocrity is a statement as unfair as it is untrue. One day spent at the New Hospital in London (entirely officered and managed by women) would completely disillusion Dr Batchelor if he would go to it with an open mind. … The true crux of the whole question is the trained mind. The best training for any walk of life is that which teaches a boy or girl sound reason and good judgement.[154]

Of Drs King and Batchelor, Dr Agnes Bennett would later reflect: 'I consider those two men were the greatest obstacle to women's progress and emancipation that New Zealand has known.'[155]

Although the views of King and Batchelor were to prove outdated when women took on all facets of war work at home and abroad, they were nevertheless listened to by their contemporaries at the University of Otago. Those initially opposed to all higher education of women changed tack, and sought to ensure that if women were to insist on university study, then the university should offer programmes more specifically designed for them, both as women and as future teachers of domestic science. At Otago, this resulted in the introduction of New Zealand's only academic programme in home science. The sponsor of an endowed chair in the subject was Mr John Studholme, a South Canterbury farmer. He had first offered it to Canterbury University College in 1907. When they turned down the idea, he turned to the University of Otago Council in 1909 and offered £200 for three years, with a government subsidy

*Professor Winifred Lily
Boys-Smith (Tripos 1895),
Professor of Home Science,
1911–1920.
Recruited from England,
she was New Zealand's first
woman professor.*

of an equal amount, topped up by the indefatigable King and Batchelor, who pledged to equal Studholme's contribution. It was thought that a suitable person might be found in the United States for £500–600 per year.[156]

The proposal did not go unchallenged by staff or students, and the reactions of the council members were mixed. However, the motion to accept Mr Studholme's offer was carried by six votes to four in June 1910. The chair in home science and domestic arts was duly appointed, and the incumbent became the first woman appointed to a professorship in a New Zealand university. She was Winifred Boys-Smith, aged forty-five, a Girton College graduate with a Natural Science Tripos, who was recruited from the prestigious Cheltenham Ladies' College, where she had been the science lecturer in the training department.[157] She was offered £500 per annum for four years, and authorised to engage a lecturer assistant at £250.[158] Professor Boys-Smith chose well. Helen Rawson had excellent qualifications in science from Cambridge University and a postgraduate diploma from King's College London. In 1911, these two women began to teach a degree and diploma course in home science, with permission to offer individual subjects without further commitment,[159] the latter no doubt having the full approval of sponsors King and Batchelor.

Significant numbers of women took up home science from the time it was available in 1911, and as the annual lists of graduates document, many chose to take diplomas in the subject rather than full degrees. It is for this reason that the numbers of women graduates in the subject appear rather low in the period to 1920. What is notable, and perhaps a consequence of introducing the domestic science programme, is that after 1911, the number of women with degrees in science declined, and as a consequence, fewer Otago women science graduates were available to teach the subject in schools.

Professor Helen Rawson (BSc TCD 1919) succeeded Professor Winifred Boys-Smith in 1921. She had earlier been appointed a lecturer in the School of Home Science (1916–1920). When she married Professor Noel Benson in 1923 she resigned as Professor of Home Science. She was a founding member of the Otago branch of the New Zealand Federation of University Women and national office holder over many years.

HOCKEN COLLECTIONS, UARE TAOKA O HAKENA, UNIVERSITY OF OTAGO S08-006A

From 1871 until the establishment of the Bachelor of Science degree in 1885, students could select one of two programmes of study as part of a Bachelor of Arts: a literary or a scientific course. The literary course consisted of the following subjects: first year—junior Greek, junior mathematics, mental philosophy (in 1871), natural science (from 1872); second year—senior Latin, senior Greek or English, senior mathematics, natural science or mental science (including political economy); third year—Greek or English, moral philosophy (including political economy), natural philosophy. The scientific course consisted of: first year—Latin, mathematics, and natural science (including chemistry, geology, mineralogy, and palaeontology); second year—Latin, mathematics, natural science, and mental science; third year—natural philosophy and natural science. Unless students progressed to a master's degree, where their specialty was recorded upon graduation, the Bachelor of Arts qualification shown in the records could have been in either specialty.

After the Bachelor of Science degree was introduced in 1885, the first woman BSc graduate was Jessie Polson (BA 1895, BSc 1896), who added an MA specialising in electricity in 1896. Prior to 1920 there were eighteen women science graduates. Of the first twenty-three MSc students there were twelve MAs (in either electricity; electricity and magnetism; chemistry, mathematics, and physics; or zoology) and eleven MScs. All but six of the total number of science graduates in this period went on to teach science in schools, predominantly at Otago Girls', Waitaki Girls', Timaru Girls', and Wellington Girls'. Four women scientists of this period, all former pupils of Otago Girls', were destined to be school principals: Mary Fraser (MA heat and electricity 1889); Catherine Ferguson (MA chemistry 1892); Christina Cruickshank (MA mathematics and physics 1896, MSc 1900); and Margaret Samuel (MSc mathematics 1914). What is clear from an analysis of subjects studied to 1920 is that the University of Otago produced more women graduates in mathematics and science than the other three university colleges, and that over 75 percent of these were taught at Otago Girls' High School by former pupils of the school, including: Mary Fraser (MA 1889), 1890–1893; Helen Alexander (BA 1891), 1894–1913; Susannah McKnight (MA 1902, MSc 1907), 1903–1916; and Margaret Gellatly (MA 1895), 1917–1928.

Women scientists were also destined to take up lecturing posts at the university. For example, Gladys Cameron (MSc 1919, BHSc 1914) had attended Otago Girls' High School, where she was dux in 1906. Gladys completed degrees in science and home science before going to Wellington Girls' High School to teach for four years. She then returned to Otago and completed an MSc before being appointed to the staff, where she taught bacteriology until 1928. She died suddenly at thirty-nine years of age.[160] Another to secure a university position was Mary Betts (m.Aitken) from Nelson Girls' College, who won both Junior and Senior University Scholarships before graduating with an MSc with first class honours in botany in 1917. She was appointed as a lecturer in botany in 1919, a position she held until 1923, when she resigned on her marriage and departure for Scotland.[161] Someone who stayed longer was Agnes Blackie (MSc 1919). She had attended Otago Girls' High School and gained a University Entrance Scholarship to Otago in 1914. Her subject was physics, and she held a number of full-time and part-time positions in the Faculty of Science over many years, before retiring in 1957.[162] Another Otago graduate, Marion Fyfe, won a University Entrance Scholarship, graduated with a BSc in 1919 and, some twenty-six years later, gained an MSc. Marion Fyfe lectured in zoology at Otago until 1957.[163] In 1951, the Portobello Marine Institute was taken over by the University of Otago, and a former science student, Dr Elizabeth Batham (MSc 1940, PhD 1948), was appointed lecturer-in-charge.[164]

The Home Science School at Otago employed a number of women scientists, most from outside New Zealand. Helen Rawson succeeded Winifred Boys-Smith as professor and dean of the faculty in 1920, but resigned in 1924 upon her marriage to Professor Benson. American Professor Mrs Ann Strong (BSc 1904) was a divorcee when she took up both leadership positions in the Home Science School; she remained in charge until 1941. During her stewardship she appointed Columbia University graduates on three-year contracts at £500 per annum: Gladys McGill (BSc) as lecturer in clothing and textiles, and Dr Lilian Storms (PhD) as lecturer in chemistry and nutrition. Dr Storms' subject replacement was New Zealander Dr Elizabeth Gregory (MHSc 1929, PhD 1932 London) who lectured from 1928 to 1941, before becoming the first New Zealand woman graduate to be appointed professor in a New Zealand university. She was professor and dean of home science until 1961.[165]

Students' Revue, Otago University Dramatic Society, 1927. ALEXANDER TURNBULL LIBRARY, WELLINGTON, NZ. HORACE HODGE COLL FMS-098-001

In other parts of the university, there were few women academic staff. One of the first, however, was Mary Turnbull (MA 1917). She had attended Otago Girls' High School, and was both an entrance scholar and a senior scholar at the University of Otago. Having gained a first class MA in Latin and French in 1917, she was appointed to lecture in Latin in that year. Her thirty-four-year career ended in 1951 when she retired as senior lecturer in classics.[166] It took much longer to appoint women to senior academic positions in other parts of the University of Otago. For example, Dr Margaret Dalziel (MA Canterbury 1937, DPhil Oxon), formerly a reader in English, was promoted to professor in 1966.[167]

The total number of students remained small in the early years; for example, when Caroline Freeman first enrolled in 1879, there was a total of 111 students; when statistics were first separated by gender in 1891, there were 177 men and thirty-six women; ten years later, there were 203 men and fifty-four women. The impact of the flow-on effect of free places in secondary schools meant that the first increase in women students appeared in 1905, when 117 women (61 percent of students) were enrolled—a proportion never since exceeded save for the World War One years; for example, there were only five fewer women than men among the students in 1918.[168]

Despite the generally smaller numbers of women students, a large number of them did not stop at one degree. Dorothy Page calculated that of the fifty-eight women graduates to 1900, over half proceeded to master's degrees, compared with 37 percent of male graduates.[169] Of the women graduates to 1920, a number took out multiple degrees in arts and sciences; for example, Violet Greig (MA 1900, BSc 1905) and Annie Inkster (MA 1908, MSc 1909).

However, Susannah McKnight topped all of these with a total of five degrees over twenty-five years. She had attended Otago Girls' High School, where she was dux in 1897, and having gained a University Entrance Scholarship, she began her studies with a BA, graduating in 1901, then adding an MA in 1902, and a BSc in 1903. Between 1903 and 1916 she taught science and mathematics at Otago Girls' High School, and whilst there completed an MSc in mathematics and physics in 1907. Susannah McKnight (later Mrs Sinclair) then changed careers: she studied for a medical degree, graduating MB ChB in 1923.[170] In so doing, she was one of the more mature women medical students of the era, and took the term 'being an educated woman' to new heights.

Notes

91 Morrell, 1969, p. 2.
92 Wallis, 1972, p. 12.
93 Wallis, 1972, p. 23.
94 *Ibid*; Thompson, 1920.
95 Wallis, 1972, p. 230
96 *Ibid*.
97 Thompson, 1920, p. 60.
98 *Ibid*.
99 Gardner, 1979.
100 Gardner, 1979, p. 82.
101 *University of New Zealand Calendar*, 1948, p. 43.
102 *University of New Zealand Calendar*, 1902, p. 203.
103 *University of New Zealand Calendar*, 1902, p. 190.
104 Morris Matthews, 2006b.
105 Morris Matthews, 2006b. The Otago Girls' High School Jubilee magazine published
      in 1921 lists former pupil graduates and is one of the few schools to do so. Unless
      graduates feature in scholarship or dux lists, or in school or community histories, it
      is difficult to determine the secondary school attended. Hence the secondary school
      attended by seventy-six (30 percent) of the Otago graduates remains unknown.
106 *University of New Zealand Calendar*, 1888.
107 Gardner, 1979.
108 Gardner, 1979, p. 102.
109 *AJHR*, 1903, E-1; *AJHR*, 1907, E-12, p. 12; Campbell, 1930, p. 11; *New Zealand Gazette*,
      1891, p. 258; *New Zealand Gazette*, 1900, p. 1263; Ramsay, Stead, & Ludemann, 1987,
      p. 200; Stephens, 1965, p. 96.
110 Ashburton High School, 1956.
111 Page, 1992, p. 110.
112 Deaker, 1979, p. 135.
113 Page, 1992.
114 Jane later married Invercargill chemist, E. B. Jones, a widower with a family that Jane
      cared for along with their own daughter. She died aged thirty-four (Page, 1992).
115 Page, 1992, p. 103.
116 Morris Matthews, 2006a.
117 Harding, 1982; Lee, 1996; Wallis, 1972.
118 *NZSM*, October 1895, p. 35.
119 Harding, 1982; Penfold, Macdonald, & Williams, 1991, p. 37; Wallis, 1972.
120 Deaker, 1979; Wallis, 1972.
121 Wallis, 1972, p. 87.
122 Taylor, L. 1998; Wallis, 1972, p. 89.
123 *Ibid*.
124 Page, 1992.
125 Ramsay et al., 1987, p. 211.
126 Page, 1992; University of New Zealand, 1948, p. 65.
127 Page, 1992.
128 Page, 1992, p. 111.
129 *Ibid*; University of New Zealand, 1948; Wallis, 1972.

130 Mills, 1933, p. 28.
131 Ashburton High School, 1956, p. 17; *New Zealand Gazette*, 1900, p. 1266; Voller, 1982, p. 243.
132 Page, 1992.
133 Arthur & Buttle, 1950; Harding, 1982; Wallis, 1972.
134 Page, 1992, p. 111.
135 Murray, 1951.
136 Page, 1992.
137 *Ibid*.
138 *AJHR*, 1907, E-12, p. 12; Ashburton High School, 1956, p. 18; Harding, 1982; Mills, 1933, p. 136; *New Zealand Gazette*, 1900, p. 1264; Page, 1992; University of New Zealand, 1948.
139 Gillespie, 1958, pp. 17, 34.
140 Lawrence, 1980, p. 202; Penfold et al., 1991, p. 146; Ramsay et al., 1987, p. 20.
141 *AJHR*, 1907, E-12, p. 12; *AJHR*, 1909, E-12, p. 11; *AJHR*, 1913, E-6, p. 21; Harding, 1982, p. 171; *Otago Daily Times*, 1921, p. 106.
142 Labrum, 1991, pp. 75–77; Page, 1992, p. 122.
143 University of New Zealand, 1948.
144 Ramsay et al., 1987.
145 Morrell, 1969, p. 83; Morris Matthews, 2006a.
146 *New Zealand Gazette*, 1891, p. 749; Northey, 1988, p. 260; University of New Zealand, 1948.
147 Page, 1992.
148 Stephens, 1965, p. 106.
149 Page, 1992.
150 *Ibid*.
151 Deaker, 1979, p. 135.
152 Morris Matthews, 2006a.
153 Manson & Manson, 1960, pp. 63–64.
154 Manson & Manson, 1960, pp. 64–65.
155 Manson & Manson, 1960, p. 69.
156 Morrell, 1969, p. 95.
157 Macdonald, 1982; McDonald, 2007.
158 Thompson, 1920.
159 *Ibid*.
160 Penfold et al., 1991, pp. 20, 36; University of New Zealand, 1948; Wallis, 1972.
161 Morrell, 1969, p. 124; University of New Zealand, 1948; *University of Otago Calendar*, 1920–1924.
162 Morrell, 1969, p. 196.
163 *Ibid*.
164 Jillett, 2007; Morrell, 1969, p. 176.
165 Campbell, 2007; Morrell, 1969, p. 131; Taylor, 2007a, b.
166 *Otago Daily Times*, 1921, pp. 109, 174.
167 Morrell, 1969, p. 233.
168 Campbell, 1930, p. 285.
169 Page, 1992.
170 University of New Zealand, 1948; Wallis, 1972, pp. 80, 175.

CHAPTER 4

Leading the way at Canterbury
(1873–1945)

Canterbury College, Christchurch.

MACMILLAN BROWN LIBRARY, UNIVERSITY OF CANTERBURY, R. P. MOORE PHOTOGRAPH, UNIVERSITY OF CANTERBURY PHOTOGRAPHS COLL 1995/3, NEG NO. 257B

The first woman graduated from Otago in 1885. By then, Canterbury University College already had 'about one hundred women students',[171] and had produced eight women graduates; seven had master's degrees, and all were teaching.[172] Two of this group, the first two women with master's degrees in New Zealand, Helen Connon (1881) and Kate Edger (1882), were later to be the first New Zealand women graduates to lead girls' secondary schools—Christchurch Girls' High School and Nelson Girls' College respectively.

Indeed, Helen Connon had been the first woman to enrol at Canterbury in 1876, and was to become the college's first New Zealand woman graduate. Unlike Otago, Canterbury from the outset established the principle of equal rights to attend classes and be awarded degrees. However, the mother of sixteen-year-old Helen Connon had to negotiate directly for her admission with the newly arrived Scottish professor, John MacMillan Brown. In later years, MacMillan Brown commented that 'I gave my ready consent as far as lectures were concerned and said that I would do my best to gain the same privileges in the lecture rooms of the other professors.'[173] The language used reflects MacMillan Brown's attitude that higher education was not a right but a privilege. His unique blend of liberalism and political astuteness was right for the times in colonial Christchurch: the college needed student numbers, and male students alone were not going to keep it afloat financially. As many commentators have since agreed, Canterbury was fortunate in having Helen Connon, not only as its first woman Bachelor of Arts in English, history, and geography (shared with Australian Anne Bolton in 1880), but also as its first woman Master of Arts (with first class honours) in 1881.[174] At the time

Helen Connon (MA (Hons) 1881), outstanding scholar and first woman Master of Arts in New Zealand. Appointed principal of Christchurch Girls' High School in 1883, she continued in this role after her marriage to Professor John MacMillan Brown in 1886, remaining in it until 1894 despite having two daughters. Helen Connon Hall is named in her honour.

MACMILLAN BROWN LIBRARY, UNIVERSITY OF CANTERBURY, P. SCHOURUP PHOTOGRAPH
MACMILLAN BROWN COLL 1991/1, NEG NO. 42K

Connon was awarded her MA at the age of twenty-two, she was already the principal of Christchurch Girls' High School. There seems little doubt that, as the 1973 history of the University of Canterbury claimed, 'Helen Connon both prepared and inspired her girls to seek degrees, and set a standard of scholarly teaching which had influence throughout the colony'.[175]

Historical evidence certainly points to the fact that Helen Connon and her Canterbury graduate staff sent ever-increasing numbers of their pupils from Christchurch Girls' High School across to the neighbouring Canterbury University College. While Gardner et al. claim that 'it seems probable that in this period (1873–1893) Canterbury College had a larger proportion of women students than any other coeducational university institution in the world',[176] they take Professor MacMillan Brown to task for his 1923 boast that Canterbury College was the first coeducational university institution in the world. As the 1973 *A History of the University of Canterbury* points out, this honour had been won by the North American institution, Oberlin College, in 1833, with its first woman student graduating in 1841. However, not to be outdone, Gardner et al. do go on to speculate that within the British Empire, Canterbury College might well have been the leader in university coeducation. In 1979, Gardner backed up this claim with the statistics that Canterbury College awarded eighty-five degrees (59 percent of the total) to women during the nineteenth century, more than any other New Zealand institution.[177] However, a rechecking of the Canterbury records for this book reveals the numbers to be even higher than this. Between 1880 and 1899, 108 women were awarded degrees at Canterbury, so the percentage of degrees going to women may well have set an all-time record for coeducational universities.[178]

Professor John MacMillan Brown, who in 1884 addressed the assembly at Nelson Girls' College saying: 'There were too many women whom it was cruel to confine to the sphere of the home, where they had no opportunity of bringing their intellect into play.'

MACMILLAN BROWN LIBRARY, UNIVERSITY OF CANTERBURY, TUTTLE & CO. SYDNEY PHOTOGRAPH
UNIVERSITY OF CANTERBURY PHOTOGRAPHS COLL 1995/3, NEG NO. 237M

A major difference between Canterbury and Otago in terms of male academic attitudes towards women's participation in higher education was highlighted at Nelson Girls' College in 1884. Principal Kate Edger had invited both Professor MacMillan Brown (Canterbury) and Professor Sale (Otago) to address the school. MacMillan Brown, who had then already taught the first seven women graduates from Canterbury, took the opportunity to advocate for equality of educational opportunity, saying: 'There were many women whom it was cruel to confine to the sphere of the home, where they had no opportunity of bringing their intellect into play.'[179] Conversely, Professor Sale, who followed MacMillan Brown as speaker, and had yet to produce a single woman graduate at Otago, expressed the opposite view, saying he '... would be extremely sorry to see the grace of womanhood sacrificed to these advanced notions of the power of intellect'.[180]

Both men would play a major role in teaching almost equal numbers of women graduates in the early years of both institutions. While Professor Sale retained his conservative views, however, MacMillan Brown was less consistent, at least back in Christchurch, where he was no doubt concerned not to provoke the anger of traditionalists. Two years earlier he was reported as greeting a group of young women from Christchurch Girls' High School, who had come to the university to sit their Matriculation Examination, with: 'Chits of girls in short petticoats! Why does the high school send them to these university examinations?'[181] This was indeed a mixed message, both for the girls whose school he had helped establish, and for which he chaired its board of governors, as well as for the school's principal, Helen Connon, who was his first graduate success and of whom he was very proud. Indeed, John MacMillan Brown remained so impressed with Helen Connon that he had proposed marriage to her in 1881. In 1884 she was still considering his offer, having told him that 'she wished to show independently what a young woman could do in life'.[182] She finally agreed, marrying MacMillan Brown in 1886. As the mother of small children, she continued leading Christchurch Girls' High School until 1894.[183]

Christchurch Girls' High School and Canterbury University College

In Dunedin, Learmonth Dalrymple had had to fight for the establishment of a girls' high school to match that already set up for the boys; but in Christchurch this was not the case: there the girls' high school (1877) was established three years before the boys' high school (1880). The reason was linked to the pre-eminent position of Christ's College, a boys' school established in 1855. The founding fathers of Canterbury province were convinced by Superintendent William Rolleston to set up a complete educational system, comprising publicly funded primary schools, secondary schools, a museum, a library, and the university college. However, Christ's College did not fulfil Rolleston's expectations of numbers of matriculated boys carrying on their studies at Canterbury College. Instead, as Gardner et al. suggest,[184] many were sent by their parents to English universities. Eager to ensure a succession plan, Rolleston supported the establishment of the girls' high school and the boys' high school under the governing auspices of Canterbury College. It was in this way that it became a key expectation of Christchurch Girls' High School to prepare students for the Matriculation and University Scholarship examinations, and parents sent their daughters to the school fully aware of this goal.

Until 1928, there were only public girls' schools in the upper half of the South Island. Between them they provided future women graduates of Canterbury University College. (Below left) Christchurch Girls' High School (established 1877) and (below right) Nelson Girls' College (established 1883).

CHRISTCHURCH CITY LIBRARIES CD17, IMG0017

NELSON GIRLS' COLLEGE

At the same time, the first group of staff decided that the school would also build a well-balanced character in each girl; she would attend for five years and, if ready, would be sent for examinations. Parents were convinced, and by 1878, 150 girls were crowded onto the original quarter-acre Canterbury College site on the corner of Antigua and Hereford Streets. The new school buildings were opened on the southern corner of Cranmer Square in 1881.

Christchurch Girls' (1877) remained the only public girls' secondary school in the town, and Nelson Girls' College (1883) was the only other public girls' secondary school in the upper South Island until the opening of Avonside Girls' High School in Christchurch in 1928. While both these schools had boarding establishments and attracted large numbers of pupils and high-calibre women graduate teachers, there was also a wide choice of private-school options for parents seeking a secondary education for their daughters. The Roman Catholic Church established convent schools for girls in Christchurch, Notre Dame des Missions (1916) and Villa Maria College (1918), as well as in Reefton (1891) and Westport (1894). The Anglican Church founded St Margaret's College in Christchurch (1910), took over Craighead (Diocesan) School in Timaru in 1926, and established Te Wai Pounamu Māori Girls' College in Christchurch in 1924. Many privately run girls' schools also operated, such as Mrs Soulsby's, Mrs Coleman's, Mrs Crosby's Montfleuri School, Girton College and the Commercial College in Christchurch, and Woodlands House in Nelson. The enduring Rangi Ruru was established and run by the Gibson family in Christchurch from 1889 to 1940, before being transferred to the Presbyterian Church.

The girls attending Christchurch Girls' in 1880 were taught by two of the University of New Zealand's first graduates. Kate Edger, the first woman Bachelor of Arts, taught English, Latin, and mathematics between 1877 and 1882, and Helen Connon taught English literature from 1878. Both made a huge impression on their pupils: Kate Edger 'for being absolutely thorough, and also as taking a great interest in the girls'; Helen Connon because, as former pupil Margaret Lorimer recalled: 'She was not a teacher in the modern sense. She seldom used the blackboard, or made any attempt at demonstrating. She merely talked quietly and interestingly, often assuming in us a knowledge which we did not possess, and thereby stimulating us to remedy any deficiencies.'[185]

In 1883, Christchurch Girls' High School first assistant Kate Edger had left to take up the position of founding principal of Nelson Girls' College, and begin a significant educational link back to Canterbury University College. Her salary increased by £50 a year to £350, and she was also provided with a residence. Lilian Edger (MA 1882), who had been fourth assistant at Christchurch Girls', went with her sister to Nelson Girls' as first assistant; she similarly improved her salary by £50 and shared her sister's house.[186] Earlier, in 1882, the salaries of the Christchurch Girls' High School teachers had been reduced and by 1884 they were cut again. This was because the land reserves allocated to the girls'

Senior pupils from Christchurch Girls' High School, including Elizabeth Milsom, attended the Canterbury University College 1882 graduation ceremony where six women graduated, including three of their teachers. Helen Connon (MA) is standing fifth from left. Seated second from left is Lilian Edger (MA). Seated fifth from left is Kate Edger (MA).

Recollections of pupil Elizabeth Milsom (m.Whyte) (MA 1887)

I think the most important school event was the presentation of diplomas to Miss Edger and Miss Connon in 1881. The senior pupils were taken to the Provincial Chambers to see the ceremony in the beautiful hall. The Chancellor of the University was there, and I remember so well seeing him put the MA hood over Miss Connon's head. The ladies were then presented with bouquets of white camellias. Very proud of our teachers were we that day. Miss Edger had been the first woman in the British Empire to receive the BA degree (1877) but Miss Connon was the first to gain the MA degree with Honours, as Miss Edger, after gaining the earlier degree, had waited a while before sitting for that of MA.[187]

Elizabeth Milsom (m.Whyte) (MA 1887) in 1887. Elizabeth taught before training as a nurse in Australia. She later worked for the Special Education branch of the Department of Education.

high school had been smaller than those allocated to the boys' high school, and only half as much income from rent was secured. For example, while Helen Connon earnt £300 with a capitation fee of £95, her contemporary at Christchurch Boys' earnt £800.[188] There were similar discrepancies regarding the assistant teachers' positions, where the highly qualified women staff earnt half the salary of their male colleagues. This land-leasing situation was certainly made worse by the economic depression, and the finances of the endowed schools continued to be the subject of newspaper articles and debates. For example, in 1894, the average cost for each pupil (apart from books that parents had to provide) was estimated to be £30 for pupils at Christchurch Boys', and £19 for pupils at Christchurch Girls'. Land-lease monies contributed £20 for the boys, but only £6 for the girls. As public debate raged in 1896, the Canterbury College Board defended its decision to differentiate between the salaries of women and men in its employ by stating:

> The Board cannot be blamed for a social system for which they are not responsible. For reasons that are tolerably comprehensible women are willing and eager to work for less wages. We should like to see the earnings of men and women equalised if this could be done not by levelling down but by levelling up.[189]

The assumption that women would accept less pay than men for the same work was an issue on which the Christchurch Girls' High School staff felt strongly. In an 1897 letter to the board of Canterbury College, they set out a case for equal pay:

1. that the same degrees are required from teachers of both schools, and that a woman in fitting herself for such a position, must necessarily spend the same time and money as a man.

2. that there are no reasonable grounds for supposing that the cost of living is less in the case of a woman than in that of a man, or that a woman has no-one but herself to provide for.

3. that the same standard of work is required from both schools.

4. that the quality of the work done is not considered inferior to that done at boys' schools is evidenced by the higher fees charged for girls.

5. that the total salaries … have decreased since 1894.

6. that the salary paid to the last appointed part-time teacher for over 10 hours' work, exclusive of that done out of school, is about equal to that of a first-year pupil teacher under the Board of Education.[190]

Student life

As Canterbury College proved so successful in attracting women students, and at times had more women students than men students, the institution and its staff came under the scrutiny of a colonial society, some members of which were not at all sure about such a trend. Neither was the college council keen to foster any kind of activity that might besmirch its image.

To help avoid any such event, the college offered few opportunities for men and women students to socialise on campus; however, graduation dances were introduced from 1896, women students' sports teams participated in the intercollegiate tournament from 1902, and the numbers of student subject clubs increased after World War One. Yet even in lecture halls, the tradition of women students sitting in the front rows while the men sat at the back was adhered to for decades.[191] Women students continued to come under special scrutiny, such as that of long-serving local politician W. H. Montgomery; years later, he appeared to have shared Truby King's view of the impact of higher education on women's physical and nervous energy. He clearly thought Professor MacMillan Brown's curriculum and 'gospel of work' was too much and reported that student life of the late 1880s meant that 'some of the girls used to read all the way as they walked to College. They never seemed to take any exercise. There was no social life that I can remember; it was all work.'[192]

Once at college, a number of measures were taken to 'protect' women students from so-called undesirable influences. For example, in 1885 Professor

Haslam was taken to task by the college council because a mildly suggestive play by Terence was considered unsuitable study material for mixed Latin classes. Although twelve women students petitioned in favour of its continued use as a text in support of Professor Haslam, the case was lost and he was forced to introduce other set reading.[193]

The following year, Professor Haslam fought back in his graduation address. Based upon his own experience of college student life at Cambridge University, he made clear his opinion that if Canterbury College aspired to be a proper university, then it would introduce more day lectures and build an academic community around the university, including student residential halls. He also took a radical view for the times in stating that 'students of both sexes can meet and learn healthily and happily from each other far more useful things than they can learn from a whole army of professors ...'[194]

This very public statement, which clearly went against the combined view of the college council, may well have been prompted because, in 1886, the college provided the nineteenth century version of a dedicated women's space/room in the form of the 'Women's Cottage'. Like their modern-day counterparts, the excluded male students, who already had their own on-campus 'Men's Club'

Diploma day parade at Canterbury College, 1905. It was on this occasion that the male students raided the Women's Cottage and took regalia. CHRISTCHURCH CITY LIBRARIES CD 9, IMG0083

and, by 1888, even got their own cottage, known by students as the 'Stud Room', protested against such exclusiveness for women. Their response was perhaps exacerbated by the university later building a fortress-style fence to encircle the female enclave. When, in 1905, the fence was breached and the women's cottage raided of its academic regalia on graduation day, Professorial Board Chair Professor Cook and local newspapers took the extreme moral view that '... we do not want any scandals at the College'.[195]

Canterbury was the only university college that adopted the practice, introduced by Professor MacMillan Brown, of the wearing of academic gowns by all matriculated students within the university grounds. Gardner et al. point out that whilst this no doubt emphasised the university atmosphere, the fact that a large proportion of the students were women wearing regalia made a powerful statement. Further, the fact that there were so many women meant that Canterbury came to have a reputation as a good behaviour institution, where women were presumably the moderating influence. Indeed, staff member Arnold Wall, upon his arrival in 1899, reported that he found 'most striking ... the quietness and decorum'[196] of the students, compared with the more boisterous group he had taught in Wales.

Not all women students fitted this mould, however. In 1894, Alice Burn, the prominent dress reformer, turned up to class wearing 'rational dress', namely knickerbockers, underneath her regalia. This 'caused some distractions' among students, and the college board decided to ban such reform dress, even though Alice protested, saying that her reform knickers were barely visible under the gown. From that time on, the board resolved that students must appear in 'customary dress'. Alice Burn did not remain a student at Canterbury. However, she later gained a medical degree overseas, and in 1910, in full academic regalia, she led the New Zealand delegation in the great London street procession to support British women's bid for suffrage.[197]

At Canterbury, the eleven degree subjects offered for the BA degree, with a specialisation in three of these, were similar to those offered at Otago, with mathematics and Latin remaining compulsory until 1911 and 1917 respectively. Students studying Stage 1 subjects were required to pass the college's three internal terms examinations in order to gain a pass. With Stage 2 and Stage 3

Canterbury women students and graduates were active members of political groups such as the Women Teachers' Association and the Women's Christian Temperance Union. Having won the right to vote in 1893, the New Zealand women's contingent marched in support of their English counterparts who, at the time of this parade in London in 1910, were still not entitled to vote. Leading the parade is former Canterbury student Alice Burn, now Dr Alice Burn. CANTERBURY MUSEUM, NEWMAN COLL 1989.43.4

Student Alice Burn, wearing rational dress, 1894. Objecting to women having to wear cumbersome skirts and corsets which limited movement for cycling and sport, Alice wore her knickerbockers to class in 1894, causing an uproar and a specific change to women students' dress code. She left the university in protest.
CANTERBURY MUSEUM, NEWMAN COLL 1989.43.3

subjects, students had to pass the college's internal examination in October before sitting the University of New Zealand examination in November. Those who gained their BA degree could sit the honours examination at the end of the following year, and if they obtained first, second, or third class honours, were entitled to the degree of MA.[198] The examination questions came from Britain and all papers were then sent to Britain for external marking. Not surprisingly, this system was not without its problems. For example, in 1898 Elsie Low's MA examination papers 'were lost at sea'; but by the time this was discovered she had already taken up a teaching position at Waimate High School. She refused to accept the second class honours offered to her, choosing instead to sit the papers again, and in 1899 she graduated with first class honours.[199] Challenges were made by staff, including Professor Wall; in 1917, he advocated local professorial control of examinations. Recalling all the difficulties, he raged, '... the faults, the injustices, the inevitable errors of "one-man" examining would fill a volume. The thing is utterly discredited.'[200] Change was slow, however. It took until 1941 for Canterbury College staff to be first to control all examinations for their own Stage 1 students; 1946 for Stage 2 students; and 1948 for Stage 3 and master's students, although these were still externally moderated by outside examiners.[201]

However, overall the numbers of successful women graduates in the period to 1920 were very similar: Otago had 241 women graduates, and Canterbury had 224. Together, they produced 60 percent of the total number of New Zealand women graduates in the period. While Canterbury produced 10 percent more master's degrees, both had very high numbers of women graduates who went on to teach (Otago with 65 percent and Canterbury with 70 percent) and the records indicate that just over 40 percent of women graduates from both institutions married.[202]

There were also key differences between the two universities. One of these was linked to the fact that Canterbury University College, established in 1873, was geographically closer to the home regions of many students than was Otago, not just for students from the middle and upper South Island areas, such as Canterbury, West Coast, Nelson, and Marlborough, but also for those from a range of regions further afield, such as Wellington, Napier, New Plymouth, and even Auckland. This was important, given that it was to be another ten years before the establishment of Auckland University College in 1883, and another sixteen years before Victoria University College began classes in Wellington in 1899. Thus, Canterbury drew a larger number of students from a wider range of schools than did Otago, and in turn, some of its women graduates returned to teach in their home regions. However, the dominance of Christchurch Girls' High School former pupils among Canterbury's first women graduates is striking, as it produced nearly 50 percent (110) of the 224 women graduates in the period to 1920.[203]

Women graduates of Canterbury University College 1883–1920

Secondary principals

Helen Connon	MA	Christchurch Girls' High School	1883–94
Kate Edger	MA	Nelson Girls' College	1883–90
Beatrice Gibson	MA	Nelson Girls' College	1890–1900
Clementine Harrison	MA	Wanganui Girls' High School	1891–93
Lilian Edger	MA	Ponsonby College for Girls	1894–97
Maria Marchant	MA	Otago Girls' High School St Mary's Diocesan, Stratford	1895–11 1915–17
Mona Elise Allman Marchant	MA	Otago Girls' High School St Mary's Diocesan School St John's Collegiate, Invercargill	1896–11 1915–17 1918–19
Mary McLean	MA	Timaru Girls' High School Wellington Girls' High School/College	1898–1900 1900–26
Mary Gibson	MA	Christchurch Girls' High School	1898–28
Althea Tendall	MA	Nelson Girls' College	1900–05
Jerome Spencer	BA	Napier Girls' High School	1901–10
Nina Greensill	BA	Queen Victoria School for Maori Girls, Auckland	1903–04
Margaret Lorimer	MA	Nelson Girls' College	1906–26
Esther Baber	MA	Fitzherbert Terrace School for Girls, Wellington (later Samuel Marsden Collegiate School)	1907–31
Mary (Molly) Barker	MA	Nga Tawa Diocesan School for Girls, Marton	1912–20
Mother Mary St Domitille (Mary Hickey)	MA DLit	Sacred Heart College, Christchurch	1916–39
Clara Mills	MA	Palmerston North Girls' High School Nelson Girls' College	1921–26 1927–31
Alithea Batham	MA	Wellington East Girls' College	1925–37
Kathleen Gresson	MA	Avonside Girls' High School, Christchurch	1928–42
Mabel Connon (m.Rhodes)	MA	Palmerston North Girls' High School	1929–33

First women academic staff at Canterbury University College

Elizabeth Herriott	MA 1905	Assistant Lecturer, botany Lecturer, botany	1916–27 1927–34
Alice Candy	MA 1911	Lecturer, history Senior Lecturer, history	1921–41 1941–48

First women on the Canterbury University College Board

Emily Chaplin	BA 1899	1924–38
Emma Cull (m.Clark)	MA 1905	1924–33
Helen Richmond (m.Simpson)[204]	MA 1920	1939–51

Students in a zoology class dissecting crayfish, Canterbury College, 1926. CHRISTCHURCH CITY LIBRARIES CD 14 IMG0082

Another key difference between Canterbury and Otago was the fields of study preferred by women students. As the preceding chapter showed, Otago produced a number of Bachelor of Science graduates and Bachelor of Arts graduates who had included some science and mathematics papers in their degrees. This blended-subject approach was no doubt welcomed by school principals seeking expertise across the curriculum. While the same BA and BSc statutes of the University of New Zealand applied at Canterbury, with the opportunity to take papers for the BA and MA in pure and applied mathematics, physical science, chemistry, and natural science, it appears these were less popular options there. Only nine of the first 224 women graduates at Canterbury graduated with a Bachelor of Science; using master's subjects at graduation as a guide, the majority of the 112 master's graduates between 1880 and 1920 specialised in languages and literature.[205] While Canterbury's record in science did not significantly improve until the 1970s, what is particularly noteworthy is that for many years Canterbury retained its distinction of winning the highest number of first class honours in arts awarded by overseas examiners.[206] By 1944, Canterbury had produced 730 women graduates (29 percent) out of a national total of 2600.[207]

Funding a university degree

A final key difference between Otago and Canterbury was that, unlike Otago, Canterbury College was not a day university catering for full-time students. There were possibly two reasons for this. Many of the early students were teachers, who could attend classes only before or after school, and because of there being few staff, many chose subjects such as Latin, Greek, English language and literature, history, and political economy. All these subjects were taught by Professor MacMillan Brown, who began lectures at 7.45 am so that the Christchurch-based teachers might begin their own teaching day at 9 am. He and his college colleagues then ran a series of lectures in the evenings and a full day's programme on Saturdays, so that country teachers could attend. It was important to the college to secure these students, and free rail passes were granted to students in 1876.[208] The abilities and the efforts of teachers did not go unrecognised by Professor MacMillan Brown, who got to know his students well over the four to five years it usually took them to complete degrees part time. He did much to raise teachers' morale and status by praising them publicly. For example, in his 1884 graduation address, he drew attention to the fact that half the students financially supported themselves throughout their studies, saying that 'the instances here are not rare of young men and women, who, at risk of ill-health, have supported their relatives and themselves by daily and severe work, and yet have, at the same time, pursued their College course without flinching'.[209] MacMillan Brown and his Canterbury College colleagues also knew that a group of Canterbury founders and administrators who could well afford the fees of their local college continued to send their sons to British universities.[210]

The second reason was linked to the cost of study at the college; a full course of study was beyond the means of most settler parents, with full-time tuition fees around £18, and board around £50 a year. The very few women who won a University Junior Scholarship at £40 a year for three years, and perhaps a Canterbury College Exhibition Prize at £20 a year for one year, might just manage to eke out a student existence. It was not surprising, therefore, that at one guinea per term per course, attending for two hours a week while living at home, a part-time student might more easily be funded by parents and/or from their own teacher salary.

Lack of funds was doubtless the reason why students took up teaching to augment their studies, or took time out to gather funds for future study. Some obviously dropped out altogether for this reason. Some insights into the fraught student lives of early Canterbury women graduates were provided by the women themselves at the time. For example, in the 1880s, Lilian Williams (m.Blyth) (MA 1890) recalled the case of a woman friend, a student of Professor C. H. Cook's. Apparently, she 'would have had to leave the College because she had run short of money, if Cook and his wife hadn't taken her into their house as a boarder without paying'.[211] Indeed, Professor and Mrs Cook were generous sponsors of more than one woman student. Mary McLean, later principal of Timaru Girls' High School (1898–1900) and Wellington Girls' (1900–1926)

Mary McLean (MA 1890) completed two degrees part time while teaching. She was later principal of Timaru Girls' High School (1898–1900) and Wellington Girls' College (1900–1926).
WELLINGTON GIRLS' COLLEGE

was one of these. Although her father was a physician and surgeon in Timaru, and presumably could afford to support his daughter in Christchurch, Mary McLean began her university studies as an exempt student for several years while teaching at Timaru Girls' High School. She boarded with the Cooks in 1886 when she first came up to Canterbury College, then completed her BA in 1888 and MA (Latin and English) in 1890 while a resident teacher at the private Montfleuri Girls' School in Christchurch.[212]

Those parents committed to their daughters' advanced education, but with low incomes, included a number of clergy. For example, the Rev C. H. Garland had secured prestigious secondary schooling for his two daughters Ella and Myrtle at Prince Albert College in Auckland in 1901 and 1904 respectively. This was because Prince Albert had been established especially for children of Methodist clergy, and fees were subsidised.[213] However, when both girls contemplated university study at Canterbury, the Rev Garland told them, 'I won't have anything to leave you, but I'll pay your college fees.'[214] His daughters did not let him down. Both graduated with Master of Arts degrees, in 1911 and 1912 respectively, and both went teaching. Later, both married Gunson brothers. The Rev T. N. Griffin was less magnanimous; he paid the college fees of his daughters Annie and Isabella on the condition that they paid him back once they were earning salaries as teachers.[215] It is likely they did so. Annie Griffin gained her BA at Canterbury in 1908 and taught in turn at Southland Girls' High School, Napier Girls' High School, and Palmerston North Girls' High School. Her sister, Isabella Griffin, gained a BA (1907) and an MA (1908), and taught at Southland Girls' High School until her marriage.

Mrs Connon, mother of graduates Helen, Maria, and Mabel, saw early on that her husband's earnings from his carpentry business were not going to cover university tuition or examination fees for her daughters. The family did their best for the first two years of Helen's university course, but in her third year, in 1878, Helen joined the teaching staff of Christchurch Girls' High School, no doubt in a bid to help fund her own studies. Meanwhile, Mrs Connon took into the family home women students, including Junior University Scholars Edith Searle and Elizabeth Milsom, as boarders for a year.[216] Once she became a principal, Helen Connon bought a house where she lived with her sisters, and supported each in turn to go through university.[217] Maria and Mabel both won Junior Scholarships, and with no lodgings to pay for, were able to enrol as full-time students. Maria graduated with a BA in 1893 and Mabel with

Mary St Domitille Hickey (Mother Mary St Domitille) (MA 1916, DLit 1925 Canterbury)

The most important virtue is Common Sense, but often it is the least commonly found.

Mary Hickey grew up on a farm in Opunake, Taranaki, becoming a pupil-teacher at the Opunake School (1898–1901) and then the West Infants' School in New Plymouth (1901–1903). She gained her teacher's certificate while teaching at the Stratford District High School in 1904, and the following year moved to Christchurch to join the Sisters of Our Lady of the Missions. As Sister Mary St Domitille, she attended Canterbury University College part time while teaching at Sacred Heart Girls' College, graduating with a BA in 1914. Having won a Senior Scholarship in history in 1915, she moved on to postgraduate study, gaining an MA with first class honours in history in 1916. This was also the year she was appointed principal of Sacred Heart College, a position she held until 1939. Pupils benefited from her strong personality, deep human interest, and lively faith. Her school

an MA in 1902. Like her older sister Helen, Mabel also became a secondary school principal, of Palmerston North Girls' High School (1929–1933). This was towards the end of her thirty-year teaching career, beginning at Ashburton High School prior to her marriage, and then (as Mrs Rhodes) at Taihape District High School (1913–1916) and Christchurch Boys' High School (1917–1921). She also held positions as assistant and senior mistress at Palmerston North Girls' (1922–1928).[218]

While the Connon family lived within reach of secondary schooling and university classes in Christchurch, this was not the case for Christina Henderson from Ashburton. At seventeen years of age, she was a pupil-teacher at Ashburton School, then won a scholarship to Christchurch Normal School to finish her teacher training, which she did by attending teacher-training courses before and after school and on Saturday mornings. As a certificated teacher she went to Springston School (1883–1885), from where she studied part time at Canterbury College. By 1886, she had gained a position at Christchurch Girls' High School, not only because she needed to increase her salary to help support her widowed mother and eight children, but also to more easily attend university classes. It took her eight years to complete her BA, but she did this in 1891. Christina Henderson remained at Christchurch Girls' until her retirement in 1912. Throughout her life she was a political activist for women's causes: 'She saw capitalism as cruel and unjust, especially to the "weak disorganised masses" of women workers.'[219] She became the founding president of the

assemblies became forums where she exhorted and flattered students into an understanding of local and international affairs.[220]

Mother Mary St Domitille's love of scholarship led to her writing a doctoral thesis on the history of Canterbury Province to 1857, and she graduated DLitt in 1925, the first woman to do so within New Zealand. In that year, she also travelled to England as delegate to the congregations' chapter, and whilst there met with Maria Montessori, the founder of the Montessori school movement. Back in Christchurch, she set up a Montessori school. Throughout her career, Mother Mary St Domitille wrote for Catholic teacher journals and was a well-known commentator on girls' schooling. Following her retirement as principal, Mother Mary St Domitille was Prioress (1939–1943) and then Provincial (1943–1945) of her order. She was twice awarded a Coronation Medal for her services to education.[221]

North Canterbury Women Teachers' Association (1901); legal and political superintendent of the WCTU (1913–1938); president of the Canterbury branch of the WCTU (1926–1946); and president of the National Council of Women's Christchurch branch (1919–1924).[222]

A popular option for students at Canterbury College was to undertake studies as an exempt student. Those who lived in Wellington before the establishment of Victoria University College in 1899 did so. In this way, many women students enrolled in subjects at Canterbury College and, with only reading and self-teaching, sat the university examinations. It required ability and determination to gain a degree in this way. Maria Marchant was one example of a person who studied as an exempt student and went on to be a successful teacher.

Completion of degrees then was often dependent upon precarious financial circumstances and total commitment to success. There was little space or energy for frivolous distractions, as Alice Candy later recalled. During her student days she lived in a mixed boarding house in Christchurch, took little part in

Maria Marchant (MA 1894)

Maria Elise Allman Marchant (MA 1894), principal of Otago Girls' High School 1895–1911, c. 1911. She later worked for the Anglican Church as superintendent of the Ponsonby Girls' Orphanage; and was founding principal of St Mary's Diocesan School, Stratford, 1915–1917 and St John's Diocesan Girls' School, Invercargill, 1917–1918. HOCKEN COLLECTIONS, UARE TAOKA O HAKENA, UNIVERSITY OF OTAGO S08-006D

While Maria Marchant's family could no doubt have financially supported her studies, her father became Surveyor General and Secretary for Crown Lands in Wellington. Maria wanted to become a teacher. Having attended Wellington Girls' High School and been dux there in 1887, she went straight to teaching at Fitzherbert Terrace School for Girls (1888–1889), before returning to the staff at Wellington Girls' (1890–1895).[223] All the while she took at least one university subject per year from Canterbury, graduating with a BA in 1892 and an MA in 1894. Her combined teaching/study strategy proved its worth when, in 1895, at the age of twenty-six, she was appointed principal of Otago Girls' High School, complete with a £400 annual salary and free accommodation. By all accounts, Maria Marchant was a formidable young woman, and not easily

any student activities there were during the week, and returned to her parents' home in Oxford most weekends. For the women teachers, just balancing a full-time job, complete with class preparation and marking, and university study left little room for other activities.

For those women who did participate in university life, things were not easy. Edith Searle (m.Grossmann) (MA 1884) wrote that as one of the first group of women students at Canterbury, she had encountered 'abuse and ridicule'. This had manifested itself in 1881, when Helen Connon led a women's debating team on the topic of higher education for women as part of the activities of the College Dialectic Society. So rude was the male student response that Connon and her good friend Searle did not participate ever again.[224] The city seems to have been proud that Canterbury had produced the first numbers of graduate women, but, as Lilian Williams later recalled, 'the city looked on the university as something outside, I think. It was very proud of Misses Connon and Edger, but in the main it thought going to university [for women] was a rather faddy, although harmless, sort of thing.'[225]

intimidated by her male board of governors, who, in the early years of her sixteen-year stewardship, often deferred consideration of her ideas for school reform. She has been described as someone who:

> … set a high standard for both her staff and pupils. She was an admired figurehead for the school, always composed and well dressed, she was an accomplished public speaker and debater and woman of considerable intellectual bearing.
> … On Saturday evenings the boarders would gather in her sitting room sewing while she read to them, usually from Dickens. After an extensive overseas trip in 1901, she also entertained them with accounts of her travels.[226]

A dynasty for girls' education

The Gibson women

One family in Christchurch was committed to higher education for their ten children, and its advanced thinking ensured the financial security of their eight daughters. Captain Frederick Gibson had met passenger Mary Fox Rodd while taking a ship from England to Australia. They had married in New South Wales and arrived in Lyttelton in 1863. Nine of their ten children were born there, and for a short time around 1877, Captain Gibson was the port harbourmaster, until ill health forced him to retire. The three elder daughters boarded at Mrs Crosby's private school for two years while the Gibson family were in Dunedin between 1884 and 1886. The couple sent their daughters to Christchurch Girls' High School, no doubt made easier by their moving to live on the South Town Belt in Christchurch (later Moorhouse Avenue) from around 1886. Five of their daughters and one of their sons went on to graduate from Canterbury College. Three of these daughters became principals of girls' schools. When their third daughter, Helen, began her own school

in 1889 at Arawa House in Papanui, the family moved there. However, the following year Captain Gibson purchased a site on the corner of Papanui Road and Webb Street for £640 on which he built a large house, including two rooms to be used as schoolrooms. It was in this way that Rangi Ruru School for Girls was established by the Gibson family. The family took in a few boarders at £18 per term, with Mrs Gibson supervising the house, although she was a talented musician and fluent in French and German. However, the immediate success of the school may well have had much to do with the fees that day pupils were charged for tuition, as well as the family atmosphere, which appealed to many parents. In the early days and until the introduction of free places in the public system, the Gibson family were able to offer fees very competitive with those of Christchurch Girls' High School; because of the academic calibre of the Gibson daughters, they could also offer the same subjects to pupils.[227]

Rangi Ruru School for Girls, founded in 1889 and run by the Gibson sisters until 1940 when it was sold and managed by the Presbyterian Church. CANTERBURY MUSEUM, *WEEKLY PRESS* PHOTOGRAPH, F.C. BISHOP COLL 1923.53.535

Mary Victoria Gibson b.1864 d.1929 (MA 1888)

Mary Gibson (MA 1888), eldest of the Gibson sisters of Rangi Ruru. She was principal of Christchurch Girls' High School 1898–1923.

The eldest daughter, Mary, did not teach at Rangi Ruru because, by the time it was underway, she had an established teaching career: she had begun teaching at Sydenham Primary School while a student at Canterbury College, then became headmistress of the girls' side of the large Christchurch East School, a position she held from 1889 to 1898. However, Mary lived with her family at Rangi Ruru all her life, and often supervised the homework of the boarders. She may have been the only principal of a public school in New Zealand to own a private girls' school at the same time, as she did in the four years between inheriting it from her mother in 1919 and selling it in 1923. She was principal of Christchurch Girls' High School between 1898 and 1928, the year she retired. Mary Gibson 'immersed herself in the life of her school. She strongly encouraged sporting and social activities, and regularly played the piano at school parties. An expanding roll—from 126 in 1898 to over 600 by 1926—did not prevent her from continuing to take a personal interest in her pupils and their subsequent careers.'[228] All the while, her sister Helen presided over Rangi Ruru; with their sisters, they influenced the education of thousands of girls in Canterbury for over fifty years. Mary Gibson died in 1929 in Oamaru while acting as principal at Waitaki Girls' High School.[229]

Beatrice Esther Gibson b.1866 d.1958 (MA 1888)

Beatrice Gibson was taught by Kate Edger and Helen Connon at Christchurch Girls' High School, was head girl in 1883, and that year also won a Junior Scholarship and Exhibition Prize in English. Her stellar academic record continued with her holding exhibitions in four subjects in 1885, the same year that she began teaching as an assistant mistress at Christchurch Girls' High School. She went on to win the John Tinline Scholarship in 1886 and at the same time was awarded a Senior Scholarship in English and Latin. In this way, Beatrice funded her own studies while living at home at Rangi Ruru. She graduated with a BA in 1887 and an MA with first class honours in English and Latin in 1888. In 1890, she followed in the footsteps of Kate Edger when she succeeded her as principal of Nelson Girls' College. She held this position for ten years until her marriage to Dr Alfred Talbot of Nelson.[230]

Helena Fanny Gibson b.1868 d.1938

Helen Gibson, as she was usually known, attended Christchurch Girls' High School and took private lessons to fund her studies at the School of Art in 1887. She did not graduate from Canterbury College but combined a variety of teaching activities. For example, she continued studying art for over ten years until 1897, while principal of Rangi Ruru, and was then employed to teach drawing both at Christchurch Girls' High School until the end of 1900 and at the School of Art until at least 1906. Helen Gibson taught English, history, geography, mathematics, botany, divinity, and painting to generations of girls. She led Rangi Ruru for over fifty years, assisted by her younger sisters.[231]

Alice Gertrude Gibson b.1869 d.1928

Alice Gibson attended a private school in Lyttelton and then moved with her parents to Dunedin, where she went to Otago Girls' High School. Like her mother, Alice was a talented musician and took lectures in music at Canterbury College between 1891 and 1893. She lived at Rangi Ruru and assisted Helen Gibson with teaching, but in 1894, because of her ill health and asthma, she left Christchurch and held several positions as governess. At some point she returned to Christchurch, and was matron of the Sumner School for the Deaf until she had to give this up because of poor health. The Gibson family built her a house at Sumner where Alice lived with her younger sister Winifred.[232]

Lucy Gibson and friends, Canterbury University College students, 1890s. Standing, left to right: E. Atkinson; K. Inglis; G. T. Weston; Kathleen Gresson (MA 1898), later founding principal of Avonside Girls' High School (1928–1942); Clara Mills (BSc 1897, MA 1898), later principal of Nelson Girls' College (1927–1931). Sitting, left to right: Samuel Atkinson; Beatrice Richmond (MA 1898), later the owner, along with her sister, of Fitzherbert Terrace School for Girls, Wellington, which became Samuel Marsden Collegiate School; Lucy Gibson (m.Rutherford) (BA 1897); Mary Newton (m.Lady Rutherford). MACMILLAN BROWN LIBRARY, UNIVERSITY OF CANTERBURY, UNIVERSITY OF CANTERBURY PHOTOGRAPHS COLL 1995/3, NEG NO. 286-41

Lucy Margaret Gibson b.1875 (BA 1897)

Lucy Gibson attended West Christchurch School until 1888, when she won a scholarship to Christchurch Girls' High School. She then taught music and history at Rangi Ruru and lived there while studying at Canterbury College. After she graduated from university, she remained teaching at Rangi Ruru until her marriage in 1907 to Mr L. A. Rutherford, and went to live near Hawarden in North Canterbury.[233]

Ethel Marianne Gibson b.1877 (MA 1900)

Ethel Gibson also won a scholarship to Christchurch Girls' High School, and was head girl there in 1895, the same year as she gained an Entrance Scholarship to Canterbury College. She lived and taught at Rangi Ruru throughout her university studies, graduating with a BA in 1899 and an MA in English and French the following year.

Perhaps because there were other sisters to teach at Rangi Ruru by 1901, and also perhaps to be near her older sister Beatrice, Ethel went to teach at Nelson Girls' College for three years. However, when her sister Ruth became ill and could not continue teaching at Rangi Ruru, Ethel returned to Rangi Ruru to teach for the rest of her career. Ethel made a trip to Europe in 1927 where she climbed the Swiss Alps. Both she and her sister Winifred were keen mountaineers.[234]

Ruth Constance Manning Gibson b.1879 (MA 1902)

Like her two older sisters, Ruth Gibson gained a scholarship to Christchurch Girls' High School from the West Christchurch School, and was head girl in the same year she won a Junior University Scholarship. Ruth Gibson lived and taught at Rangi Ruru throughout her university studies, graduating with a BA in 1901 and an MA in English and French in 1902. Although plagued by bouts of ill health, Ruth continued to teach at Rangi Ruru for the rest of her life.[235]

Winifred Graeme Gibson b.1882

The youngest of the Gibson children, Winifred spent some of her secondary schooling at Nelson Girls' College, staying with her sister and school principal Beatrice Gibson, before returning to Rangi Ruru. She then attended Mrs Gard'ner's cooking and domestic science school, passed the examination set by the London Kensington School, and taught part time for Mrs Gard'ner for a number of years. Winfred also helped her mother run the house and boarding establishment at Rangi Ruru, taking over this role completely upon Mrs Gibson's death in 1919. She helped teach art, music, and swimming at the school, and when living with her sister Alice at Sumner, travelled into Rangi Ruru each day.[236]

Rangi Ruru colleagues

As the school roll increased, the Gibson teaching team was augmented by an impressive set of colleagues, no doubt hand-picked because of the Gibson family connections to Christchurch Girls' High School and Canterbury College. For example, Agnes (Kitty) Merton had been a pupil at Christchurch Girls' High School, from where she won a Junior Scholarship in 1907 to Canterbury College. She joined the staff at Rangi Ruru after gaining her BA in 1910, teaching the middle and junior forms until 1915. Kitty Merton taught in turn at Nelson Girls' College (1917–1919) and Christchurch Girls' High School (1921–1923), was principal of a girls' Presbyterian school at Berwick in Victoria, Australia (1924–1930), and returned to Christchurch Girls' as Deputy Principal (1931–1947).[237]

When Kitty Merton left Rangi Ruru, she was replaced in 1916 by Helen Richmond, who taught there while undertaking her university studies.

The strong links between Christchurch Girls' High School, Canterbury College, and Nelson Girls' College forged by Kate Edger and Helen Connon were continued through a formidable succession of Canterbury graduates. For example, the first five principals at Nelson all held Master of Arts degrees from Canterbury College. The first principal, Kate Edger, had her equally highly qualified sister working alongside her at the school for the first two years; when Lilian Edger left, she was replaced by Clementine Harrison (MA 1885), who completed two degrees as an exempt student based at Auckland. When Beatrice Gibson took over as principal at Nelson in 1890, another Canterbury graduate joined the staff. Ellen Gribben (BA 1888), a former pupil of Nelson Girls', stayed for seventeen years as resident mistress and later as first assistant, until her marriage to Mr Dunne. The principal, Margaret Lorimer, later wrote of her colleague that 'she was a great enthusiast, a wise and helpful *censor morum*, who watched the girls' conduct carefully, and supplied the principal

Helen MacDonald Richmond (m.Simpson) (MA 1920; PhD London 1923)

Dr Helen MacDonald Richmond (m.Simpson), first New Zealand woman PhD from an English university.

Helen Richmond was born in Wellington in 1890, the daughter of solicitor Maurice and his wife Flora Richmond, who sent their daughter to Esther Baber's Fitzherbert Terrace School. Just why Helen went to Canterbury College in 1916, rather than the local Victoria College, is not clear, but it is likely that it had something to do with Helen being employed as a part-time teacher at Rangi Ruru (1916–1917), where she was also able to live.[238] Helen graduated with a BA in 1919, followed in 1920 with a first class MA in English and French. She then won a prestigious scholarship to study at the University of London, from where she wrote her thesis on the work of Scottish author Henry Mackenzie,

graduating with a doctorate in philosophy in 1923. Upon her return to New Zealand in 1924, she taught again at Rangi Ruru before being appointed in 1925 to the Christchurch Training College as assistant lecturer in English and history. Helen married schoolmaster Arthur Simpson in 1927 and the couple spent a year travelling in England and Europe. After her return she taught English and English literature at Canterbury College as assistant lecturer to Professor Arthur Wall until she resigned in 1932 in order to spend some time in England, France, and Germany. A progressive thinker and pacifist, Helen Simpson wrote for the Christchurch *Press* and the left-wing periodical *Tomorrow*, and served from 1939 to 1951 on the Canterbury University Council. Her book, *The Women of New Zealand*, was published in 1940 as one of the government-funded centennial publications, and remains an insightful and comprehensive work on women's lives in the first century of colonisation.[239]

with valuable caveats to be used at Lecture on Monday mornings. She had an attractive personality, a good deal of Irish wit and humour, and was loved and admired by her pupils.'[240] Ellen Gribben was replaced by another former pupil, Marie McEachen (MA 1899), while Florence Kirton (MA 1899), also a former pupil, became senior resident mistress.

The high academic calibre of the staff was essential, because although Nelson Girls' was a relatively small school, it had another mission attached to it, as Beatrice Gibson explained: 'Victoria College had not yet come into being when I went to Nelson. Girls who wished to take degrees preferred to work as exempted students of Canterbury College rather than try for a Junior Scholarship; a scholarship, even if won, did not go far to cover University expenses.'[241] It was in this way that young women in Nelson could live at home and access university study through three grades of classes, First Year Terms, First Section BA, and Final BA, taking paid classes and tuition from the Nelson Girls' staff until the 1920s. Writing in 1933, Beatrice Gibson remembered this university section of her school as 'a particularly pleasing and intelligent row of bright faced girls: ... so responsive and so grateful for the help given to them ... In the University calendar is a list of names that all Nelson College girls can

TERMS:

For Girls over 12 years of age.
Tuition fees and school stationery..............3 3 0
Board and residence in the College,
     including washing....................12 10 0
Dinner only..............................2 10 0
For Girls under 12 years of age.
Tuition fees and school stationery..........2 2 0
(other charges as above)
Instrumental Music, Drawing, Singing, Dancing.
Board during Mid-summer or Mid-winter holidays 20s per week.
Young ladies wishing to supplement previous education in any particular branch may receive instruction in one language or subject on payment of a fee of one guinea per quarter and for every additional subject half-a-guinea, and may attend the Music, Drawing, or other extra classes at the school rates.
Arrangements are being made for the foundation of annual and other scholarships.
The College will be open for the reception of pupils at the expiration of the Christmas holidays.

N.B.—Tuition Fees and Boarding Charges are payable quarterly in advance to the undersigned, who alone is authorised to receive them. Before removal of a boarder a quarter's notice must be given to the Secretary in writing, or a quarter's fees and charges paid.

Oswald Curtis, Secretary.

Above, *Nelson Girls' College, 1883.* NELSON GIRLS' COLLEGE
Left, *Nelson Girls' College advertises for pupils, 1883.*
NELSON GIRLS' COLLEGE

113

point to with pride, as "Our University degree girls"!'[242] Margaret Lorimer, who succeeded Beatrice Gibson as principal, was equally proud of the academic record at Nelson Girls'. In the twenty-year period of her stewardship, she later reported the winning of eighteen Junior University and Senior National Scholarships, and seventy-one university degrees.[243]

Canterbury University College was proud of its women graduates, and they are included in both its histories. James Hight and Alice Candy's 1927 *Short History of Canterbury College* features many women graduates and their achievements. Both authors were early Canterbury graduates who later became members of staff. The book shows their recognition of the accomplishments of other women, which was rare within university histories then and later. The centennial publication *A History of the University of Canterbury*, coauthored by W. Gardner, E. Beardsley, and T. Carter in 1973, includes some mention of women as students and their subsequent careers, but in the main, highlights the accomplishments of the male students. W. Gardner's own research interest in the first women graduates of Canterbury and Otago universities to 1914

Alice Candy (MA 1911)

CANTERBURY MUSEUM 1987.62.3

Alice Candy (MA 1911), New Zealand's first woman academic historian.

Alice Candy is an example of a young woman whose family wanted her to have educational opportunities, but for whom secondary schooling and beyond on her father's blacksmith's income seemed impossible. It is not clear whether Alice was a pupil-teacher at Oxford in North Canterbury where her family lived; but when she was fifteen years old she won enough scholarship money to enable her to travel from there to attend Christchurch Girls' High School for three years from 1903 to 1906. Alice then continued to mainly self-fund her studies by winning a Junior Scholarship to Canterbury College in 1907, Exhibition

Prizes in economics and political science in 1908, and another in economics in 1909. She boarded in Christchurch throughout her studies, returning home to Oxford at the weekends. She graduated with a BA in 1910, and in that year also won a Senior Scholarship in economics that no doubt paid her postgraduate student fees in 1911. She graduated in that year with a first class honours MA in political science.

Like many of her contemporaries, Alice Candy then embarked upon a teaching career in girls' secondary schools and by 1920 was senior mistress at Chilton St James School in Lower Hutt. At the end of 1920, she was appointed assistant lecturer in history at Canterbury College, the first academic woman to be appointed in arts (Elizabeth Herriott (MA 1905) had been appointed assistant lecturer in biology in 1916). Alice Candy's position was to assist Professor James Hight, who, as a lecturer

became the focus of his 1979 publication, *Colonial Cap and Gown*.

Social reformers and political activists

Canterbury College produced a number of early women graduates who made significant contributions to New Zealand social, religious, and educational movements.

A very early graduate and outstanding scholar was Edith Searle (m.Grossmann) (MA 1885). She was an entrance scholar from Christchurch Girls' High School, had boarded with Mrs Connon, and was a Senior Scholarship and Bowen Prize winner. According to her friend Elizabeth Milsom, both at Christchurch Girls' and at Canterbury College, Edith was 'the

Edith Searle (m.Grossmann) (MA 1885), journalist and writer.
MACMILLAN BROWN LIBRARY, UNIVERSITY OF CANTERBURY 1991/1 39 D

in history and political science, had taught Alice throughout her university studies. By all accounts, 'Hight was a shy man, and Candy, a lively and outgoing person, did much to break down his reserve—to the great benefit of Hight, the department and the college. Besides carrying a heavy and varied burden of teaching, Candy had to fill in for Hight, who was often involved in college, university and government affairs.'[244]

The other role Alice Candy assumed at Canterbury College was that of informal dean of women students, at a time when 25–33 percent of the students were women, and the university remained highly sensitive about scandal. As a former student and long-serving staff member, Alice Candy knew hundreds of college women, and this knowledge was put to good use in the 1927 jubilee history. She had by this time already set up, in 1921, the Canterbury Women

Graduates' Association (later the Canterbury branch of the Federation of University Women), of which she was president in 1926–1927. While national vice-president in 1928–1929, she was exchange lecturer at Bedford College for Women at the University of London, and in that year also represented New Zealand at the meeting of the International Federation of University Women. Her effectiveness in all these roles no doubt led to her formal appointment as warden of Helen Connon Hall from 1936 to 1951, a position she combined with her academic position. She was promoted to senior lecturer in 1941 and retired from Canterbury College in 1948. Even then, she remained associated with the college, serving as a member of the university council between 1954 and 1957.[245]

115

most clever of all; she was a reader and a thinker far in advance of those she came in contact with'.[246] After graduating with a BA in 1884, Edith taught for two years at Christchurch Girls', gaining her MA with first class honours in English in her first year of teaching. She then spent five years as second assistant at Wellington Girls' High School prior to her marriage to former university student friend and Christchurch teacher J. P. Grossmann, a brilliant economist appointed to the Canterbury College staff in 1896. However, he misappropriated money and shares entrusted to him by two university colleagues, and in a scandal Canterbury wanted to forget, he was sent to prison in 1898 for two years.[247] Edith returned to Wellington and in 1901 was teaching at Wellington Girls'.[248] Separated from her husband, she forged a new career as a journalist and remained a writer, novelist, and commentator all her life.[249] Her writing about women and women's issues provides welcome insights into the lives of sister graduates, such as in her 1905 tribute to her friend and colleague, *Life of Helen MacMillan Brown*, and her 1908 article in *Westminster Review* on the New Zealand women's movement, where she wrote:

> The objects of Feminism, some of which are already partially gained, have been to free women from artificial or barbaric restrictions …; to give them fair opportunities and equal legal and political rights; to develop their talents instead of suppressing them; to put an end to the theory that one half of the human race ought to be systematically exploited by the other half.[250]

Elsie Low (m.Dohrmann) (MA 1899) was active in the WCTU as president of the Waimate Branch, national treasurer, and national corresponding secretary between 1903 and 1908. Even though she had a young daughter, born in 1905, Elsie travelled from her farm at Studholme Junction to public meetings 'where she impressed listeners with her command of the subject and charm of manner. As controversy over liquor reform intensified, she met opposition calmly and confidently.'[251] Mid campaign in 1909, Elsie died of an attack of rheumatic fever, at the age of thirty-four.[252]

Intrepid mountaineers

Perhaps more than any other college, Canterbury had groups of women students and graduates with an abundance of adventurous spirit. Locally, climbing parties were launched from Christchurch to the Southern Alps, but like the Gibson sisters of Rangi Ruru, many ventured further afield to Europe and the Swiss Alps. Mountaineering was considered a radical, yet healthy, undertaking for women, but the women themselves clearly relished the independence and challenge associated with climbing and hiking. It also offered salaried teachers opportunities to travel within New Zealand and to Great Britain and the continent. School holidays offered chances to undertake local explorations, and it was not uncommon for women teachers to apply for a year's leave of absence, allowing them to combine official visits to girls' schools with mountaineering expeditions, as Nelson Girls' College principal Margaret Lorimer did in 1923.

Another who taught and climbed was Eileen Fairbairn (BA 1915), who had walked the Milford Track with her family by the time she was thirteen. Upon graduating, Eileen returned to teach at her former school, Christchurch Girls' High School, and in 1927 went to Newnham College, Cambridge, to gain a

Margaret Lorimer (MA 1888)— 'The Mighty Atom'

NELSON GIRLS' COLLEGE

Margaret Lorimer (MA 1888) ('The Mighty Atom'), principal of Mt Cook Girls' School Wellington, 1897–1905; principal of Nelson Girls' College, 1906–1926.

Margaret Lorimer funded her university studies by teaching part time at Christchurch Girls' High School, where she herself had been a pupil. In this way she was taught by Helen Connon, and later became her colleague. Once she had completed her MA, Margaret Lorimer became a full-time teacher at Christchurch Girls', where she was in charge of mathematics for eight years until 1897, when she was appointed headmistress of Mt Cook Girls' School in Wellington. There she served on many national committees and between 1901 and 1905 was particularly involved in advocating equal pay for women teachers. Under her stewardship, the large Mt Cook school went from strength to strength, and her outstanding reputation led to her next appointment as principal of Nelson Girls' College in 1906. During her twenty-year stewardship, she regularly escaped from her small, cramped living quarters amidst her boarders and headed for the mountains, basing herself at Graham's Hotel at Waiho or the Hermitage at Mt Cook.

Initially, she climbed many peaks of the Southern Alps with guides Peter and Alexander Graham, but 'she showed her independent spirit by making a number of unguided ascents in the company of Horace Holl'.[253] Her love for mountaineering endured and she was an active member of the New Zealand Alpine Club and the Ladies' Alpine Club, London. Still climbing in later life, she ascended Mt Cook in 1918 at the age of fifty-two.[254]

postgraduate diploma of geography and climb in Europe. By 1929 she was back at Christchurch Girls' teaching geography. She introduced fieldtrips to the mountains for the girls in her classes, as well as a number of new teaching techniques such as relief models. In later years she commented that these 'were introduced in the face of departmental opposition which now seems ludicrous'.[255]

Christina Henderson (BA 1891), who had taught full time throughout her university studies and had to financially support her mother and numerous siblings, had strong socialist leanings and belonged to a Christchurch socialist club in the 1880s. She knew first-hand just what equal pay for equal work as a teacher would mean for her and her family, saying that, 'it is quite true that a

Helen Connon Hall

Another first for women at Canterbury College was the opening of New Zealand's first women's residential hall in 1918. Appropriately named Helen Connon Hall, it attracted women students from outside Christchurch and was, according to Gardner et al., one of the reasons why numbers of women students from the North Island chose to study at Canterbury instead of Auckland or Victoria. Students at Helen Connon Hall soon made their mark, organising socials and dances (which required chaperones until 1923) and establishing traditions such as the female equivalent of the haka party, a graduation procession float, and the production of revues and plays.

Helen Connon Hall students, 1924. MACMILLAN BROWN LIBRARY, UNIVERSITY OF CANTERBURY WAS YB GB

woman manages to live on less than a man because her wants are fewer, but it is equally true that her wants are fewer because her earnings are less'.[256] Christina became the first president of the first Women Teachers' Association, formed in North Canterbury in 1901, and continued throughout her career to lobby for better salaries and conditions for women teachers. In Christchurch she was also very much involved in the National Council of Women (NCW), arguing for women's right to serve as police officers, members of parliament, jurors, and justices of the peace. She served as national secretary of the NCW between 1900 and 1905. At the same time, she was very active in the Prohibition League and held national positions within the WCTU; after her retirement, she was national secretary and president in turn of the Presbyterian Women's Missionary Union of New Zealand. Between 1923 and 1946 she edited the union's magazine, and continued to support her missionary sister in China.[257]

Maria Marchant (MA 1894) was also an educational and religious reformer. After retiring in 1911, aged forty-two, as principal of Otago Girls' High School, she pursued her idea of establishing an Anglican women's teaching order in New Zealand. Following a trip to England to visit a range of church training organisations, she became the superintendent of the Anglican Children's Home in Ponsonby, Auckland, for a year in 1914, before helping to establish and become founding principal of the Stratford Church School for Girls (later

Drama at Canterbury

Canterbury's reputation for drama soared to new heights in 1941, when Ngaio Marsh (later Dame Ngaio Marsh) produced the first of a series of twenty Shakespearian productions for the Dramatic Society, ending in 1964. Ngaio Marsh was educated at St Margaret's College Christchurch, and studied at the Canterbury College School of Art. Both her drama contributions and her international recognition as a writer of detective novels were recognised by the University of Canterbury in 1963, when she became the first woman there to be awarded an Honorary Doctorate of Literature. The university later named its new Student Union Theatre on the Ilam campus in her honour.

Ngaio Marsh, school prefect, St Margaret's College.
IMAGE SUPPLIED BY CHRISTCHURCH CITY LIBRARIES CD17 IMG0040; REPRODUCED WITH PERMISSION OF ST MARGARET'S COLLEGE

Seated centre, Jerome (Bessie) Spencer (BA 1895) as principal of Napier Girls' High School, 1901. NAPIER GIRLS' HIGH SCHOOL

St Mary's Diocesan School) between 1915 and 1917. She was then needed in 1917 to help set up Bishopscourt in Christchurch, an Anglican hostel for women students, and at the same time to advise on and establish a girls' school in Invercargill (later St John's Collegiate). She was acting principal there in 1919, and about to return to Dunedin to realise her dream of running a religious teaching order, when she died suddenly of a cerebral haemorrhage, at the age of fifty.[258]

The founder of the New Zealand Country Women's Institute was a Canterbury College graduate, although she undertook all her university studies from Napier as an exempt student while teaching there. Jerome (known as Bessie) Spencer (BA 1895) was the daughter of Dr William Spencer, a Napier surgeon, and attended Napier Girls' High School. She became a pupil-teacher at the school, studied extramurally, and was an independent thinker all her life. She founded the Napier Theosophy Society and was interested in a range of religions, while remaining a committed Anglican. She became first assistant at Napier Girls' High School in 1898 and three years later was appointed principal, a position she held until 1910. She retired early from teaching to plant an orchard and run an apiary, but three years later went to live and work with her lifelong friend Amy Hutchinson and Amy's husband Frank at 'Omatua', Rissington, in rural Hawke's Bay. During World War One she travelled to England, where her brothers and sisters lived, in order to undertake war work. She began in 1916 by nursing shell-shocked victims in London, and by 1918 had joined the women's international street patrol. In England she was inspired by the work of the Women's Institute, and once back in New Zealand, she held an inaugural meeting of the Rissington Women's Institute in 1921. Four years later there were six Country Women's Institutes in Hawke's Bay; by 1964 there was a national federation, with 38,000 members. Not content with a rural women's network,

Jerome Spencer set about establishing an urban women's equivalent group, and in 1932 founded the Townswomen's Guild, later becoming national president (1938–1944). Jerome Spencer also played an important role in reactivating the NCW in Hawke's Bay in 1924, becoming its first president. In 1934, she was the only woman on the Napier High School Board of Governors. She received an OBE in 1937.[259]

Canterbury University College women graduates predominated in arts subjects through to 1945. The large numbers of outstanding women graduates who entered the teaching profession in turn influenced another generation of young women in the arts. In the main, these teachers remained in the Canterbury/Nelson and Wellington region, dominated by the Christchurch Girls' and Nelson Girls' networks. Such a distinctive pattern did not emerge with the Auckland University College women who are the focus of the next chapter.

Notes

171 Gardner, Beardsley, & Carter, 1973, p. 157.
172 *Canterbury University College Calendar*, 1880–1886.
173 MacMillan Brown, J., 1923, 'Early Days and Early Students', *Lyttelton Times*, 12 May 1923, cited in Gardner, 1979, p. 83.
174 *University of New Zealand Calendar*, 1902–1903, p. 190.
175 Gardner et al., 1973, p. 157.
176 *Ibid.*
177 Gardner, 1979, p. 82.
178 Morris Matthews, 2006a.
179 Gardner, 1979, p. 71.
180 *Ibid.*
181 *Ibid.*
182 Airey, 1991, pp. 151–154.
183 *Ibid*; Hankin, 1993; Lovell-Smith, 2004.
184 Gardner et al., 1973.
185 Peddie, 1977, p. 30.
186 Mills, 1933; Morris Matthews, 2006a.
187 Canterbury College, 1927, p. 21.
188 Peddie, 1977.
189 Peddie, 1977, p. 54.
190 *Ibid.*
191 Gardner et al., 1973.

192 *Ibid*.
193 *Ibid*.
194 Gardner et al., 1973, p. 160.
195 Gardner et al., 1973, p. 158.
196 *Lyttelton Times*, 12 May 1923, p. 17, cited in Gardner et al., 1973, p. 151.
197 Coney, 1993, pp. 35, 112–113; Gardner, 1979.
198 Gardner et al., 1973.
199 Low, 1993.
200 Gardner et al., 1973, p. 242.
201 Gardner et al., 1973, p. 249.
202 Morris Matthews, 2006a.
203 *Ibid*.
204 Helen Simpson not only proved her worth at meetings with 'cool judgement, wit and sincerity', but also wasted no time in admonishing board chair Schroder for decisions she clearly disagreed with by writing him a short sharp note and signing it with a picture of a cat.
205 Morris Matthews, 2006a.
206 *Ibid*.
207 Gardner et al., 1973, p. 266.
208 *Ibid*.
209 *Lyttelton Times*, 29 August 1884, cited in Gardner et al., 1973, p. 142.
210 Gardner et al., 1973.
211 Gardner, 1979, p. 99.
212 Arnold, 1996.
213 Prince Albert College MS Collection MET 067/1/00/1 (Prince Albert College Prospectus) Methodist Archives, The Kinder Library, St John's Theological College, Meadowbank, Auckland.
214 Gardner, 1979, p. 99.
215 *Ibid*.
216 Christchurch Girls' High School, 1928, p. 21.
217 Lovell-Smith, 2004.
218 *AJHR*, 1914, E-6, p. 21; *AJHR*, 1924, E-6, p. 5; *AJHR*, 1925, E-6, p. 21; *AJHR*, 1926, E-6, p. 21; Ashburton High School, 1956, p. 18; Palmerston North Girls' High School, 1962, p. 24; *New Zealand Schoolmaster*, 1904, p. 187; *University of New Zealand Calendar*, 1903, 1948, p. 191.
219 Sargison, 2007.
220 Wright, 1996.
221 *Ibid*.
222 Sargison, 2007.
223 Carpenter, 2003; Harding, 1982; Lee, 1996; Murray, 1967.
224 Grossmann, 1905.
225 Gardner, 1979, p. 100.
226 Lee, 1996.
227 Belcher, 1964; Britten, 1988.
228 *AHJR*, 1928, E-6, p. 7; *New Zealand Gazette*, 1891; 1900, p. 1262; Peddie, 1977; Wilkie, 1993.

229 *AJHR*, 1928, E-6, p. 7; Britten, 1988, p. 23; Canterbury College Electoral Register, 1898; *New Zealand Gazette*, 1891; 1900, p. 1262; Macdonald, 1982; Peddie, 1977, pp. 109–110.
230 Belcher, 1964; Britten, 1988; Mills, 1933; Peddie, 1977; Voller, 1982.
231 Britten, 1988; Canterbury College Electoral Register; Peddie, 1977; Wilkie, 1993.
232 Belcher, 1964; Britten, 1988; Canterbury College Electoral Register.
233 *Ibid*; Canterbury College Electoral Register.
234 Britten, 1988; Canterbury College Electoral Register; Mills, 1933.
235 Britten, 1988; Canterbury College Electoral Register.
236 Britten, 1988; Voller, 1983.
237 *AJHR*, 1918, E-6, p. 22; Britten, 1988; Canterbury College Electoral Register; Peddie, 1977; Voller, 1983.
238 Belcher, 1964; Britten, 1988; Labrum, 2000.
239 Britten, 1988; Canterbury College Electoral Register; Carpenter, 2003; Murray, 1967; Wilkie, 1993.
240 Mills, 1933, p. 36.
241 Mills, 1933, p. 28.
242 *Ibid*.
243 Mills, 1933, p. 38.
244 Gardner, 2007.
245 *Ibid*; Canterbury College Electoral Register; Canterbury NZFUW, 1972; Gardner et al., 1973.
246 Christchurch Girls' High School, 1928, p. 21.
247 Gardner et al., 1973.
248 Harding, 1982.
249 McLeod, 1991a; Roberts, 1993.
250 Cited in Else, 1993, p. 58.
251 Low, 1993.
252 *Ibid*.
253 Voller, 1996.
254 *Ibid*.
255 Eileen Fairbairn 1893–1961, in *Herstory*, 1989.
256 Sargison, 1993.
257 *Ibid*; Else, 1993.
258 Lee, 1996; Wallis, 1972.
259 Else, 1993; Upton, 1998.

CHAPTER 5

Always an Aucklander

(1883–1945)

Auckland University College, c. 1910. ALEXANDER TURNBULL LIBRARY, WELLINGTON, NZ. AUCKLAND STAR COLL G-2884-1/1

The story of advanced education for girls and women in Auckland begins in 1877, when Kate Milligan Edger obtained her BA from the University of New Zealand. As Chapter 4 indicated, Edger would later provide a crucial link among many of the first women graduates, through her roles in girls' and women's education in Christchurch, Nelson, and Wellington.

As there was then no university college in Auckland, Kate Edger undertook her university studies at Auckland College and Grammar School, a boys' secondary school affiliated to the University of New Zealand.[260] It is not known whether any woman had previously applied for a place there and been rejected. What is known is that Kate Edger, supported by her University of London graduate father, Samuel Edger, obtained permission to study with the boys' class. 'As the only girl in the school, she was required to enter with downcast eyes, and seldom spoke to her classmates, who, she later said, treated her courteously.'[261]

Kate Edger proved an able scholar, especially in mathematics; in her application to the University of New Zealand for an Entrance Scholarship in this subject, she set out her academic and personal details, but did not specify her gender. It is not clear whether this ruse won her the scholarship, or whether her success stemmed from the fact that her father was an unorthodox and vocal Baptist minister, but it seems the university was keen either to avoid controversy, or to increase student numbers, or both. On 11 July 1877, Edger became the first woman in New Zealand, and in the British Empire, to be awarded a BA. Her graduation was attended by a crowd of nearly 1000, and the Bishop of Auckland presented her with a white camellia, representing 'unpretending excellence'.[262] The *New Zealand Herald* reported the occasion by saying, 'Let us hear no more of the intellectual inferiority of women. For generations their education has been neglected ... . The sex has too long been deprived of that opportunity to excel without which excellence is scarcely possible.'[263]

The graduation ceremony of Kate Edger, along with that of fellow Auckland College and Grammar School student Robert Rattray (BA LLB) in 1880, provided ammunition for those wanting to establish a university college in Auckland. Sir Maurice O'Rorke had been trying to do so since 1872, when, as a cabinet minister, he argued strongly for a university college in the North Island, located in Auckland. This was also a view shared by the Royal Commission on Grammar Schools in 1879; having considered the contributions of such schools to teaching university classes, it concluded that, 'It is evidently impossible successfully to combine school and university work in the same institution',[264] and recommended that university colleges be established at both Auckland and Wellington. Auckland University College opened in 1883.

While Kate Edger rightfully received acclamation for her achievement, her younger sister Lilian followed quickly and directly in her footsteps, also supported by her father and an Entrance Scholarship. In 1882, both sisters graduated with Master of Arts degrees from the University of Canterbury, while teaching at Christchurch Girls' High School—they were not able to undertake postgraduate study in Auckland. Both were destined to be principals of girls' schools: Kate Edger (m.Evans) of Nelson Girls' College (1883–1890), and Lilian Edger of Ponsonby College for Girls in Auckland (1894–1897), and the Hindu Girls' School in Benares, India (1913–1919). Lilian Edger was also the first woman to serve on the Auckland University College Council, between 1893 and 1895.[265]

Kate Milligan Edger (m.Evans) (BA 1877, MA 1882) and Lilian Edger (MA 1882)

Kate Milligan Edger (m.Evans) (BA 1877, MA 1882), first woman graduate in New Zealand.
MACMILLAN BROWN LIBRARY, UNIVERSITY OF CANTERBURY 1991/1 39C

Lilian Edger (MA 1882), first woman to serve on the Auckland University Council (1893–1895).
MACMILLAN BROWN LIBRARY, UNIVERSITY OF CANTERBURY 1991/1 39G

Because Auckland University College was not yet established, both Kate and her sister Lilian completed their undergraduate studies through the Auckland College and Grammar School, one of a number of secondary schools affiliated to the University of New Zealand. Both graduated with MA degrees at Canterbury in 1882.

Girls' secondary schooling in Auckland

Auckland provided public secondary schools for girls later than Dunedin and Christchurch. Although some girls attended the Auckland Girls' High School earlier, it was not until 1888 that Auckland Girls' Grammar School was established on the same site as the boys' school, Auckland Grammar School in Symonds Street, with overflow classes held in the crypt of St Paul's Church. Even then, the girls' and boys' sections of the school began and ended the school day at different times to prevent any contact between the sexes. It took until 1909 for the new Girls' Grammar School buildings to be opened on the Howe Street site in Newton.[266]

In 1906, when Auckland Girls' Grammar was at last to become a separate school on its own site, the Auckland Grammar School Board was seeking a headmistress with a British university education. It instructed the New Zealand High Commissioner in London, William Pember Reeves, to select an unmarried woman with teaching experience, the salary to be £400. One month later, the board changed its mind and decided to make a direct offer of appointment to Anne Whitelaw.[267] She later wrote:

Anne Whitelaw (MA TCD 1896)

Anne Whitelaw, aged ten, at Ponsonby Primary School.
AUCKLAND GIRLS' GRAMMAR SCHOOL

Anne Whitelaw, an outstanding scholar in mathematics, was the first New Zealand graduate from Girton College, University of Cambridge, 1896.
AUCKLAND GIRLS' GRAMMAR SCHOOL

Born in Scotland, Anne Whitelaw arrived in New Zealand on the Endymion at the age of three, accompanied by her mother Grace Whitelaw, her older sister Barbara, and her baby brother James, to join her father James, an accountant with the Bank of New Zealand. Six older children followed later when the family could afford it, and three more were born in New Zealand. The family settled at 'Rosenheim' in Cameron Street, Ponsonby.[268] Along with her brothers and sisters, the young Anne Whitelaw attended the local Ponsonby Primary School. In 1888, Anne's father died, leaving Grace to raise the children alone. All were encouraged to further their education, and that year Anne began as a foundation pupil of Auckland Girls' Grammar School, when it was established on the same site

I remember well the perfect spring morning in Buckinghamshire when with great surprise I read a cable from Mr Tibbs telling me that the Girls' Grammar School was to be separated from the Boys' School and the Board of Governors wished me to be their first head Mistress. It was a great day for me. I felt proud to have been asked, and it seemed so direct a call that there could be only one possible answer.[269]

The headmaster of Auckland Grammar, Mr J. Tibbs, the Oxford-trained mathematician who had taught Anne Whitelaw, may have recommended her to the board; certainly his enthusiasm for the appointment was later evident in his annual report: 'I should have had misgivings in handing over my charge to a stranger, but I can resign it without hesitation, though not without regret, to so distinguished a pupil of the school.'[270]

It seems that while the board was quick to secure a most suitable headmistress, they were less well organised when it came to providing the new school. Anne Whitelaw had clearly been led to believe that her school in 'splendid new buildings'[271] would be ready. She was therefore dismayed to discover that 'the building was barely started so I became headmistress to a group of girls in the crypt of St Paul's Church, and another group who were still with the boys at the Grammar School in Symonds Street'.[272]

in Symonds Street as the boys' school, Auckland Grammar.[273] During her four years there she achieved especially well in mathematics, and won numerous prizes, including a Junior University Scholarship.[274] This led to her completing her medical preliminary year at Auckland University College in 1893.[275] She did not continue with medicine, but instead set sail for England in 1894 to study at Girton College, Cambridge, where she achieved the female equivalent of an MA in mathematics in 1896.[276]

In 1906 she was invited to be principal of Auckland Girls' Grammar.[277] Anne Whitelaw was headmistress for a mere three and a half years. Yet her legacy was profound, as the annals of the school show. One of her former pupils wrote of her 'forceful yet lovable personality, her unswerving standard of excellence in both work and behaviour, her stimulating and inspiring leadership, and her clear insight into the potentialities of her charges'.[278] Fifty-six years later, the recently retired headmistress, Rua Gardner, wrote 'What she was and what she stood for still influence the school … in all worthwhile things … . This is the measure of her greatness.'[279]

*Appointed foundation principal of Auckland Girls'
High School in 1906, Anne Whitelaw ran the school
across two temporary premises at the boys' school site in
Symonds Street and the crypt of St Paul's Church until
the new school was opened in Howe Street in 1909.*
AUCKLAND GIRLS' GRAMMAR SCHOOL

For two years she contended with having to conduct classes in the crypt, with a red curtain hung down the middle to separate the two classes being taught on either side of it, and the Lower Sixth Form crammed into a far corner. At the end of the first year, Anne Whitelaw may have despaired of her environment but was clearly impressed with her colonial charges. She commented that 'the standard attained was very creditable, and compared favourably with that reached in schools of the same standing in England.'[280] Indeed, she thought the standard of achievement in mathematics to be even higher.

The girls of the Lower Sixth remembered the bleak surroundings, but also their first impressions of Miss Whitelaw: 'She was disgusted with the feeble way we cheered and used to give us practice.'[281] However, as they also found out, 'apart from all the new horizons in learning she helped open up for us, she also taught us the right way to sew on a button'.[282] As well as a range of languages, the sciences, and commercial subjects, Anne Whitelaw was determined to introduce domestic science as a new course of study, and was disappointed when only three students initially took it up. 'It is the absolute importance of all women being able to grapple with the entire management of a home; never was it more important to raise it to a plane above the level of drudgery, to which it is so often and so falsely regarded.'[283] In addition to her philosophy that not all girls were destined for higher education and should be prepared for a domestic world, she

*Epsom Girls' Grammar School opened in
1917, providing a second public girls' school
in Auckland.*
SPECIAL COLLECTIONS, AUCKLAND CITY LIBRARIES (NZ) 4-2874

also saw other advantages of teaching domestic science. As she had noticed in England, it offered the prospect of a new university-trained profession for women. 'Who would dare to say', she challenged, 'that a Chair in domestic science is not as necessary for a country's development as a Chair for music?'[284] When the school finally moved to the new buildings in Howe Street, Newton, in 1909, Anne Whitelaw was equally determined to transform the surrounding raw clay slopes, her 'chasm of emptiness', into landscaped grounds. It is testimony to her vision that the attractive grounds remain to this day.

Apart from Auckland Girls' Grammar, the only other public secondary school for girls in Auckland before 1920 was Epsom Girls' Grammar, established in 1917. With the Auckland population boom from the 1950s, coeducational schools were favoured there, and only two more state girls' secondary schools were established: Westlake Girls' High School in 1962, and Kelston Girls' High School in 1963.

It was left to the private schools to provide the bulk of separate girls' secondary education in Auckland. The Catholic Church was early to do so, with the Sisters of Mercy, led by Mother Mary Cecelia, opening 'a school for young ladies' in Wyndham Street in 1851, and later adding a boarding school. Girls from all denominations were welcomed. By 1855, the Sisters of Mercy had also established St Anne's, a Māori girls' boarding school, on Mount St Mary in Ponsonby. They ran this school for seven years before handing it over to the French order, the Congregation of the Holy Family. However, the French sisters left New Zealand a short time later, and Mother Mary Cecelia moved her convent from Wyndham Street to Mount St Mary, establishing in 1862 what is now known as St Mary's College.[285] Another long-established Catholic girls' school, Baradene College of the Sacred Heart in Victoria Avenue, was opened in 1909, and Marist College by the Marist sisters in 1928.

It was perhaps because of her own secondary schooling experience in Auckland that Lilian Edger set up Ponsonby College for Girls in 1894, and ran it for three years until ill health forced her to close. Meanwhile, across town in Remuera, Mrs Moore-Jones founded Ladies' College at Melrose Hall, and at about the same time Miss C. Law opened her own School for Young Ladies in Portland Road. These two schools merged in 1900 and provided schooling for girls, known as Cleveland House, until 1934.[286] The Anglican Church established two girls' schools in Auckland in quick succession: Queen Victoria School for Māori Girls in Parnell

Four of the private schools providing girls' secondary schooling in Auckland in the early 1900s

Baradene College, Victoria Avenue, 1909.
SPECIAL COLLECTIONS, AUCKLAND CITY LIBRARIES (NZ) 435-C6-22A

Auckland Diocesan School for Girls, Epsom, 1904.
AUCKLAND WAR MEMORIAL MUSEUM DU436.1235 M928

Cleveland House (1900–1934), Garden Road, Remuera, combined the former Ladies' College Remuera at Melrose Hall with Miss Law's School for Young Ladies from Portland Road.
SPECIAL COLLECTIONS, AUCKLAND CITY LIBRARIES (NZ) 7-A11223

St Cuthbert's College, which opened in 1914, incorporated one of the largest of the private girls' schools in Auckland, namely the Miss Bews' Mt Eden College.
SPECIAL COLLECTIONS, AUCKLAND CITY LIBRARIES (NZ) 35-R237

opened in 1903, followed by the Epsom-based Auckland Diocesan School for Girls in 1904. Other privately owned and operated girls' schools opened at the end of the nineteenth century and ran for several years, including the Girls' College at Devonport, Mrs Hanna's Melmerely Collegiate School in Parnell, and Miss Bews' Mt Eden College.[287] This school, run by May Bews and her sisters Kate and Alice, grew to 210 pupils by 1912, and was for many years the largest private girls' school in New Zealand. In 1914, the school was sold, becoming St Cuthbert's College.[288]

Prince Albert College for Girls (1896–1906)

Although short-lived, this institution was remarkable for a number of reasons. In the 1890s, the Methodist Church came under pressure from its own clergy and missionaries to provide secondary schooling for their children. Unusually, it opened the girls' and boys' sections of Prince Albert College, including superior boarding and teaching facilities, on adjacent sites in upper Queen Street in 1896.[289] Secondly, it set out to employ the best university graduates it could find, and offered perhaps the most comprehensive curriculum of any New Zealand secondary school of the time, providing an alternative to Auckland Grammar (which was then attended by both girls and boys).

The student roll was comprised mainly of the daughters of Methodist clergy and Methodist parishioners, although those of other denominations were admitted from time to time as places became available. While Methodist clergy no doubt had the

Prince Albert College, upper Queen Street (right foreground) ran separate classes for girls and boys of Methodist clergy from 1896 to 1906. The girls' college employed a series of New Zealand's first women graduates and produced, in turn, a great many more.
SPECIAL COLLECTIONS, AUCKLAND CITY LIBRARIES (NZ) 1-W1

Prospectus—Prince Albert College for Girls, 1898

E. Rainforth MA Headmistress

Day pupils—over 13 years of age—3 guineas per term

Weekly boarders—over 13 years of age—50 guineas per annum

Languages—Latin and Greek, French and German

English

History

Geography

Mathematics—arithmetic, algebra, Euclid, trigonometry

Elementary science—chemistry, botany

Shorthand, book-keeping, drawing, singing[290]

fees subsidised, it was not cheap to send one's daughter to Prince Albert, especially as a boarder; nevertheless, eighty-three girls were enrolled by 1897, and 116 girls by 1898.[291] Prince Albert College both employed and produced some outstanding women, and consequently it provides a unique Auckland case study.

All ten of the former Prince Albert College girls who gained a degree took up teaching. For example, Isobel Robertson (MA Victoria 1905) taught at Wellington Girls' (1905, 1911–1914), Nelson Girls' College (1906–1908), and Auckland Girls' Grammar (1916–1924). She also served as a missionary in New Guinea.[292] Rhoda Collins (BA Otago 1907) and her sister Edith (BA Auckland 1907) were also career teachers. When Prince Albert closed, Rhoda Collins took up her second teaching post at Wellington Girls' High School (1908–1922). During this time, both she and Isobel Robertson had their former headmistress, Emma Rainforth (MA Otago 1893), as a colleague (1912–1927). Rhoda then taught for a year at Wellington Girls' (1924) and Wellington East Girls' (1925) before ending her career back in Auckland, teaching alongside her sister at Epsom Girls' Grammar (1926–1928).[293] Edith Collins began her thirty-two years of teaching at Hamilton West District High School (1908–1910), and was there when the school became Hamilton High School. She was a senior mistress until 1920, then moved back to Auckland, where she was senior mistress at Epsom Girls' Grammar from 1923 to 1940.[294]

Lela Button (BA Auckland 1903) and Ella Garland (MA Canterbury 1911) taught for a year only, at Prince Albert and Auckland Girls' Grammar respectively,[295] before marrying, while Jessie Smith taught for four years at

Graduate staff members and pupils of Prince Albert College

Staff

1896	Rachel McKerrow	MA 1896	Otago	Headmistress
1896–1903	Emma Rainforth	MA 1893	Otago	Headmistress 1897–1903
1897–1900	Mabel Salmond	BA 1896	Otago	
1898–99	Christina Cruickshank	MA 1896	Otago	Later principal of Southland Girls' and Timaru Girls'
1901–04	Olive Cunningham	BA 1900	Otago	
1901–06	Marion Thomson (m.Thompson)	MA 1899	Otago	Headmistress 1903–06
1901	Mabel Crump*	MA 1897	Auckland	
1902–07	Rhoda Collins*	BA 1907	Otago	
1903	Lela Button*	BA 1903	Auckland	
1906	Annie Ironside*	MA 1907		Later principal of Girton College, Bendigo

*former pupils

Pupils

1896	Isobel Robertson	MA 1905	Victoria
1896	Rhoda Collins	BA 1907	Otago
1897	Lela Button (m.Taylor)	BA 1903	Auckland
1897	Jessie Hetherington	BA 1902	Auckland
1900	Edith Collins	BA 1907	Auckland
1900	Elsie Griffin	MA 1906	Auckland
1901	Jessie Smith (m.O'Shea)	BA 1918	Otago
1901	Ella Garland (m.Gunson)	MA 1911	Canterbury
1904	Myrtle Garland (m.Gunson)	MA 1912	Canterbury
1904	Teresa Tompkins (m.Thomas)	MA 1914	Auckland

Otago Girls' (1918–1921)[296] and Teresa Tompkins for five years at Hamilton High School (1914–1919)[297] prior to each marrying. Myrtle Garland (MA Canterbury 1911) taught at Nelson Girls' College (1912–1919) prior to her marriage, but returned to teach part time (as Mrs Gunson) between 1924 and 1949.[298]

The remaining two women from the Prince Albert College group both graduated from Auckland University College, and are worthy of closer attention. Jessie Hetherington went on to study at Girton College, Cambridge, converting two Tripos Certificates in History and Law to an MA from Trinity College, Dublin, and also completing a Diploma in Education from the University of London. During her career she was a headmistress in Australia, a university lecturer in Wellington, and the first woman secondary inspector of schools in New Zealand. Her full educational and career profile can be found in Chapter 7.

The career of Elsie Griffin (MA (Hons) 1906) took a different direction. She lived nearly all her life in Auckland, devoting most of it to tireless work within a range of women's community organisations.

Elsie Griffin (MA (Hons) 1906)

Elsie Griffin was sixteen by the time she enrolled at Prince Albert College, but that year her Methodist minister father moved the family to Onehunga in Auckland from Leeston in Canterbury, where she had been attending the local district high school.[299] When she went on to Auckland University College, her interest in botany had already been stimulated by teacher Emma Rainforth. She graduated BA in 1905 and MA with first class honours in botany in 1906.[300] Elsie Griffin went straight from university to teach botany at Auckland Girls' Grammar between 1906 and 1910.[301] There she proved to be a popular, progressive, and effective teacher, and her ambitious fieldtrips with pupils into the Waitākere Ranges to collect specimens became legendary. 'Tall and large, she dressed oddly, and was inclined to indulge in some boisterous good fun. This endeared her to her younger charges, who knew her as "Griff", but was apt to raise eyebrows amongst her staider colleagues.'[302]

Elsie Griffin had already set up a study group among sister graduates in Auckland, under the auspices of the Young Women's Christian Association (YWCA), by the time she left Auckland Girls' in 1910. Her strong Methodism, as well as her belief in the strength of organised community-based education for women, led her to a lifelong involvement with women's community organisations. She began by answering the call from the International YWCA for university-educated women to volunteer for regional administrator positions, serving as secretary for the Dunedin YWCA between 1912 and 1915.[303] She then travelled to the YWCA training school in New York, where she spent two years studying social work, returning in 1917 to take over as the

Auckland University College

When Auckland University College opened in 1883, the first young women to attend came directly from Auckland Girls' High School, later Auckland Girls' Grammar. (The school is referred to from this point on as Auckland Girls'.) This tradition continued, and by 1920, of the 103 women graduates to that time, at least 57 percent had attended Auckland Girls'. The Bachelor of Science degree was introduced at Auckland in 1887, but as at Canterbury,

Auckland University College library.
SPECIAL COLLECTIONS, UNIVERSITY OF AUCKLAND LIBRARY 5-97/5.6.2/15A

women graduates in science were rare, with only seven of the 103 graduates between 1887 and 1920 holding BSc degrees. However, women did proceed to master's degrees, with fifty-seven of the 103 gaining MAs by 1920. As at Otago and Canterbury, a large number (61 percent) of all women graduates from

secretary of the Auckland branch of the YWCA. Her biographer, Sandra Coney, summarises Elsie's contributions:

> She is credited with modernising the Auckland YWCA, so that it was fully part of the secular world while retaining its Christian roots. Contemporaries noted her business sense, her organisational flair and her ability to get people working for her on a task. In 1918 the YWCA moved to imposing new Queen Street premises, and by 1919 could boast 2,500 members.[304]

While in the United States, Elsie Griffin had observed the power of women's club movements and the ways in which women from all walks of life could be politicised to 'take a live interest in municipal matters'.[305] This was part of her philosophy about making educational opportunities available to women at the community level, and

encouraging women to actively participate. She was a key force in the establishment and growth of the YWCA of New Zealand. Between 1924 and 1934 she was the National General Secretary of the YWCA in Australia and New Zealand, with an international profile. During these years she spent much time in Australia and travelling further abroad.

She was also active in a range of other women's organisations, including the founding of the Auckland branch of the Federation of University Women; the Pan-Pacific and South East Asia Women's Association; the Lyceum Club; the National Council of Women, where she served on the national executive; and the Food Value League, a group that gave advice on nutrition in relation to food rationing during World War Two. When Elsie Griffin died in 1968, she left bequests to the YWCA and the University of Auckland.[306]

Auckland University College geology/ biology laboratory.
SPECIAL COLLECTIONS, UNIVERSITY OF AUCKLAND LIBRARY 2-LTOPB

Auckland went teaching. As far as records indicate, one-third of the women graduates from this period married.

The first women to graduate from Auckland University College in 1889 were Mary Hill (m.Cole-Baker) (BA), Louisa Durrieu (m.Hill) (BA), and Edith Adams (m.Buchanan) (BA, also first MA 1890). All three had attended Auckland Girls', and all three went teaching prior to marriage. In 1906, the first woman to graduate in law was Ellen Melville (LLB), later long-serving Auckland city councillor and National Council of Women stalwart. The following year, the first woman to graduate in music was Edith Webb (MusB). The first woman to graduate in science at Auckland was Mona Brown (m.Osborne) (BSc) in 1908.

Student life at Auckland University College was later described by Christina Gray (quoted by Keith Sinclair), who had come from Auckland Girls' to study between 1906 and 1908,[307] and graduated with a BA in 1909:

> The course I took kept me in the main building which had been the original rooms of the Provincial Parliament. Downstairs there was a small Library with fairly well-stocked shelves, great leather tables, in winter time large glowing fires of Westport coal, and a general air of quiet dignity. One day when I was rejoicing in the comfort of the fire I was told that it was kept glowing so continuously not for the students but to preserve the old leather covered books. The general decay of the building was such that books would soon deteriorate, if the atmosphere had been kept damp.[308]

Christina Gray continued to take an interest in the university college long after she left. For example, in 1917, when she was teaching at Auckland Girls', she attended a predemolition ceremony organised by the students' association to mark the farewell to the old college building, which students had named the 'shedifice'. Also present were Kate Edger (now Mrs Evans) and her sister Lilian Edger. Christina Gray 'thought that with their "dowdy" "Holland outfits", their old-fashioned hats, their hair up in buns and heavy shoes, they typified the best of early Auckland—plain living had to accompany every effort at high thinking'. She thought that 'in them in this old wooden building there was the spirit of a true university'.[309]

Although many Auckland students were part time, women students did take part in student activities such as the Women's Korero Club, a debating and discussion group (1898), which, according to Sinclair, became the Women's Common Room Club in 1901. Three women students were able to go to the first student Easter Tournament in Christchurch in 1902, not least because two of them had brothers who acted as chaperones. These women were Rita Pickmere, Cecil Hull, and Marion Metcalfe. All three had attended Auckland Girls', and all became teachers.

Marguerita (Rita) Blomfield Pickmere won a University Entrance Scholarship in 1897. By the time she went to the Christchurch Tournament in 1902, she had graduated with a BA, and completed an MA at the end of that year. She went straight from university to teach at Wellington Girls' High School from 1903 to 1904, and from there to Nelson Girls' College, where she taught until 1906.

This is likely to have been the year she married Alan Mulgan, a journalist and writer. Their son was the writer John Mulgan, also a graduate of Auckland. Their daughter Dorothea (Turner) later gained her PhD from Victoria at the age of eighty-one. Rita Mulgan was an active member of the Federation of University Women, serving as president of the Auckland branch between 1925 and 1929. As national vice-president, she led the New Zealand delegation to the 1926 conference in Amsterdam.[310]

Cecil Lena Hull also won a University Entrance Scholarship. She was involved in student activities, and was on the editorial committee of the student publication *The Collegian*. She graduated with a BA in 1903 and an MA in 1905. She went back to teach

Marguerita (Rita) Blomfield Pickmere (m.Mulgan) (MA 1902).
SPECIAL COLLECTIONS, UNIVERSITY OF AUCKLAND LIBRARY
5/6/1/1/3

Graduates, Auckland University College, 1905. ALEXANDER TURNBULL LIBRARY, WELLINGTON, NZ. AUCKLAND STAR COLL 9-2871-1/1

at her former school in 1915 and remained on the staff for eighteen years. During this time, Cecil Hull was an active member of the Federation of University Women, serving on the national executive between 1925 and 1929.[311]

Marion Hannah Metcalfe graduated with a BA in 1905. Between 1910 and 1913 she taught at Waihi District High School, returning in 1914 to teach at Auckland Girls'. As Mrs Walker, she resumed teaching in 1923 at Epsom Girls' Grammar, and was on the staff there for twenty years.[312]

First women on the students' association executive

The Auckland Students' Association was founded in 1891. The first vice-president was Catherine Donaldson Grant (MA 1893), and the 1893 executive included Annie Morrison (MA 1893) and Winifred Picken (MA 1895). All three had attended Auckland Girls': Annie Morrison and Winifred Picken were the first winners of University Entrance Scholarships at the school, in 1888 (when Annie came ninth in New Zealand) and 1890 respectively, and Catherine Grant and Annie Morrison were the first former old girls to graduate with MAs.[313] All three would be future leaders of New Zealand girls' secondary schools.

Women continued to be politically active at Auckland, and in 1908 women comprised four out of eleven members of the students' association. All would graduate with Bachelor of Arts degrees in 1909.

In his history of Auckland University, Keith Sinclair makes the point that for this vibrant generation of young scholars within a small college, especially those who were full time, many of whom were 'either women or scholarship winners, or both', it was 'an intimate and intense society. Everyone knew just about everybody else.'[314] Strong friendships were forged, and anxieties for fellow students ran high during World War One, when 689 former Auckland University College students were on active military service. At least 141 were killed, and many more were wounded. The impact was unprecedented, as Sinclair stressed: 'it would be hard to exaggerate the effect of the toll of deaths and wounded in that war'.[315] The other three university colleges were similarly devastated; according to Sinclair, 20 percent of those who served abroad were killed. This toll of young men, through death or disablement, affected their families and their young friends, both women and men. Many of the first generation of women graduates lost sons; the second generation lost husbands or young men to whom they were betrothed.

There were other effects too. Numbers of Auckland women graduates were appointed to boys' public secondary schools for the first time, to help replace male staff who were on active service, or who had been killed. Married women were among this group. The smaller provincial town schools were the first to be affected. Waitaki Boys' High School in Oamaru appointed three women graduates to its staff between 1916 and 1919. They were Georgina McMullan (BA 1914), Catherine Copland (BA 1913), and Henrietta Woodhouse (MA 1914).

Catherine Donaldson Grant (MA 1893)

Catherine Donaldson Grant (MA 1893) resigned as principal of New Plymouth Girls' High School to join the war effort in London and Egypt.

It is likely that Catherine Grant went from Auckland Girls' to Auckland University College as a part-time student, while teaching in a local primary school, as she was already registered as a teacher by 1890. In 1891, when she was vice-president of the students' association, she was completing a BA, graduating in 1892. The following year, she completed an MA in political science; by then she was based in Wanganui, where she was presumably teaching until 1897, when she won an appointment as senior teacher to the girls' side of New Plymouth High School. After the girls' and boys' sections of the school were separated, Catherine Grant became the first principal of New Plymouth Girls' High School in 1913. During her second year as principal, World War One was declared, and she decided to serve overseas in the Women's Auxiliary Forces. Initially she worked in Egypt, 'serving the forward-going troops in the railway station canteens ... visiting them in hospital when they returned wounded, writing their letters home for them ...'.[316] By 1917 she had joined the New Zealand War Contingent Association in England, and continued her work there until the end of the war. By the early 1920s she had returned to Auckland, where she was an active member of the Federation of University Women, representing the Auckland branch in 1923 as delegate to the New Zealand Conference in Dunedin. Catherine Grant died in 1926.[317]

Timaru Boys' High School recruited Janet McLeod (MA 1908) in 1917 and she remained until 1921. Emmie Billens (BA 1911) went to New Plymouth Boys' High School for one year (1917–1918). By 1917, the first of the larger urban boys' schools had also begun to seek women teachers: Otago Boys' High School appointed Mrs Cora Longton (MA 1901) and Evelyn Whitehead (MA 1911) from 1917 to 1918; Christchurch Boys' High School employed Mrs Mabel Rhodes (MA 1902) between 1918 and 1919; and from 1917 to 1921 Auckland Boys' Grammar appointed an unprecedented five women: Mabel Freeman (MA 1912), Dorothy Holmden (MA 1913), Elizabeth McCulloch (MA 1916), Mary Terry (MSc 1916), and Eva Lynch (MA 1904). Of all these women, only

Annie Morrison (MA 1893)

Annie Christina Morrison (MA 1893), foundation principal of Epsom Girls' Grammar School 1917–1929.

It is only the live fish that swim against the current; drifting is easy, it is always downward.[318]
(*Korero*, 1929)

Annie Christina Morrison was born in Auckland in 1870. After four years in the New Hebrides (Vanuatu) with her missionary parents, she returned to attend Auckland Girls', where (as noted above) she was the first pupil to win an entrance scholarship to Auckland University College in 1888; she combined university study and primary school teaching until she graduated with a BA in 1892. She then returned to Auckland Girls' as a part-time teacher, and in 1893 served on the students' association executive while completing her master's degree in mathematics and physics.[319]

When Auckland Girls' was established separately from the boys' school in 1906, Annie Morrison transferred there, and by 1914 was senior mistress. When Epsom Girls' opened in 1917, she became its foundation principal, a position she held until her retirement in 1929. At the end of her first year as principal, she wrote that her hope for her first 170 pupils was 'to maintain all they have found good and helpful in its routine and work and to hand down to those who will follow them a tradition of industry and good conduct as a trust to be guarded and preserved'.[320]

She cemented early the academic reputation of Epsom Girls', and no one knew better than her the formidable record of rival school Auckland Girls'. For the thirteen years she was principal, the substance of her message within annual reports was 'learning is good, combined with character it is better'.[321] Annie Morrison believed that girls needed to be able to step up to examinations 'without fuss or complaint … very little anxiety should be felt about them … a girl who cannot produce her knowledge when required is likely to fail in other emergencies of life, and cannot be considered so valuable a citizen as the one who can keep her head and rise to the occasion'.[322]

In retirement, Annie Morrison lived in Auckland. She served on the Auckland Federation of University Women's Trust Board from 1939 to 1950.[323]

four were first-time teachers; the two married women were very experienced teachers, and the others had taught in small rural district high schools or, in one case, a provincial private school. This latter group may well have found it difficult to obtain a position in the highly sought-after girls' secondary schools, but having the experience of teaching in a boys' school did not harm their careers. Indeed, all those who continued teaching after the war secured their next teaching posts in girls' secondary schools.

Among them were two Auckland University College graduates of 1912, Mabel Freeman and Dorothy Holmden. Both took up their initial teaching posts in district high schools—Mabel Freeman went to Pukekohe, and Dorothy Holmden to Waihi, both between 1913 and 1917. During this time a number of their fellow students at Auckland had been killed on overseas service, including two members of their graduation group—the Rhodes Scholar Alan Wallace, and J. C. Brook. Another, Frank Taylor, president of the students' association in 1912, was badly wounded and would receive a Military Cross.[324] For Mabel Freeman and Dorothy Holmden, returning to Auckland after five years, and arriving at Auckland Grammar, must have been particularly poignant. Both taught there for two years before they were appointed in 1920 to nearby Epsom Girls' Grammar, where they found a sister graduate, Hilda Kirkbride (MA), who worked there from 1917 to 1943. Together they remained at Epsom Girls' for the rest of their careers, until 1944.[325]

By the 1920s, student numbers at Auckland had more than doubled to 1321, with 142 extramural students. Of the full-time students, one-quarter were women; but even in 1920, all women students were relegated to one side of

Winifred Picken (MA 1895)

Like Annie Morrison, Winifred Picken went straight from Auckland Girls' to Auckland University College, armed with an Entrance Scholarship, but as a full-time student, and graduating BA in 1894. The following year she added an MA with honours in mathematics and physics, and in 1896 she was back at Auckland Girls' teaching alongside Annie Morrison. Unlike her friend, however, Winifred Picken spent her entire thirty-year career at the school. By 1916 she was third assistant, and between 1917 and 1920 was senior mistress. She was also an active member of the New Zealand Federation of University Women, serving as president of the Auckland branch in 1920. Her leadership skills were already evident to the Grammar School Board, and in 1921 she was appointed principal of Auckland Girls', a position she held until her retirement in 1925.[326]

the library—there was to be no fraternising between the sexes or between the books.[327] Outside classes and the library, there was a women's common room, but the meagre facilities were limited to a gas ring and a sink. Still, they seem to have tried to make their own fun within their own space. The 1933 University College jubilee book reported:

> The more athletic amazons are reputed to have been able to make a tour of the walls without touching the floor. The noise that accompanied this game was often such as to annoy the Professor of English and he is believed to have entered the room on one occasion only to discover that the offender was his own daughter.[328]

The 1933 jubilee book, written by E. H. Blow, did include some references to women students; but in terms of acknowledging more fully the contributions of women students, it fell well behind the Canterbury jubilee book, written by Alice Candy and James Hight. For example, at the end of the Auckland publication, short biographical profiles of forty-one distinguished students appeared, but only four were women.

The first was Kathleen Maisey Curtis (MA 1915, DSc London 1919), whose contributions to New Zealand science would later be more widely recognised. The entry keeps to a standard formula of qualifications, scholarships, and career. Kathleen Curtis went to university from Auckland Girls', and in the final year of her BA in 1913 was the Senior Scholarship winner in botany. In 1915 she graduated with an MA with first class honours in botany, and that year became the first woman at Auckland to win an Exhibition Scholarship for overseas study. Having gained a doctorate in botany from the University of London, and spent some time overseas, Kathleen Curtis returned to New Zealand to take up an appointment as a mycologist at the Cawthron Institute in Nelson. She specialised in plant diseases, and the Royal Society of New Zealand recognised her research by making her the first woman Fellow (later Senior Fellow) of the Society, in 1936.[329]

The second woman selected by Blow was Mary Edith Clarke (BA 1910, MA 1911), who, under her married name of Mary Scott, was by 1933 a well-known New Zealand writer[330] (and was active in the students' association). Mary Scott was to become a much more renowned author after 1933, when the jubilee history appeared. In 1991, a much fuller account of her life was written by Heather Roberts for *The Book of New Zealand Women*. This account, as well as additional research, shows that Mary Clarke attended Auckland Girls', and earned first class honours in English literature and French before going teaching. Her first post was as the only woman staff member at Thames High School, between 1912 and 1913. According to Roberts, she also taught at Gisborne and Christchurch. She met Walter Scott in Gisborne while nursing her mother, married him in 1914, then lived on a farm at Pirongia, west of Te Awamutu, until 1958. The couple had four children and while they were at school in Te Awamutu, Mary Scott worked in the town library and began contributing columns and stories to newspapers. These were combined into four books produced between 1936 and 1954. Her thirty-five other books were written between 1953 and 1978, including the famous *Breakfast at Six*, which was reprinted twice and, like many of her other books, was translated into other languages. Her novels appealed to New Zealanders, as they were set in rural New Zealand and focused on farming families and communities. Mary Scott died at the age of ninety-one in 1979.[331]

The third woman selected by Blow in 1933 was Annie Tizard, who, by that time, had just retired from a sixteen-year teaching career in girls' secondary schools. Another Auckland Girls' pupil, she was the college's Senior Scholar in botany in 1915, the same year she graduated with a BA. Her MA in 1916 was earned with first class honours in botany, and during that year she also taught at St Cuthbert's. The following year she joined the staff at Auckland Girls' and taught there until 1921. Her next move was to New Plymouth Girls' High School (1922–1926), although Blow suggests she travelled to India and England in 1925. Hamilton High School appointed her senior mistress in 1927, a position she held until 1931, when she became principal of Wanganui Girls' High School (1931–1938). In Hamilton she was copresident of the Waikato branch of the New Zealand Federation of University Women.[332]

The last of the women students selected by Blow is inspiring, both because she was blind and because, if Blow had not chosen her, the record of her life at Auckland may well have been lost. May Roussell first went to Auckland University College as an undergraduate in 1919, and completed a major part of her arts degree there. One can only imagine the difficulties she experienced. However, by 1925 she had transferred to Victoria University College, where she completed an MA in 1926. According to Blow's account, she then 'took up massage as a profession', and secured the distinction of first place in the Dominion in the massage examination at the medical school in Dunedin. In 1993, the authors of *Redbrick and Bluestockings: Women at Victoria 1899–1993* included May Roussell in their account, pointing out that 'she was blind from the age of four, studied classics at Victoria but then worked as a physiotherapist, one of the few careers open at that time to someone with her disability'.[333]

The first woman was appointed to the academic staff at Auckland University College in 1924. Dora Lilian Miller had graduated from Auckland two years earlier with an MA in French, and had recently returned from the Sorbonne in Paris with three diplomas. Her first position was as assistant lecturer in French, officially to assist Professor Walker; but in reality, according to Sinclair, 'for many years she did much, perhaps most of the teaching, and was Walker's devoted helper, admirer and protector. She was a very good teacher. Auckland students of French had rarely won a Senior Scholarship. Now they won it ten times in eleven years, which was an impressive achievement.'[334]

Dora Miller was employed by the university until 1941, by which time she was a senior lecturer. Her resignation was connected with Professor Walker. His very tough marking of French matriculation scripts had recently been challenged—his median mark was twenty-three, rather than the examination board's preferred median of forty-three. Indeed, the board suspected that he had not marked the scripts with due diligence, and sent them for re-marking to Professor Boyd-Wilson and lecturer Dr A. C. Keys of Victoria University College, who assigned much higher marks. As a result, Professor Walker was dropped as an examiner for the matriculation examinations. When he died in 1940, his replacement, Dr Keys from Victoria, asked Dora Miller to continue in her role. However, she was so displeased with the results of his re-marking of Professor Walker's scripts that she refused, and resigned in protest.[335]

Auckland women graduate teachers

As at Otago and Canterbury, students living more than ten miles from Auckland University College could be exempted from attending lectures, but sat annual examinations. Auckland's exempt students, later called extramural students, were able to sit their exams in regional centres, including Napier, New Plymouth, Nelson, and Wellington.[336] This group of students was important to Auckland University College, as they swelled the still relatively small student population. For example, in 1883, ninety-five students were attending lectures; by 1901, this had risen to only 156 students.[337] Of those attending lectures in 1901, four were graduates and fifty-one were undergraduates, but most of the students (101) were unmatriculated; they had gained entry to the university through being over the age of twenty-one, and were given provisional admission until they had passed a number of degree units.

Another feature of the early Auckland student population attending lectures was that the majority were part time, as many were teachers or training to be teachers at the nearby Wellesley Street Auckland Training College. These students did well: in the second year of classes at Auckland University College, three training college students won three out of four of the scholarships offered by the university, and others excelled in the end-of-year examinations.[338] By 1893, just over half of all Auckland graduates were teachers; by 1901, forty-one out of 114 graduates that year were teachers.[339] Keen to gather as many students as it could, Auckland University College held most classes after

The original Auckland Teachers' Training College, Wellesley Street, Auckland.

6 pm. However, as the headmaster of Thames High School pointed out in 1890, this meant that full-time students had to wait all day for classes, whereas in Canterbury classes were held throughout the day.[340]

Initially, Auckland, like Canterbury, had adopted the Otago model for the academic year. Based on the Scottish system, it comprised just two fourteen-week terms, the idea being that poorer students could work to earn money in the other half of the year. By 1892, following a committee report examining the terms system, the Council of Auckland University College moved to install the English three-term academic year, essentially adding forty-seven days to the teaching year. Not surprisingly, perhaps, this proposal was totally opposed by the professors. However, they suggested that if this system was to be adopted at Auckland, three-week vacations should follow each of the first two terms, with another ninety days' holiday over the summer, and that the third term should include the end-of-year examinations. This system was introduced at Auckland, albeit with three extra teaching weeks added, and became the common model for New Zealand and Australian universities. However, it meant that the University of New Zealand was forced to change its examining procedures to cope with a longer teaching year.[341]

The Auckland Teachers' Training College, Epsom. SPECIAL COLLECTIONS, AUCKLAND CITY LIBRARIES (NZ) 1-W680

At least two Auckland women graduate teachers sought alternative ways of augmenting their income, publishing advertisements for their professional services at a time when such a practice was considered 'not proper' for women. In 1894, Lilian Edger (MA 1882) announced in the New Zealand teachers' monthly journal, *The New Zealand Schoolmaster*, that she was available to 'prepare public candidature for matriculation, Civil Service, teachers and other examinations'. Those interested were asked to enquire about terms by correspondence to her at Ponsonby College for Girls, Auckland, the school she owned and operated for several years.[342] Three years later, Mabel Crump (MA 1897) went a step further, advertising more publicly in the *New Zealand Herald* as a coach for a range of examinations.[343] She had earlier taught at Prince Albert College in 1901, and was later to teach with her sister at Clarendon College in Ballarat, Australia.[344]

The name of Elsie Shrewsbury was to become synonymous with early teacher training in Auckland, due to her influence on hundreds of teachers. She had attended Auckland Girls' and went on to study part time at Auckland University College while teaching at a local primary school. Having gained her BA in 1892, she won a Senior University Scholarship to enable her to complete an MA with first class honours in political science in 1893. This higher degree with honours meant that Elsie Shrewsbury automatically became a Class A graded teacher in the primary school service,[345] the first to do so in Auckland. With this grading, she was also the highest paid woman primary teacher in the region for a number of years. However, Elsie Shrewsbury was also an outstanding teacher. In 1897, while on the staff of the Wellesley Street School, she was appointed by Chief Inspector Donald Petrie to take Saturday morning classes in mathematics with local pupil-teachers.[346] She left Wellesley Street School for two years in 1904 to join the staff at Parnell Primary School, where her A1 grading earnt her the meagre sum of £105. However, she raised her salary to £200 in 1905, when she was appointed to head the secondary department of the Auckland Normal School, formerly known as Wellesley Street School. In 1909 she received a salary increase to £245, but by 1913 it was only £20 more. Indeed, it took until 1918 for Elsie Shrewsbury's salary to match that of a senior mistress in a girls' secondary school. That year she finished her teaching career with a salary of £350. Aware of the many professional issues and difficulties of primary teachers,

Elsie Shrewsbury joined the New Zealand Educational Institute (NZEI) early in her career. For many years she was the Auckland representative at NZEI conferences, and at the 1901 conference in Wellington she was very aware that the Auckland teachers she represented were named by President Grundy as the poorest paid in the country: compared with all the other education board pay rates, the Auckland Board paid less. Elsie Shrewsbury not only strongly identified with the plight of the average Auckland female teacher who earnt £110, compared to their contemporaries in Canterbury who earnt £200, but also took up the cause on their behalf. She was involved in the extensive lobbying NZEI undertook on primary teacher salaries. When the Hogg Commission was established by the government to investigate the inequalities that existed in the payment of salaries in schools of the same size, Elsie Shrewsbury appeared before it on Saturday 1 June 1901, representing Auckland assistant mistresses. She would have been well pleased when the commission recommended a Colonial Scale of Primary Teacher Salaries. This was introduced with the passing of the Public-School Teachers' Salaries Act in 1902.[347]

Among Elsie Shrewsbury's first students in the secondary (B) division, Auckland Training College, in 1906 were five women who already kept terms at university, three of whom would complete degrees. As training college students, they were eligible to have their university fees paid and receive an allowance of £10. However, prior to 1910 they had limited access to boarding allowances, and it is likely that, as each of them was raised in Auckland, they lived in their parents' home.

Fanny Jewel Taylor also attended Auckland Girls', then completed at least one year at university, and obtained a D teaching certificate. By the time she completed her two-year training college course in 1907, she had obtained a C teaching certificate, but not a BA, which took a further year. However, in 1909, with both a BA and C4 teaching grading, she was appointed teaching assistant at Tauranga District High School with a salary of £150, a position she held for nine years, at the end of which her grading had increased to B3. Her next school was Te Awamutu District High School (1920–1921), where she earnt a salary of £350. From there she returned to Auckland, and while on the staff of the Kowhai Intermediate School, she was also an executive committee member of the Women Teachers' Association (1939–1940).[348]

Naomi Gibbons, a contemporary of Fanny Taylor's at Auckland Girls', had a very similar academic pattern: she too left training college with a C teaching certificate and took another year to complete her BA, graduating with Fanny Taylor in 1909. She also headed for a rural district high school to take up her first appointment, at Paeroa in 1910, where her salary was £135. Naomi Gibbons is not recorded as a teacher in official records after 1910, and the reason may well have been that she married—university listings included her with the married name of Sisam.[349]

Of the three initial teacher graduates from the training college, Edith Charlotte Collins became a career teacher. Born in 1886, she attended Newton East School in Auckland before being enrolled at Prince Albert College in Queen Street in 1900. She had already passed a number of university units at Auckland University College by the time she began the teachers' training course in 1906, because in 1907 she graduated with both a BA and a C teaching certificate. Her first teaching position was as assistant at Hamilton West District High School in 1908, where her salary was £125. When Hamilton West became Hamilton High School in 1911, she continued her employment there, becoming senior mistress. It is not clear why she left Hamilton High in 1920, or where she was based until 1923, but in that year she began a seventeen-year tenure at Epsom Girls' Grammar School, initially as an assistant and then as senior mistress. In 1926 she held an A grading and earnt a salary of £354.[350]

While working towards a degree at the same time as undertaking teacher training could result in having university fees paid, those women who were already graduates and wanted to go teaching generally went directly into teaching positions from university. For them, there was no teacher training. In Auckland, the first one-year postgraduate teacher training course was offered in 1911, although those eager to train in the secondary department could do so. It was in this way that Elizabeth Tooman (BA) became the first woman graduate to complete teacher training in Auckland in 1910. The following year, the first MA graduate, Ruby Morrison, did so too.[351]

Elsie Shrewsbury ran the secondary training until 1911, but because there had been so few graduates entering teacher training, a special course for graduates was not offered again until after 1930. Even then, there was no guarantee that there would be positions available in secondary schools, and graduates also spent some teaching practice time in local primary schools. Secondary training took on new impetus under the guidance of Dr John Murdoch, who arrived in 1935 to head the programme at the Auckland Training College. Three years later, he was joined by Olga Adams, the doyenne of Auckland secondary science teachers. Olga Adams attended Auckland Girls', and proceeded to study science at Auckland University College. In 1918 she won the Sinclair Scholarship.[352] She joined the staff of Takapuna Grammar School in 1928 and completed her master's degree in science part time at Auckland University College, graduating in 1930. She specialised in biology, and was later described as having 'the gift of lucid and interesting exposition that led to pupil enthusiasm'.[353] Many former pupils at Takapuna Grammar were quick to acknowledge her teaching as instrumental in their careers; they included Professor G. T. S. Baylis, Chair of Botany at the University of Otago, Professor N. G. Stephenson of the University of Sydney, Miss Jean Crosher (MSc 1937), headmistress of St Hilda's Collegiate School, and Dr E. J. Godley, Director of the Botany Division of DSIR. To them she was a 'tremendous teacher, an inspiring teacher; when you left her class you already knew Stage I University botany'.[354] Olga Adams was not only a popular teacher and colleague at Takapuna Grammar, she was also much appreciated by teacher trainees who spent their teaching practice at the school. Similarly, her graduate students at the Auckland Training College benefited from her teaching for the twelve years she was on the staff. Olga Adams died suddenly in 1950.[355]

Auckland University College produced many outstanding women scholars in the years to 1945. While the influence of those who taught in Auckland City girls' schools endured, there were many others who spent their careers in town schools outside Auckland. It was in this way that young rural women in the upper North Island were taught for the first time by young women scholars within a secondary school setting.

Notes

260 Wellington College and Nelson College were also affiliated to the University of New Zealand for teaching. The University of New Zealand was responsible for the examinations.
261 Hughes, 1993; Hughes & Ahern, 1993.
262 Hughes, 1993.
263 *New Zealand Herald*, 11, 12 July 1877.

264 *AJHR*, 1879, H-1; *AJHR*, 1880, H-1; Reichel & Tate, 1925, pp. 1–90.
265 Sinclair, 1983, p. 306.
266 McCulloch, 1988; Northey, 1988; Trembath, 1969.
267 Northey, 1988.
268 O'Connor, 1967.
269 Flint, 1989, p. 14.
270 Flint, 1989, p. 30.
271 *Ibid.*
272 *Auckland Girls' Grammar School Archives*, 1963, interview.
273 Northey, 1988; Trembath, 1969.
274 *Auckland Girls' Grammar School Archives*, school rolls, school lists 1888–1893.
275 *Ibid.* Prizes awarded 1888; 1889; 1890. She completed her Medical Preliminary
    at Auckland University College and in the same year re-sat Junior Scholarship,
    improving her position from the previous year and coming 17th in New Zealand.
276 *Girton College admission register, 1894; Girton College admission register, 1897.*
277 Northey, 1988.
278 O'Connor, 1967, p. 25.
279 *Ibid.*
280 *Auckland Girls' Grammar School Archives*, 1963, interview.
281 *Auckland Girls' Grammar School Archives*, Former Pupils of the Lower Sixth Remember
    Miss Whitelaw, September 1963.
282 *Ibid.*
283 *Auckland Girls' Grammar School Archives*, Report of the Headmistress, 1908.
284 O'Connor, 1967, p. 17.
285 Delany, 1990; Sisters of Mercy, 1952.
286 Winkelmann Collection, Auckland City Library 7-A11074; 7-A11223; 7-A4483; *New
    Zealand Graphic*, 1 March 1903; 23 July 1904.
287 *New Zealand Graphic*, 23 July 1904.
288 McClean, 1993.
289 MET 067/1/00/1; Methodist Archives, Prince Albert College, The Kinder Library, St
    John's Theological College, Meadowbank, Auckland.
290 *Prince Albert College MS Collection*, MET 067/2/00/2.
291 *Prince Albert College MS Collection*, MET 067/2/00/1.
292 *AJHR*, 1907, E-12, p. 24; *AJHR*, 1909, E-6, p. 35; Harding, 1982, p. 170; Northey, 1988,
    p. 242; *Prince Albert College MS Collection*, MET 067/1/1/4/9/1896.
293 *AJHR*, 1924, E-1, p. 4; *AJHR*, 1929, E-6, p. 4; Arthur & Buttle, 1950, p. 39; Gambrill,
    1969, p. 107; Harding, 1982, p. 171; *Prince Albert College MS Collection*, MET 067/2/1,
    MET 067/1/1/ 19/9/1896.
294 *AJHR*, 1909, E-6, p. 20; *AJHR*, 1921–1922, E-6, p. 13; Epsom Girls' Grammar, 1967, p.
    52; Hamilton High School, 1971; *Prince Albert College MS Collection*, MET 067/1/1/
    12/2/1900.
295 Arthur & Buttle, 1950; Northey, 1988, p. 241; *Prince Albert College MS Collection*, MET
    067/2/.
296 *AJHR*, 1919, E-6; *AJHR*, 1922, E-6, p. 15; *Prince Albert College MS Collection*, MET
    067/1/1/ 4/1/1901.
297 *AJHR*, 1915, E-6, p. 53; *AJHR*, 1921/1922, Vol 2, p. 13; Hamilton High School, 1971;
    Prince Albert College MS Collection, MET 067/1/1/ 25/4/1904.
298 *Prince Albert College MS Collection*, MET 067/1/1/ 8/2/1904; Voller, 1982, p. 243.

299 *Prince Albert College MS Collection*, MET 067/1/1/ 4/6/1900.
300 *Auckland University College Calendar*, 1906, 1907.
301 Northey, 1988.
302 Coney, 1991, p. 261.
303 Coney, 1986.
304 Coney, 1991, p. 187.
305 *Ibid.*
306 *Ibid*; Coney, 1986.
307 Northey, 1988.
308 Sinclair, 1983, p. 60.
309 Sinclair, 1983, p. 62.
310 Harding, 1982; Mills, 1933, p. 136; Penfold et al., 1991, p. 43; Sinclair, 1983, pp. 66, 162.
311 Blow, 1933, p. 29; Northey, 1988, pp. 54, 89; Penfold et al., 1991, p. 43.
312 *AJHR*, 1911, E-6, p. 21; Epsom Girls' Grammar, 1967, p. 27; Northey, 1988, p. 241.
313 Blow, 1933; Northey, 1988.
314 Sinclair, 1983, p. 72.
315 Sinclair, 1983, p. 73.
316 Cole Catley, 1985, p. 15.
317 *AJHR*, 1906, E-12, p. 14; *AJHR*, 1914, E-6, p. 29; Cole Catley, 1985, pp. 15, 273; *New Zealand Gazette*, 1891, p. 749, 1900, p. 1262; *NZSM*, 1903, May, p. 157; Northey, 1988, p. 260; Penfold et al., 1991, p. 37.
318 *Korero*, Epsom Girls' Grammar, 1929, cited in Epsom Girls' Grammar, 1967.
319 Stenson, 1996.
320 *Ibid.*
321 Epsom Girls' Grammar, 1967, p. 16.
322 Epsom Girls' Grammar, 1967, p. 17.
323 *AJHR*, 1928, E-6, p. 4; Epsom Girls' Grammar, 1967, pp. 6–9; *New Zealand Gazette*, 1900, p. 1266; Northey, 1988, p. 54; Penfold et al., 1991, p. 80; Stenson, 1996.
324 Sinclair, 1983, pp. 73–74.
325 *AJHR*, 1914, E-6, p. 19; *AJHR*, 1917, E-6, p. 35; *AJHR*, 1921/22, Vol. 2, p. 13; *AJHR*, 1929, E-6, pp. 4, 13; Epsom Girls' Grammar, 1967, p. 52; Northey, 1988, p. 48.
326 *AJHR*, 1926, E-6, 19; Northey, 1988, p. 54; Penfold et al., 1991, p. 86.
327 Blow, 1933, p. 66; Sinclair, 1983, p. 139.
328 Blow, 1933, p. 66.
329 Blow, 1933, p. 81; Northey, 1988, pp. 54, 257; Rhodes, 2007.
330 Blow, 1933, p. 88.
331 *Ibid*; *AJHR*, 1914, E-6, p. 28; Northey, 1988, p. 260; Roberts in Penfold et al., 1991, pp. 589–592.
332 Blow, 1933, p. 90; Hamilton High School, 1971; Northey, 1988, pp. 54, 241; Penfold et al., 1991, p. 174.
333 Blow, 1933, p. 93; Hughes & Ahern, 1993, p. 68.
334 Sinclair, 1983, p. 129.
335 Sinclair, 1983, pp. 149, 318.
336 Sinclair, 1983.
337 *Ibid.*
338 Shaw, 2006.
339 Sinclair, 1983, p. 83.

340 *Ibid.*
341 *Ibid.*
342 *NZSM,* March 1894, p. 125.
343 *New Zealand Herald,* 15 February 1902, p. 2.
344 Arthur & Buttle, 1950, pp. 29, 48.
345 *NZSM,* October 1894, p. 39 reported 1887 Regulations.
346 Shaw, 2006, p. 29.
347 *AJHR,* 1907, E-12; *AJHR,* 1909, E-6, p. 19; *AJHR,* 1914, E-6, p. 19; *AJHR,* 1919, E-3, p. 32; *NZSM,* January, 1901, p. 83; Shaw, 2006.
348 *AJHR,* 1910, E-6, p. 21; *AJHR,* 1913, E-6, p. 20; *AJHR,* 1917, E-6, p. 35; *AJHR,* 1921, E-6, p. 26; Northey, 1988, p. 260; Shaw, 2006, p. 38.
349 *AJHR,* 1911, E-6, p. 21; Northey, 1988, p. 260; Shaw, 2006, p. 38.
350 *AJHR,* 1909, E-6, p. 21; *AJHR,* 1921, E-6, p. 20; Epsom Girls' Grammar, 1967, p. 52; Hamilton High School, 1971; *Prince Albert College MS Collection,* MET 067/1/1/; Shaw, 2006, p. 38.
351 Shaw, 2006.
352 Northey, 1988, p. 256.
353 Minogue, 1977, p. 27.
354 Minogue, 1977, p. 28.
355 *Ibid;* Shaw, 2006, p. 101.

CHAPTER 6

Victorious in Wellington
(1899–1945)

Victoria University College, Wellington. J.C. BEAGLEHOLE ROOM, VICTORIA UNIVERSITY OF WELLINGTON LIBRARY 2/189

Wellington was late to provide a university compared with the Otago, Canterbury, and Auckland regions. A university in the capital city was regarded by many as long overdue. Attempts had been made to establish one prior to 1897. By that time the Middle District, comprising the former provinces of Wellington, Taranaki, Hawke's Bay, Nelson, and Westland, had a rapidly expanding population, a large number of secondary schools, and more University Entrance students between them than any other district.[356] That year, the premier, Richard Seddon, attended the English celebrations for the Diamond Jubilee of Queen Victoria; he was also given an honorary doctorate and appointed privy councillor at the University of Cambridge. These events led Seddon to take matters into his own hands and produce the Victoria College Bill later that year. Matters moved fast, and Victoria University College was affiliated to the University of New Zealand in 1899.[357]

Until Victoria began, those in the lower half of the North Island seeking university study either moved away from home to one of the three established colleges, or embarked on a degree as an exempt student. Even after Victoria University College was established, the majority of its early students were part-time, as in Auckland. By 1901, 20 percent of the total student body at Victoria still did not set foot on campus, because of their exempt status.[358]

Victoria University College thus became known as a 'night school' for Wellington-based teachers and civil servants, with most classes having to be held between 5 pm and 9 pm. Moreover, when the university college opened in April 1899, these classes were spread over two locations: arts and law at Wellington Girls' High School[359] in Thorndon, and science at Wellington Technical High School in Mount Cook. There were seventy-eight students and four professors, but no library and no common room.[360]

Early days at Victoria

While the board of Wellington Girls' High School was initially happy to make three rooms available free of charge for the University College arts and law classes, they were less keen to agree to the secondment of another room in 1900 for use as a library. The board agreed with the principal, Miss Hamilton, who argued that there had been certain occurrences in the first year of occupation which the university council needed to deal with, namely 'the conduct of some of the students such as smoking and spitting in the classrooms, disfiguring of desks and mantelpieces, and twisting up a poker so [as] to make it unfit for use'.[361] She wanted 'some stringent rules to keep unruly students within bounds'.[362] Once this was promised, she agreed to release the additional room, but with the proviso that 'should I suffer any annoyances such as I have this year experienced, and the offenders remain unpunished,

Between 1899 and 1905 Victoria University College taught arts and law classes at Wellington Girls' High School.
WELLINGTON GIRLS' COLLEGE

I shall feel myself at liberty to withdraw this consent'.[363] After two years, the board began charging the university council rent: £50 a year at first, rising to £100 during 1904, the final year of classes at the school.[364] From 1905, Victoria College of the University of New Zealand was located on the hill above the city at Kelburn.

From the outset, women students were enrolled in the same way as men at Victoria. Over one-third of the students in 1899 were women, and there was growing concern for their wellbeing, especially in relation to the standard of accommodation for those who had come to Wellington from provincial areas. In 1905, the Wellington Presbytery and the Anglican Church combined to open the first women's student hostel, later known as Victoria House. One of its key instigators, Margaret Wallace, wife of the Bishop of Wellington, wrote in the June 1907 edition of *Spike* about the advantages of having a comfortable house located on The Terrace, close to the university, for women students; but she also alluded to the pioneering nature of the hostel, saying 'We shall not only be supplying a real want in Wellington, but shall be setting a noble example to all the other university colleges, who only want to be shown the way in order to do it for themselves. Forward, Wellington!'[365] By 1910, thirty-three women students lived there for about £1 a week, including one hot meal a day and laundry. In what would have been a very progressive move, a telephone was provided for conversations and messages from 12.30 pm to 2.30 pm, and from 9 pm to 10 pm.[366] From 1915 to the early 1930s, the Society of Friends also ran a hostel in The Glen, Kelburn, for women students of the teachers' training college.

Despite being the last of the four university colleges to be established and affiliated to the University of New Zealand, Victoria produced more women graduates than the other three university colleges in the period 1899–1920.[367] Overall, 185 women graduated with bachelor's degrees and seventy-nine (43 percent) of these also gained master's degrees. Even in the period 1926 to 1939, the total number of women graduates remained relatively high at 387, or 40 percent of the total number of graduates.[368] The numbers of women taking pure science degrees over this period—a total of nine—were about the same as at the other three colleges. At Victoria, women students mainly studied arts subjects. The high percentage who went teaching (110, 59 percent) was also comparable with the other three colleges. In the period 1899–1920, at least 28 percent of Victoria's women graduates married.[369]

Were there more women proportionately attending Victoria University College than the other three colleges in the period to 1920, and was this the reason why the number of women graduates was higher? This is not easy to calculate, as not all colleges kept annual records of student numbers by gender, especially prior to 1900, and Victoria's own statistics began to be recorded by gender only in 1910. At that time, women comprised 37.6 percent of student numbers, rising to 39.4 percent in 1915 and to 42 percent in 1920. This level would not be reached again until 1980.[370] Another factor that probably influenced the overall numbers of women enrolled at Victoria was the provision for exempt students. Those who did not live within easy access of the university typically combined full-time paid work with reading one unit per year; in this way, many women teachers in the lower half of the North Island struggled through a degree course over many years, completely on their own. The pattern was to pay the course and examination fee, be provided with a reading list, and at the end of the year turn up and sit the supervised examination held in a regional town centre.

In the case of Olive Rose Sutherland, this was in the town of Masterton in the Wairarapa. Born in Masterton, Olive was sent to Wellington Girls' for her secondary schooling. Like many others, she began studying for her degree at Wellington Teachers' Training College (1909–1910), but despite a huge effort of taking four units in her second year, she still had at least half a BA to complete when she took up her first teaching post at Lansdowne School in Masterton (1911–1913). She moved to Fernridge Primary School in 1913, before taking up a new position in 1914 at Masterton District High School, where, teaching a class of eighty pupils, she completed her BA.[371] Olive Sutherland then kept teaching and completed an MA through Victoria in 1917. Her teaching career spanned forty-six years. She taught at Masterton District High School until 1922, transferring to the newly established Wairarapa High School in 1923, where she was a long-serving senior mistress until her retirement in 1951.[372]

First women graduates at Victoria

Aware of the many gains made by Victoria women, Beryl Hughes and Sheila Ahern, both retired academic historians from Victoria University of Wellington, researched and wrote the only book focusing exclusively on women within one New Zealand university, *Redbrick and Bluestockings: Women at Victoria 1899–1993*. The book appeared in 1993, the centenary of women's suffrage. The first half of their book traces the period from when the university was established in 1899 to 1949, highlighting various aspects of university women's education during these years. It is not the intention of this chapter to replicate that work, but rather to reference aspects of it where applicable to the themes being developed here in relation to girls' and women's education within Wellington and throughout the Wellington region.

Even Hughes and Ahern found it difficult to identify Victoria's first women graduates. According to University of New Zealand records, the first Victoria women to graduate in 1901 were Alexandra Brown, Mary Greenfield, and Margaret Ross. However, identifying them as the first women graduates from Victoria was not straightforward. The 1903 Listing of University of New Zealand Graduates includes all three names for 1901, but in the 1948 publication listing all graduates, two of the three appear under their married names, one with the wrong graduation date. As was suggested in Chapter 1, the transposing of names by hand and even from printed lists as they were accumulated meant that omissions occurred. These three women graduates comprised a third of Victoria's first batch of graduates. To graduate with bachelor of arts degrees just two years after the college opened meant that all had earlier passed a number of university subject examinations, from another university college, and in 1899 or 1900 had either transferred as exempt students to Victoria, or had attended lectures in Wellington.

Little is known about Alexandra Brown either before or for some time after her graduation. She first appears in 1913 as an assistant teacher at Masterton District High School, where she was paid £135. She left in 1922, with a salary of £333, when the District High School was disestablished to make way for the new Wairarapa High School. Between 1922 and 1924, Alexandra Brown was senior mistress at Featherston District High School, with a salary of £343. By 1925 she had moved again to Carterton District High School, where, as senior mistress, her salary was recorded as £365.[373]

Mary Greenfield had attended Wellington Girls' High School, where she was dux and gold medallist in 1894.[374] The intervening six years add weight to the argument that she was an exempt student, perhaps at Canterbury or Auckland, before enrolling at Victoria in 1899. In 1903, she appears on the University of New Zealand list of graduates under her family name of Greenfield, but she is on the University of New Zealand 1948 list under her married name of Rose.

Also from Wellington Girls' High School came Margaret Cleland Ross; she was winner of the 'Mary' Scholarship there in 1898, and is likely to have been a full-time university student, given that she graduated BA in 1901. She was one of the first women in the Students' Society (later the Students' Association) when it was formed in 1902, and would become one of a select group to be made a life member of the Victoria Students' Association. Margaret Ross was also the first Victoria woman to graduate MA (in Latin and English), which she did in 1902. The following year she took up a teaching position at Marlborough High School and left there in 1910, presumably to marry. She is listed under the name of Price in 1948, and her graduating date is given as 1902.[375]

Two of the first women to graduate in science from Victoria went on to complete medical degrees at the University of London. Mary Blair went straight from Wellington Girls' High School to study science at Victoria. The first woman vice-president of the Students' Society, she graduated with a BSc in 1902. She left New Zealand to study medicine in London and did not return. She set up in general practice in London, served with the Scottish Women's Hospitals in Serbia during World War One, and in World War Two supervised two air-raid shelters in central London.[376]

Victoria College Hockey Club First Eleven, 1904, with Fanny Irvine-Smith as captain (seated centre).

Mary Barkas came to Wellington in 1906 from Christchurch Girls' High School, where in 1905 she had been head girl, dux, and earned fifth place in the Junior University Scholarship examinations. A full-time student, she graduated with a BSc in 1908 and an MSc in chemistry in 1910. After a couple of years keeping house for her father, she left for England and qualified as a physician and surgeon from the University of London in 1918. She also qualified in psychological medicine, and spent some years working in psychiatric hospitals and studying psychoanalysis in Europe. However, senior positions in English public psychiatric hospitals were difficult for women to secure, and she opted in 1928 to become superintendent at a private asylum in Lincoln. Mary Barkas returned to New Zealand in 1932, but never practised medicine here. Instead she spent the next thirty years living at Tapu on the Coromandel Peninsula.[377]

Maude Mary Rigg was the first woman at Victoria to graduate with two double degrees (BA 1904, MA 1905, BSc 1907, MSc physics, chemistry, and mathematics 1907). She had been dux and gold medallist at Wellington Girls' High School in 1900. While completing her science degrees, she taught at Newtown District High School (1905–1907), where her salary was £135 in 1907. Her next move was to Southland Girls' High School (1908–1909), but by 1910 she had returned to Wellington Girls' to teach until the end of 1911. This may have been the year in which she married and became Maude Dale.[378]

Harriet Vine was thirty-seven years old when she became the first woman to graduate in law from Victoria (LLB 1913). She was also the first woman to complete a master's degree in law in 1914. From that time until her death in 1962, she worked in the Whanganui law firm of Treadwell and Gordon. She was also an active member of St John, and was made a Dame of the British Empire for this work. The Harriet Vine Kindergarten now stands on the site of her former property, which she bequeathed to Wanganui City Council.[379]

Elsie Millicent Johnston (MA 1910) is perhaps the best known of the Victoria graduates who became principals of girls' schools. She moved from England to Wellington when she was a child, and attended Petone Primary School from 1893 to 1901. In her final year she gained the highest marks in the Wellington Education Board Scholarship examination. This scholarship of £15, plus travelling allowance, enabled her to attend Wellington Girls' High School.

Victoria University College graduates who became school principals 1899–1945

Ada Eastwood	MA 1907	Southland Girls' High School	1932–1940
Ida Tennant (as Mrs Cleghorn)	BA 1908	Archerfield Girls', Dunedin St Matthews', Masterton St Hilda's Collegiate, Dunedin	1919–1932 1933–1945 1951
Elsie Johnston	MA 1910	Southland Girls' High School Auckland Girls' Grammar School	1924–1925 1926–1944
Nora Issac	MA 1912	Wellington East Girls' High School	1937–1949
Eliza Edwards	BA 1913	Waikato Diocesan School for Girls Auckland Diocesan School for Girls	1929–1932 1933–1952
Esma North	BA 1915	Wellington Girls' College	1938–1950

At the end of the third form, she was allowed to sit the junior University Entrance examination, a highly unusual occurrence, given that this was normally reserved for pupils in their final year at secondary school. Elsie Johnston did not disappoint her teachers: she was placed nineteenth overall, and first in English. As a fourth former she was dux of the school in 1904, and as a fifth former gained fifth place overall in the University Entrance Scholarship. By 1908 she was teaching at her old school while studying for her BA, and in 1909 undertook relief teaching at Chilton St James, a private girls' school in Lower Hutt. In 1909 she was Victoria's Senior Scholar in French and Queen's Scholar, and the following year she gained her MA with first class honours in French and English. She went teaching for three and a half years, firstly to Auckland Girls' Grammar (1910–1911) where she worked with principals Anne Whitelaw and Blanche Butler in turn, then back to Wellington Girls' and her own former principal, Mary McLean (1911–1914). She was en route to England when war was declared in 1914, preventing her continuing; she then chose to spend the war years teaching at Durban Girls' High School in South Africa. Going on to the University of London in 1919, she completed the one-year postgraduate teacher training course in one term, and for this effort won a first class University of Cambridge Teachers' Certificate. She then taught for one year in England at Redditch Secondary School in Worcester. By 1921, Elsie Johnston was back at Wellington Girls' as Head of Languages, but left at the end of that year to go to the Christchurch Technical College as senior

Elsie Johnston (MA 1910) was principal of two girls' schools: Southland Girls' High School (1924–1926) and Auckland Girls' Grammar (1926–1944). She also studied and taught overseas.
AUCKLAND GIRLS' GRAMMAR SCHOOL

mistress and Head of English and Languages. She was not there long, as in 1924 she became the principal of Southland Girls' High School (1924–1926). Although her stewardship at Southland Girls' was also brief, she made a big impression: she introduced 'a system of self-government whereby matters relating to the conduct and discipline of the girls were decided under her supervision by a school council elected by the girls themselves ... By her strict but just discipline she had in two years greatly raised the tone and scholarship of the school.'[380]

In 1926 Elsie Johnston was appointed principal of Auckland Girls' Grammar (AGGS), a position she would hold until her retirement in 1944. She inherited a school roll of 559, and made it her business to know each girl's name and something about her, even when the roll reached 800. All third formers were interviewed by her, and on the basis of the interview, an IQ test, and primary school reports, she allocated each to a form. She often intervened in a pupil's choice of academic programme; for example, she contacted the parents of Louise Gardner, and persuaded them not to let their daughter pursue a commercial course. Miss Johnston's concern and guidance resulted in Louise Gardner excelling at school and at university; later she would herself become the school's principal (1967–1978). Elsie Johnston's influence on the girls was to last for a very long time. As she had at Southland Girls', she promoted self-government and responsibility 'by the custom of each form electing a form representative and a games captain, who were responsible for discipline in the classroom when teachers were not present. Prefects and games captains were elected by fifth and sixth form girls ... she set up literary and debating societies in every third form ... for half the year one English period a week was set aside for this purpose, and Miss Johnston herself was always present.'[381] Another practice which was unusual for the time, but one that

166

many pupils came to value in later life, was Elsie Johnston's training in meeting procedures through regular formal class meetings, including speaking 'clearly and articulately, summing up arguments and keeping logically to the point'.[382] While Elsie Johnston upheld the highest academic standards and patterns of behaviour, she was also keen on fostering cultural and community pursuits for the girls. 'I make no apology,' she said, 'for mentioning what are often called "outside activities", as these play an important part in the life of the school. The orchestra and Literary Club, the Helping Hand Circle, the Toy Circle, the Thursday visits to the public hospital, the hospital choir, the Tramping Club, the life-saving classes.'[383] Elsie Johnston retired to England, returning to New Zealand in 1963 for the school's 75th jubilee celebrations. There former pupil Dorothy Fowler (m.Winstone) summarised the three hallmarks of girls' education at AGGS in the Elsie Johnston era as 'in service, in scholarship and in good citizenship'.[384]

Eliza Rutland Edwards (MA 1923) was raised on the Lower Moutere, Nelson, and went to Nelson Girls' College, where she won a University Entrance Scholarship in 1907. She may well have been an extramural and part-time student for at least some of her undergraduate years, as she did not graduate with her BA from Victoria until 1913. At that time she was teaching at Nelson Girls' College. In 1915 Eliza Edwards was appointed to Christchurch Girls' High School, when Mary Gibson was principal, and remained there until 1922 when she travelled to England to study at Cambridge University. The trip and the not insignificant tuition and boarding costs were presumably self-funded. At Cambridge she attended Newnham College, graduating with an MA in mathematics and geography in 1923. She spent the next two years in England teaching at King Edward Girls' Grammar School in Louth, Lincolnshire (1924–1926), and returned to New Zealand in 1927 to take up the position of senior mistress at Nelson Girls'. By 1929 she was on the move again, this time to become the founding principal of Waikato Diocesan School for Girls in Hamilton. When the principalship of Auckland Diocesan was advertised in 1932, Eliza Edwards applied and was appointed. In the nineteen years she led Auckland Diocesan School for Girls, she was renowned for her inspirational speeches and for being the kind of principal who knew all the girls by name,

Eliza Edwards gained her MA from Cambridge in 1923 and taught in England before becoming principal in turn of two Diocesan Schools for Girls (Waikato, 1929–1932; and Auckland, 1932–1952). DIOCESAN SCHOOLS FOR GIRLS AUCKLAND

having taught most of them. She inherited a school with firmly entrenched English school traditions, as laid down by English graduates Miss Pulling and Miss Sandford in turn; while she respected these, she also made evident her own philosophies for girls' education. An early step was to introduce a period of physical work/education for each form each day, as, according to Miss Edwards, 'the body must have its place on the timetable. To leave physical training to choice, and also to after school hours is not enough.'[385] Perhaps sensing parental resistance to compulsory physical education, Miss Edwards went on to emphasise that in English girls' schools, it was common for girls to have between two and five afternoons dedicated to games. Both health and academic achievement benefited: 'English Upper Sixth girls reach a high standard of scholarship with a buoyancy of health that astonished me,' she said, adding that 'we are giving one period daily to each class for drill, games and singing, and two for divinity'.[386] Part of her thinking was obviously linked to how extracurricular activities and the full school curricula could be covered in three years, so that girls could be prepared 'for a generous pass in the University Entrance Examination'. Few girls from Diocesan schools had graduated from university before Eliza Edwards took over, and she wanted to change that. Clearly, she also thought that three years' secondary schooling was just not enough; at the end of her first year, she decreed that 'we are returning to the four years' course for University Entrance and after this year girls will sit only when such a course has been covered'.[387] That examination was the most suitable for girls to aim for: 'as this is at present almost essential as an open sesame into the professional and business world, it seems to me right to encourage girls to work towards it'.[388]

Eliza Edwards no doubt realised that for the parents of some Diocesan girls, academic attainment and the ability to be financially independent were less valued than a good general Christian preparation for life, and that three years seemed quite adequate, perhaps even too long during the economic depression of the 1930s. As far as parents were concerned, therefore, she left nothing to chance, telling them, 'we want hard work, and are grateful when parents co-operate with the school in providing a silent room with good lighting and other conveniences for home-work'. She also told them what she did not want: 'children should not be taken out on week-day evenings except on rare occasions to something of great educational value … An afternoon away, an evening out, may seem trivial things, but they undermine a girl's attitude towards her work, and if there is no keenness sharpened by just a touch of ambition, how is the school to help that child to make progress?'[389]

From the girls themselves, Eliza demanded high standards of 'service, ungrudging loyalty, initiative and enterprise … as a training for life she sought to give as many girls as possible experience of responsibility'.[390] Outside school, she maintained contact with others interested in education. She was active in the Auckland branch of the New Zealand Federation of University Women, serving as president in 1940. After retiring in 1952, Eliza spent two years travelling before returning to Auckland, where she lived for the rest of her life.

Esther (Esma) North (BA 1915) was a prominent figure in the education of Wellington's girls. She was the foster daughter and niece of Isabel Ecclesfield (BA Auckland 1891), who taught at Wellington Girls' between 1892 and 1910. Not surprisingly, Esma was sent to Wellington Girls' too, then studied full time at Victoria University College from 1912. An outstanding speaker, she was president of the Women's Debating Society. Esma North graduated with a BA in 1915.[391] After a year as a pupil-teacher, in 1916 she completed the graduate one-year course at Wellington Teachers' Training College. At this point it is likely she went teaching in the Wellington area. In 1921 she won a Postgraduate Scholarship from the University of New Zealand Senate to enable her to travel and study in Europe. She spent a year as a resident at Bedford Women's College in London, gaining a Diploma in Pedagogy, followed by two years at the Sorbonne in Paris, adding certificates in French. In 1924, she returned to teach for two terms at Wellington Girls' College, before being appointed a foundation staff member at Wellington East Girls' College (1925–1926). Between 1927 and 1930 she taught at several girls' colleges—in Australia in

Esma North (BA 1915) went on to study in London and Paris. She was principal of Wellington Girls' High School 1938–1950. WELLINGTON GIRLS' COLLEGE

1927 and at New Plymouth Girls' High School in 1928. In 1931, she was off travelling again, and in 1932 was back teaching at Wellington East Girls' for five years, prior to taking up the principalship of Wellington Girls' College in 1938. When she retired twelve years later, she acknowledged that because of the war years and limited funding, implementing innovative educational ideas had not been possible. While she was disappointed that she had not been able to achieve some of 'the projects that I cherished dearly at the beginning',[392] commentators on the North era praised her wise selection of an almost completely new staff, who, like many of their predecessors, would remain at the school for at least twenty years. Outside school, Esma North wrote poetry and was active in the Federation of University Women, including being Wellington branch president in 1943 and 1944. She was also an advocate for the preservation of native forests, and in 1957 gave some of her Silverstream property, known as the Ecclesfield Reserve, to the Forest and Bird Society.[393]

Women staff at Victoria

World War One impacted upon students and staff at Victoria as it did in the other university colleges. For a start, the numbers attending lectures fell, and by 1917 women students (172) outnumbered men students (148). By the end of the war, 25 percent (150) of the 600 students and former students of Victoria had died.[394] It was one of the most controversial events at Victoria in the early part of the war that led to the appointment of the first two women lecturers. The government required the university to remove the Professor of Modern Languages, George von Zedlitz, from his post, following the passing of the Alien Enemy Teachers Act of 1915. The university council refused to bow to government and public pressure to get rid of their 'popular professor: an energetic supporter of student clubs and a spellbinding lecturer'.[395] Further, he had the full support of the professorial board, as well as of past and present students, who wrote and presented testimonials in his favour. All knew the facts: Professor von Zedlitz had renounced his German citizenship, had not been in Germany since he left at the age of fourteen, and had been raised by his English-born mother. He was, however, not a British citizen, and anti-German sentiments led to accusations of all kinds. In the end, the government warned the university council that if they did not sack the professor, then it would enact legislation to do so. It was in this way that Mrs Margaret McPhail and Miss Mary Baker were employed to take over his teaching when he was forced to resign in 1915.[396]

Margaret McPhail, a Scottish widow, did not have a degree, but had been assistant to Professor von Zedlitz since 1911. She took over most of the teaching of French as a lecturer when he left in 1915, and was on the staff when she died three years later, at the age of fifty-eight.[397] In 1916, Mary Baker, a graduate from the University of Melbourne, was appointed as a lecturer in German, to take the classes previously taught by Professor von Zedlitz. Mary Baker was also the first woman to have a seat on the professorial board. She represented modern languages until 1919, when she left the university. Both Mrs McPhail and Mary Baker were paid a salary of £300.[398]

The first New Zealand woman graduate to become a lecturer at Victoria appears to have been Hilda Heine, a Victoria graduate (MA 1923), who was first employed in 1928 as an instructor in economic history and statistics in the commerce faculty. Hilda Heine, a former Senior University Scholar in English and German, won a University of New Zealand Travelling Scholarship in order to study for her PhD from the University of Berlin. She was later promoted to a lectureship, and when she retired in 1953 she held a senior lectureship. Hilda Heine was the first woman on the staff to gain a doctorate.[399]

It took until 1965 for the first woman professor to be appointed, other than in home science, in any of the New Zealand universities. Professor Janaki was appointed Professor and Director of the Asian Studies Centre at Victoria; later she became Professor of International Relations.[400] In 2006, there were 121 women (14.8 percent) out of 696 university professors nationwide.

Other than the women mentioned above, the first women on the staff at Victoria were mainly former students who were employed initially as professors' assistants, instructors, and demonstrators. The first four of these women were listed in 1911: Evelyn Watson, assistant in English (MA Victoria 1907); Bertha Reeve, assistant in mathematics (MA Victoria 1911); Margaret McPhail, assistant in modern languages; and Phoebe Myers (BA Canterbury

Phoebe Myers (BA 1890)

Phoebe Myers was born in Nelson and went to primary school in Motueka before her successful merchant father moved the family to Wellington in 1879, where she attended Wellington Girls' High School; her progressive Jewish family then supported her so that she could live and study full-time at Canterbury University College, there being no university in Wellington at that point. With her BA completed in 1890, Phoebe Myers returned to Wellington to teach at Marsden Collegiate (1890–1900), enrolling at Victoria in its first year of operation in 1899, although she did not complete another qualification. Two primary-school teaching posts followed, at Roseneath Primary (1901–1902) and Mt Cook Girls' (1903), before she took up her first district high school position at The Terrace District High School (1904), followed by four years at Petone District High School (1905–1908). The rest of her school teaching career was spent at Hutt District High School (1909–1921).[401]

Myers has been described as 'a formidable and tenacious woman whose ability as a teacher and political activist ensured that women's interests became better represented in the New Zealand education system'.[402] While at Mt Cook Girls' School in 1903, she helped to found the Wellington branch of the Women Teachers' Association, out of concern for the lack of representation of the interests of women teachers in decision-making bodies, and the rights of women and children in general. In 1914, while at Hutt District High School, she helped organise the first meeting to

co-ordinate the activities of a number of women teachers' associations around New Zealand. This resulted in the establishment of the New Zealand Women Teachers' Association, of which Phoebe Myers was the founding president (1914–1916).

Her ideas for the reform of health and education institutions in New Zealand were published in booklet form in 1914, where she argued for women's perspectives to be represented on local authorities and in regional and national government. She was one of the first (along with Nellie Coad and Emily Chaplin) to be elected by women teachers to represent women's interests on the Council of Education, which she did until 1920. The Women Teachers' Association also wanted the issues affecting the education of girls and women represented to the Minister of Education, as they believed these were being ignored by their male-dominated teacher union, the New Zealand Educational Institute (NZEI). Of major concern were inequities for women teachers in terms of salary and promotion. Every year they lobbied the minister, sending a deputation to outline their concerns.

Phoebe Myers was active during the war years, working for the New Zealand branch of the Red Cross and the Women's National Reserve of New Zealand, and she was also founding president of the Wellington Crippled Soldiers' and Sailors' Hostel. In September 1929 she went as a delegate to the League of Nations to discuss issues on the welfare of women and children. She was awarded an MBE in 1947, just prior to her death.[403]

1890), demonstrator in biology. The roles of these women were to mark examination papers and to prepare work for the professor. From 1920, full-time assistants were employed by the emerging 'departments' to undertake some teaching in addition to marking, for which they were paid a salary of £300. Hughes and Ahern devoted an entire chapter to women staff in their history of women at Victoria; that they could do so is testimony to the fact that more women were employed earlier at Victoria University College than at the other three colleges, albeit in a range of sublecturer positions. This was the case for Phoebe Myers, who, as the first woman demonstrator in biology at Victoria, combined this work with teaching science in district high schools in the Wellington region. Although her name is first listed in the College Calendar from 1911, other sources indicate that Phoebe Myers was actually the first woman on the staff at Victoria, having been employed in 1906. Phoebe Myers was also an activist for educational reform, and in 1929 was the first woman to represent New Zealand at the League of Nations in Geneva.

In the main, it was the full-time students who took active roles in student activities at Victoria, such as the clubs and students' association. The Tennis and Hockey Clubs were particularly popular with women students, as was the Women's Indoor Basketball Club from 1918, and the Tramping Club from 1921. Another club that appealed to women, at least initially, was the Debating Society; in its first year, Annie Down spoke to the motion 'that women should take an active part in public life'. For a variety of reasons, women students set up their own debating club between 1908 and 1916, insisting that it be the *Women's* Debating Club. The reason was made clear in the October 1911 edition of *Spike:*

> We carefully called ourselves 'women',
> And felt very proud of the name.
> But still we're referred to as 'ladies',
> A title we *never* did claim:
> For we thought of its misapplications—
> 'Char-ladies, 'drunk ladies' and such.
> So please will you just call us women?
> You see, we'd prefer it so much.

In addition to debates, the Women's Debating Society held readings, literary discussions, and oratory competitions.

Because of the law school, debating was introduced early at Victoria, and the society was modelled on the Oxford Union. Prizes were awarded after the annual debates held in the town hall, the Union Prize going to the best debater, and the Plunket Medal for the best oration on a famous person in history. The women students chose female subjects, and in their own club competitions practised style and delivery. Staff members such as Mrs McPhail and Phoebe Myers offered support and feedback, while Dr Agnes Bennett sometimes acted as adjudicator. In 1913, the winning women's club speech on Joan of Arc was by Marjorie Nicholls. She then entered the city competition with a speech on the same subject, and came away with the Plunket Medal, one of five women to win it before 1948.

Victoria University College graduates 1914. Back row, left to right: B. Blake, E. Fitzgerald Eager, C. Bevendesen, C. H. Gibb, L. Griffiths, K. Ross, F. Wolters. Second row: Nellie Coad, Elizabeth Piggott, C. H. Taylor, Fanny Ross (m.Hogg), C. Heine, Mary Clachan, J. C. McDowell, Mary McKenzie, Ethel Duff. Sitting: Jessie Tolley, E. O. Hercus, Dorothy Hueston, G. G. Watson, Elizabeth Shirer (m.Bisley), E. G. Gondringer, Isabella Still. Front: G. S. Strack, F. T. Clere, P. V. Armstrong, L. M. Moss, A. C. Nathan. Eight of the ten women went teaching. Mary Clachan (MA 1915) was music teacher at Queen Margaret's College 1919–1949 and Fanny Ross became principal of Columba College for Girls, Dunedin.
ALEXANDER TURNBULL LIBRARY, WELLINGTON, NZ. JOSEPH ZACHARIAH PHOTOGRAPH, J. OLDS COLL F-111613-1/2

However, a large proportion of the Victoria student body remained part-time, attending lectures in the evenings after work. In 1915, part-time students comprised 82.5 percent of the student body;[404] even in 1949 the proportion was still high, at 75 percent.[405] Nellie Coad was one of the part-time students who had initially been a pupil-teacher at Thorndon School in 1903, before teaching in local primary schools and attending Victoria University College in the evenings. It took until 1914 for her to gain her MA.

Women students had their own common room from 1918, and a room was established in 1921 in the then-new northern wing of the Hunter Building. It became the norm from the beginning to have two vice-presidents of the students' association, one of whom was to be a woman. The very first Student Society Executive had five women among its twelve members, including Mary Blair, the first woman vice-president. Women were also involved with the college student review *Spike*, which began in 1902 and was produced every second year until 1931, when it was published annually. Fanny Irvine-Smith was cofounder and coeditor of *Spike* in 1902, and wrote for and illustrated the newspaper for several years. She was also active in the Ladies' Hockey Club

Nellie Euphemia Coad (MA 1914)

Nellie Coad (MA 1914) was author of three geography textbooks, president of the Women Teachers' Association, and long-serving member of staff at Wellington Girls' College.

Nellie Coad was an advocate for social reform, and in particular for girls' and women's education. She taught at Wellington Girls' College from 1917 to 1938, where she was head of the history, civics, and geography department. The three textbooks she authored were used throughout New Zealand secondary schools: *Dominion Civics*, *Geography of the Pacific*, and *New Zealand from Tasman to Marsden*. She had a reputation for

being a strict teacher, but every pupil knew just where they stood with her. As a member of her 1927 class later wrote:

> Miss Coad begins to dictate. I head up "Causes of War", underline it in red ink and in the margin neatly wrote "1". Now if Miss Coad said there were four causes of war, that was all there was. We didn't have to bother our heads thinking of any more. After "Causes" and "Events", then "Results" of the War. She believed in giving good strong signposts through the confused paths of history.[406]

Outside school, Nellie Coad pursued many interests. She was one of the few women to serve on the executive of the NZEI, was a member of the University Entrance Board, and was vice-president of the New Zealand Secondary Schools' Association.[407]

and was one of the original members of the Student Executive. In later life she would become one of Wellington's influential educators.

The first woman president of the students' association was Olive Sheppard (m.Grenfell), who was elected in 1926, having been women's vice-president in 1925. The attitudes of many of her contemporaries, made evident in a debate of that year, led the editor of *Spike* to write of her election: 'Is it a proof that the old-fashioned prejudice against women holding any public position of responsibility is dying out? ... we are afraid that there are still many seekers after knowledge in these halls who are unable to extricate themselves from this ancient web.'[408] Even so, Olive Sheppard did the job and completed her MA at the same time, graduating in 1927.

Wellington Teachers' Training College

From the outset, Victoria University College drew many of its students from the teaching profession. Some were exempt students who taught in rural areas; others from the Wellington area travelled or walked to evening classes. The original Wellington Teachers' Training College was, like the university, situated

Wellington Teachers' Training College, 1920. COLLEGE OF EDUCATION, VICTORIA UNIVERSITY OF WELLINGTON

Fanny Irvine-Smith (MA 1920)

Fanny Irvine-Smith graduated with a BA from Victoria University College in 1908, and twelve years later completed an MA in history. She taught before and after graduating, beginning her career straight from Wellington Girls' High School in 1892, when she went teaching at the Fitzherbert Terrace School. By the time she enrolled as a student at Victoria in 1901, she had also taught in New Plymouth. After she gained her BA, Fanny taught in a range of schools, including Dannevirke High School (1917–1918), where she was senior mistress, and Waipawa District High School (1919–1922), where she studied for her MA. In 1928 Fanny Irvine-Smith was appointed to the staff at Wellington Teachers' Training College, and it was here that she made a lasting impression on future generations of teachers. Colin Bailey, later Professor of Education at Victoria University of Wellington, was one of her students. In later life, he recalled:

> Fanny, though she had been appointed only two years before I got there, was already a legend. She was an original, a character, authentic and unique. Tall, gaunt, with an extraordinary large face and deep set shadowed eyes that haunted, caressed, blazed and laughed in a kaleidoscope of moods, she held us in helpless thrall, awed and enduring.[409]

At a time when neither subject was commonly taught, Fanny took classes in New Zealand history and in Māori culture, and 'her personality, as well as her brilliant teaching, enthralled students'.[410] As legendary as her teaching was her total commitment to drama, both at the college and later

Fanny Irvine-Smith (MA 1920). This photograph was taken in 1929 while she was on the staff of the Wellington Teachers' Training College. Her students described her as 'legendary'.
ALEXANDER TURNBULL LIBRARY, WELLINGTON, NZ. STANLEY POLKINGHORNE ANDREW PHOTOGRAPH, S.P. ANDREW COLL F-018605-1/1

in productions for Wellington amateur societies, as well as her fostering of new talent. Fanny Irvine-Smith intrigued her students; one commented on how 'her tall and sweeping presence at first awed us',[411] but this was accentuated by her wearing of long skirts with 'mysterious leather boots' and her hair wound around her head. After she retired, Fanny Irvine-Smith gathered data for her book *The Streets of My City* (1948) by walking the streets of Wellington. According to her biographer, she 'broke new ground in the presentation of history by portraying Wellington's past through a tour of its streets, a study of how they were named, and some interesting anecdotes'.[412] Fanny Irvine-Smith died in 1948, just as her book was published. The book proved immensely popular, and the royalties went towards buying books for the Khandallah Public Library, which she had helped to found. In the preface of her book, she wrote 'Guard well your heritage.' While the book did that, so too did Fanny, through a lifetime's teaching of history to secondary students and teachers' college students.[413]

in rented rooms in Thorndon, so it was relatively easy for a number of selected training college students to attend university evening classes until 1901. At that point they, along with civil servants and others, had to trudge up the hill to the new Kelburn-based university. Life became easier for the training college students from 1916, when their institution also relocated to Kelburn.

By 1925, the training college students comprised 21 percent of Victoria's student body; according to the Reichel-Tate Report on University Education in New Zealand, this was a much higher proportion than at the other three colleges.[414] As a result of the Reichel-Tate report, which was critical of the part-time nature of many of the university colleges, students at Victoria were asked their opinions on daytime classes. In 1925, arts classes were also held during the day, and in 1926 all science lectures and laboratories were scheduled between 9 am and 5 pm. From 1928, Stage 1 arts classes were alternated each year between an evening and a daytime slot. While these timetabling moves were undoubtedly more popular with full-time students, they did little to further

Hedwig Weitzel (BA 1920)

It was the actions of a female teachers' training college student in 1921 that focused national attention on Victoria University College as a so-called hotbed of revolutionary activity. The young woman was Hedwig (Hetty) Weitzel, born in Palmerston North, where her father was a brass-founder. It is likely that the family had moved to Wellington by the time Hetty went to Wellington Girls' High School. She first enrolled at Victoria University College in 1914, and may well have been a part-time student, as she did not graduate for another six years (BA 1920). Hetty Weitzel was a founding member of the New Zealand Communist Party, but this was obviously not known when she was accepted for the one-year teacher training course at Wellington Teachers' Training College in 1921. To her student friends, 'she was a nice quiet girl'.[415] During that year, she sold a copy of *The Communist* to an undercover police officer in the Wellington Communist Hall; she was arrested, convicted of selling seditious literature, and fined £10. Student friends supported her at court and rallied around to help pay the fine. However, she was stood down from the college and barred from teaching. The Minister of Education made clear in the *New Zealand Free Lance* his view that, 'Victoria College sadly needs purging of a Red Revolutionary and Disloyal Section',[416] insisting that the college launch an inquiry into the whole affair. The chair, Phineas Levi, could not find any evidence that Hetty Weitzel had influenced other students with her views, or indeed was influenced by others at Victoria. With her reputation and means of livelihood destroyed in New Zealand, Hetty moved to New South Wales, where she taught in Sydney schools, and for over thirty years was an executive member of the Australian Women Teachers' Federation. She remained committed to communism for the rest of her life.[417]

the interests of part-time students, particularly training college students and teachers. It is not coincidental that from 1925, when the timing of arts classes was changed, the numbers of exempt students rose rapidly to 196.[418]

In 1933, Victoria's student numbers were adversely affected by the closing of the Wellington Teachers' Training College as an economy measure. The number of women students was particularly affected, falling from 32 percent of the total student body in 1931 to 22 percent in 1933.[419] By 1935, the proportion of women was down to less than 21 percent, and remained at about this level until 1939.[420]

Regional girls' schools

Victoria students were drawn from a much wider distribution of girls' schools than students at the other university colleges. While more graduates had attended Wellington Girls' (established 1878) than any other school in the period from 1899 to 1945, other schools were also well represented, including Nelson Girls' College (1883), Napier Girls' High School (1884), New Plymouth Girls' High School (1885), Wanganui Girls' High School (1891), Palmerston North Girls' High School (1921), and Wellington East Girls' College (1925). At that time fewer girls came to Victoria from the private schools in the region. As in the other main centres, a great number of private or church girls' schools operated for periods of time in or near Wellington. A great many also endured, such as St Mary's College, Thorndon (1874); Nga Tawa—The Wellington Diocesan School for Girls, Marton (1891); Fitzherbert Terrace (later Samuel Marsden Collegiate) School for Girls, Wellington (1907); Solway College, Masterton (1916); Sacred Heart, Lower Hutt (1912); Chilton St James, Lower Hutt (1918); and Queen Margaret's College, Thorndon (1919). Perhaps because of the larger number of girls' schools in its region, Victoria enrolled more female University Entrance Scholarship winners, and a higher number of women who were dux of their school in their final year.

For example, Piati Heni Park (BA 1910) from Palmerston North was dux of Palmerston North Girls' High School in 1906. Despite her Māori name, Piati was Pākehā, the daughter of a local bookshop owner, borough town councillor, and later mayor of Palmerston North. Piati first enrolled at Victoria in 1906,

179

and when she graduated with a BA in 1910 she was the first woman from Palmerston North to do so. She also studied at the teachers' training college, returning to Palmerston North Girls' High School in 1914 to teach until 1917. At that time, she joined the Anglican church as a full-time parish sister, taking scripture lessons in schools in and around Palmerston North until 1926. She was made a deaconess of the Church of England in 1927, and from that time worked as Education Organiser for the Christchurch Diocese.[421]

Like Piati Park, many of the Victoria graduates who came from outside Wellington and then went teaching returned to schools in their home regions or other rural centres. For example, of the 105 Victoria women graduates who went teaching between 1899 and 1945, at least forty-three (41 percent) took up positions in rural high schools.[422] There are two possible reasons for this trend. First, many undertook university study as exempt students while teaching in rural primary schools. With a completed degree and several years' teaching experience, these women could significantly increase their salaries through securing a position as a teaching assistant or senior mistress in a high school located in a rural town. The other reason is that by the time Victoria's first women graduated, their peers from Otago, Canterbury, and Auckland had already won positions in the girls' schools in larger towns, and remained there, thus reducing the options for the Victoria teacher graduates. For the pupils in the rural high schools, however, being taught by such well-educated women challenged orthodoxies of female traditional roles, especially when salaries were published in local newspapers, and it became appreciated that most earnt more than the majority of local townspeople.

This was indeed the case for two former Napier Girls' High pupils, Ellen Casey and Chloe Lehndorf.[423] When Ellen Christine Casey (MA 1912) was appointed the founding senior mistress of Taumarunui District High School in 1918, she was twenty-seven years of age with an annual salary of £220.[424] Ten years earlier, she had won a University Entrance Scholarship enabling her to study full time at Victoria. She graduated with a BA in 1911 and an MA in 1912. By 1915, she was teaching assistant at Hokitika District High School on the West Coast of the South Island, and in her final year there in 1917 was earning £150. Winning the position at Taumarunui in 1918 in the central North Island

The staging of garden theatricals was an annual event in many girls' secondary schools.

Wellington Girls' College 1914. WELLINGTON GIRLS' COLLEGE

New Plymouth Girls' High School, 1913. NEW PLYMOUTH GIRLS' HIGH SCHOOL/CHRISTINE COLE CATLEY

was a great career move after three years' total teaching experience. By 1921, the numbers of pupils had increased dramatically and so had teacher salaries; the young Ellen Casey now earnt an annual salary of £340.

Chloe Ruth Lehndorf graduated from Victoria with a BA in 1915, and took up a teaching position at Patea District High School in Taranaki with a salary of £190. After three years she was appointed senior mistress at Marton District High School; by 1922, her salary had increased to £293. By 1923, Chloe Lehndorf was senior mistress at the larger Te Awamutu District High School, and nine years after graduating was earning £320. Both Ellen Casey and Chloe Lehndorf earnt more than many of their vastly more experienced town-based peers.[425]

One of these was Fanny Ruth Livingstone (m.Denham) (MA 1908), whose salary at Petone High School in 1923 was the same as Chloe Lehndorf's at £320. However, unlike Chloe, Fanny Denham had seventeen years' teaching experience, and had moved more often than most other New Zealand women graduate teachers. She had attended New Plymouth Girls' High School, graduating from Victoria with a BA in 1906 and an MA in 1908. Between 1906 and 1921 she held teaching positions at Hutt District High School, Levin District High School, New Plymouth Girls' High School, Petone District High School, Hastings District High School, Waipawa District High School, and Petone High School.[426]

Flora Hodges (MA 1901)

NEW PLYMOUTH GIRLS' HIGH SCHOOL

Flora Hodges (MA 1901), principal of New Plymouth Girls' High School 1915–1916.

'It is a perfect scandal,'[427] said the principal, Flora Hodges (MA 1901), in her speech at the 1915 break-up ceremony of New Plymouth Girls' High School. She thus ensured full and immediate press coverage of her strong views on the total inadequacy of new rented school accommodation, 'to the top floor of the new electricity substation in Liardet Street'. Reminding parents and girls that they had been promised a new school building by the board of governors (who also administered the New Plymouth Boys' High School), she did not mince words:

Isn't it time, you people of New Plymouth, that you shook off your apathy and did something for your girls? ... So far these girls have not even been treated with common justice. It is no favour we beg from the board but our legal dues. Education endowments in Taranaki are for girls as well as boys. How much have your girls got?[428]

Flora Hodges' rallying cries did not finish there, however. In what must be one of the most remarkable speeches delivered by a New Zealand woman principal, she made clearer her suspicions

First woman Inspector of Secondary Schools in New Zealand

Jessie Hetherington (MA 1909). First woman Inspector of Secondary Schools, c.1930s.

Constant lobbying for a woman Inspector of Secondary Schools did not succeed until 1926, with the appointment of the outstanding Jessie Isabel Hetherington (MA 1909) to the Department of Education in Wellington. She had earlier worked at Wellington Teachers' Training College and lectured at Victoria University College. In all, she spent twenty-seven years of her career in education in Wellington. She was the first woman to teach education at Victoria, and remained based in Wellington as Inspector of Secondary Schools for the Department of Education.

Jessie Hetherington was also the first New Zealand woman graduate to undertake postgraduate study in England, being prompted to do so after meeting and talking with Anne Whitelaw during a visit Whitelaw made back to New Zealand. Jessie's initial schooling was modest: she attended primary school and the first two years of high school in rural Thames, a town on the Coromandel goldfields, where she had been born in 1882 and where her parents ran the local draper's shop.[429] By 1896, the family could afford to send Jessie to Prince Albert College, the Methodist secondary school for girls in

about why equality of educational facilities did not exist in this rural provincial town:

> Have you some rags of the Dark Ages attitude to women clinging about you? In the rest of the world we are in the 20th century, where the education of girls is receiving ever-increasing attention, and where people have awakened to the fact that the finer the woman, the finer the race.[430]

Even though a first generation of colonial girls and women had already progressed through both a secondary school and a university education by 1915, Flora Hodges' analysis of backward attitudes extended beyond rural Taranaki, and continued to challenge the advancement of girls' education.

The new building at New Plymouth Girls' High School, c.1919.

Auckland (see Chapter 5). Jessie was dux of the school in 1898, and continued to board there while she attended Auckland University College.

Jessie graduated with a BA from the University of Auckland in 1902, then went on to study law in 1903. That was the year her father, now a widower, took his three daughters for a visit to England; while there, Jessie decided that she wanted to study law at Cambridge. This was unusual, because, as Jessie later wrote: 'In my day we did not expect our contemporary graduates to go "home" to Cambridge or Oxford Universities except at the culmination of a brilliant university career in New Zealand.'[431] However, her father was an enthusiastic supporter and funder of her studies, and Jessie entered Girton College in 1904 to read law. Here she found that because she was the only woman attending law lectures, she not only had to be chaperoned but was also excluded from tutorials altogether. The reason she was given was that 'a woman student had fainted in the chemistry laboratory and no female could be quickly discovered on the premises to look after her'! Later, she would also recall not being able to attend law lectures held in the men's colleges without having been personally escorted through the grounds by a don.[432] She gained a Law Tripos in 1905 and went on to add a History Tripos in 1906. She would graduate in person in 1907 with a BA from Trinity College, Dublin, followed by an MA in absentia in 1909.[433]

The three years at Girton were mixed ones for Jessie. While she clearly enjoyed the classes and the camaraderie of sister students, she was shocked by the attitudes of the male students towards the female students, something she had not experienced at Auckland University College. She began to take an active interest in student politics and formed strong alliances with other Girtonians, especially Dorothy Brock, who would later lead the Cambridge Training College. She was also lonely during the term holidays, when other students could go to their parental homes. However, her father turned up regularly and accompanied her to Europe on several term holidays, and in one instance funded a trip for her to study French in Paris. By then her father had remarried and spent much of the year living in England. This may have been one of the reasons that Jessie decided to stay and teach there. She explained how, 'in the last term at Cambridge, notices of teaching position vacancies were posted on noticeboards. To my dismay membership of the Church of England was almost always specified and social connection in England inferred.'[434]

Jessie suggested that this was the reason that upon leaving Girton in 1905, she, a Methodist, was appointed to Blackburn High School for Girls as an assistant mistress. She had thought Blackburn was in Liverpool, with access to a library, but instead found it to be a rather grey cotton town in Lancashire. This was the first time a New Zealand woman graduate had gained a teaching position in an English secondary school. Encouraged by her colleagues, she became involved in the women's suffrage movement, meeting Millicent Fawcett, who greatly impressed her. In 1908, Jessie had to leave Blackburn High School against her will; she became so seriously ill with pneumonia that her London-based nurse sister persuaded their father that Jessie should return to New Zealand. While recovering in Thames, Jessie saw an advertisement for the new position of Principal of Burwood Ladies' College in Sydney, and in 1909 was escorted by her father to take up this new role.

It was not all plain sailing in Sydney, as she would later explain: 'In my zeal to introduce features that had attracted me during my English experience, I incurred the criticism and veiled hostility of the senior mistress (sister of the former principal) and some of the senior staff.'[435] However, after the departure of the senior mistress to a school of her own, matters improved greatly and Jessie devoted herself to her work, so much so that she later reflected how her social life suffered: 'How dull I was! Often crying off early from dinner parties to go home and work.'[436] Despite this she enjoyed her time in Sydney very much indeed, especially hiking and visiting other parts of Australia during the school holidays.

By early 1909, however, Jessie had decided to return to England to study educational theory, and in September of that year began a Diploma in Secondary Education at St Mary's College, Lancaster Gate, at the University of London.[437] There she was taught by the inspirational Helena Powell and Professor Adams, and she also undertook practical classes at North London Collegiate School with Dr Sophie Bryant, and at the Godolphin School for Girls in Hammersmith, where she later reported that 'everyone was so kind to me'.[438] Her time at London was to cement her educational philosophy and, with impressive credentials, she was employed as an assistant lecturer at Cambridge Training College until the end of 1914.[439] As World War One took hold, however, her father insisted that she seek the sanctuary of her New Zealand home. She returned and in 1915 was appointed, initially as a tutor and then as a full lecturer, to the Wellington Training College, where she taught English, history, and teaching methods. She was the only woman on the staff, and by default became Women's Warden. Between 1919 and 1923 she was also employed by Victoria University College as a teaching assistant to teach history of education.[440]

Jessie no doubt believed that she was very well placed to win the position of Vice-Principal of Wellington Training College in 1923. However, she was told that applications from women would not be considered, and resigned from the college in protest. It was a brave move, given that she had to live on her savings and be supported by her sister for the next two years. However, she put the time to good use, researching, writing, and publishing, in two volumes in 1926 and 1927, *New Zealand: Its Political Connection with Great Britain*.[441]

In 1926, Jessie Hetherington became the first woman to be appointed a full Inspector of Secondary Schools. This meant that for sixteen years she spent about nine months of the year travelling in order to visit every girls' school and half the coeducational schools in New Zealand. She supported school principals in their bid to break the stranglehold of the University of New Zealand on the rules and regulations surrounding the senior school Matriculation Examination. She also worked hard to foster stronger links between primary and secondary schools. All the while, she took trips overseas on a regular basis, in order to obtain new ideas. For example, in 1937 she visited schools in India, Europe, and the United Kingdom.[442]

After her retirement to Auckland in 1942, Jessie continued her commitment to women and education.[443] She was a lecturer for the Workers' Education Association for two years, and an active member of the New Zealand Federation of University Women and the National Council of Adult Education. Between 1945 and 1953, she was also a member of the Auckland Grammar Board of Governors. Jessie Hetherington died in Auckland in 1971, aged ninety.[444]

Jessie Hetherington was one of a group of younger New Zealand women who studied in a range of universities in other countries. The links between scholarship and internationalism provide the focus for the next chapter.

Notes

356 Barrowman, 1999.
357 Parton, 1979.
358 Barrowman, 1999.
359 From its establishment in 1878, Wellington Girls' was known as Wellington Girls' High School. In 1905 the school changed its name to Wellington Girls' College. See Harding, 1982, p. 42.
360 Harding, 1982, p. 42.
361 Harding, 1982, p. 47.
362 *Ibid.*
363 *Ibid.*
364 *Ibid.*
365 Hughes & Ahern, 1993, p. 28.
366 Hughes & Ahern, 1993, p. 29.
367 Morris Matthews, 2006a.
368 Barrowman, 1999, p. 382.
369 Morris Matthews, 2006a.
370 Barrowman, 1999.
371 Sutherland, 1973, pp. 27–28.
372 *Ibid*; AJHR, 1924, E-6, p. 3; University of New Zealand, 1948.
373 AJHR, 1914, E-6, p. 19; AJHR, 1923, E-1, p. 26; AJHR, 1924, E-6, p. 18; AJHR, 1926, E-6, p. 19.
374 Harding, 1982, p. 180.
375 AJHR, 1906, E-12, p. 20; Hughes & Ahern, 1993; Marlborough High School, 1950, p. 91.
376 Harding, 1982, p. 184; Hughes & Ahern, 1993.
377 Hughes & Ahern, 1993; Sanderson in Penfold et al., 1991, pp. 45–47.
378 AJHR, 1905, E-12, p. 50; AJHR, 1908, E-12, p. 10; Deaker, 1979; Harding, 1982, p. 171.
379 Hughes & Ahern, 1993.
380 Northey, 1988, p. 112.
381 *Ibid.*
382 Northey, 1988, p. 114.
383 Northey, 1988, p. 7.
384 Deaker, 1979; Harding, 1982, p. 183; Northey, 1988, pp. 122–123.
385 Johnson & Jensen, 1953, p. 61.
386 Johnson & Jensen, 1953, pp. 60–61.
387 *Ibid.*
388 *Ibid.*
389 *Ibid.*
390 Johnson & Jensen, 1953, p. 62.
391 Although her name appears on earlier Victoria University College lists, she is one of a number of students, both men and women, omitted from the 1948 University of New Zealand listing: 'Noakes' is the last name on page 89, and 'O'Dea' is the first name on page 90.
392 Harding, 1982, p. 102.
393 *Ibid*; Cole Catley, 1985, p. 276; Gambrill, 1969.
394 Barrowman, 1999.
395 Barrowman, 1999, p. 36.
396 *Ibid*; Beaglehole, 1996; Hughes & Ahern, 1993.

397 Hughes & Ahern, 1993.

398 *Ibid.*

399 *Ibid;* Barrowman, 1999.

400 Hughes & Ahern, 1993.

401 *AJHR*, 1902, E-1, p. 31; *AJHR*, 1904, E-1; *AJHR*, 1905, E-1, p. 36; *AJHR*, 1906, E-12, p. 35; *AJHR*, 1909, E-6, p.19; *AJHR*, 1910, E-6, p. 21; *AJHR*, 1920, E-6, p. 29; Murray, T., 1967, p. 56; *New Zealand Gazette*, 1900, p. 1263.

402 Berman, 1996, p. 355.

403 Berman, 1996; Else, 1993, p. 214; Haggard, 1941; Hughes & Ahern, 1993.

404 Barrowman, 1999, p. 19.

405 Barrowman, 1999.

406 Harding, 1982, p. 87.

407 Hughes, 1996b.

408 Hughes & Ahern, 1993, p. 58.

409 Colin Bailey 1925–1926, Wellington Teachers' Training College, Kowhai Road, in Macaskill, 1980, p. 46.

410 Hughes & Ahern, 1993, p. 323.

411 Bremner, 1998.

412 *Ibid.*

413 Irvine-Smith, 1948; Macaskill, 1980.

414 *AJHR*, 1925, E-7 A; Barrowman, 1999, p. 78.

415 Hughes & Ahern, 1993, p. 50.

416 Barrowman, 1999, p. 92.

417 Hughes & Ahern, 1993; Taylor, 1998.

418 Barrowman, 1999, p. 382.

419 Barrowman, 1999, p. 78.

420 Hughes & Ahern, 1993.

421 *AJHR*, 1915, E-6, p. 38; Murray, 1951; Palmerston North Girls' High School, 1962, p. 23.

422 Morris Matthews, 2006b.

423 Garnham & Cowlrick, 1984.

424 *AJHR*, 1919, E-6; Taumarunui High School Jubilee Committee, 1984.

425 *Ibid; AJHR*, 1916, E-6, p. 33; *AJHR*, 1922, E-6, p. 25.

426 *AJHR*, 1909, E-6, p. 19; *AJHR*, 1917, E-6, p. 35; *AJHR*, 1920, E-6, p. 30; *AJHR*, 1924, E-6, p. 18; New Plymouth Girls' High School, 1935, p. 10.

427 Cole Catley, 1985, p. 17.

428 Cole Catley, 1985, p. 18.

429 Both Jessie Hetherington's parents came from Northern Ireland. Her father, Samuel Hetherington, was from Lurgan while her mother, Rebecca Brown, had come from Donoughcloney. Her mother died as Jessie went to school in Auckland in 1896. Her father, who became a prosperous merchant, died in 1923 (Butler & McMorran, 1948, p. 161).

430 Cole Catley, 1985, p. 18.

431 Hetherington, n.d., Ch. 5.

432 *Ibid.*

433 *Trinity College Calendar*, 1907 & 1909. With thanks to Susan Parkes, Trinity College, Dublin.

434 Hetherington, n.d.

435 *Ibid.*
436 *Ibid.*
437 Butler & McMorran, 1948, p. 161.
438 Hetherington, n.d; *Trinity College Calendar*, 1904–1907.
439 *Ibid.*
440 *Ibid*; Hughes, 1994.
441 *Ibid.*
442 *Ibid.*
443 *Ibid*; Fry, 1985, p. 290.
444 Hughes, 1994.

CHAPTER 7

Travelling trailblazers:

educated women as citizens of the world

Form V, Wellington Girls' High School, 1890. Seated centre, Rosa Lichtscheindl (m.Innes), the first New Zealand schoolgirl to graduate from a university outside New Zealand, when she gained a BA from the University of Sydney in 1893. Seated to the right of Rosa are two future Canterbury graduates and teachers: Emily Broome (BA 1894, MA 1911), front second right; and May Kebbell (BA 1895), far right, who lived in London from 1910. WELLINGTON GIRLS' COLLEGE

Janette Grossmann (MA Canterbury 1884) went to Australia to teach and was later principal of West Maitland High School and North Sydney Girls' High School.

MACMILLAN BROWN LIBRARY, UNIVERSITY OF CANTERBURY
1995/3 4-33

This final chapter highlights the intersections of university education, girls' secondary education, and the dissemination of educational ideas across international boundaries. The first section examines the career development of the women teachers who travelled and taught abroad. It draws together for the first time information about both the New Zealand and British women graduate teachers who travelled to the other side of the world to take up teaching positions. Some stayed, but most returned to their home country. It concludes that there was respective importance and value placed by the women and their employing authorities on 'centre and periphery' professional experience, within the layers of citizenship, nationhood, and Empire.

The second section traces the links between women's university education and internationalism in the period to 1945. In particular, it analyses the poorly recognised but significant role of the New Zealand Federation of University Women in networking with other educated women across nations to promote citizenship, human rights, and international peace.

Elizabeth Hewett (AA Oxford, AQC London)

NAPIER GIRLS' HIGH SCHOOL

Elizabeth Hewett (AA Oxford, AQC London), foundation principal, Napier Girls' High School, 1883–1892.

Before accepting the position of foundation Lady Principal of Napier Girls' High School in New Zealand in 1883, Mary Elizabeth Grenside Hewett (AA Oxford, AQC London) negotiated a number of matters with her new employers. The salary of £300, with dwelling and boarders' fees, was acceptable; but Miss Hewett made clear that taking up the position depended upon 'her rooms being finished', that the boarders' fees 'be set at £40',

and that 'the school be opened by a Bible reading and a prayer'.[445]

The Napier Girls' High School Board of Governors agreed. They had searched in England for the first principal of their state school, before advertising in the colonies more generally. As it happened, the twenty-six-year-old Miss Hewett, a graduate of Oxford University, with teaching qualifications from Queen's College, London, was already in New Zealand, acting as principal of Otago Girls' High School in Dunedin.[446] She was well placed to both identify and insist on her conditions of employment. Napier Girls' High School thus gained the English university qualifications and teaching experience they sought; but as it turned out, Miss Hewett was also well

Teachers at home and away

The professional lives of those independent women graduates who travelled to the other side of the world raise a number of questions. For example, what was their motivation? For those going out to the colonies of the British Empire, was it missionary zeal? Was it part of an exciting adventure for antipodeans, who fitted teaching around 'seeing the world'? What did it mean for the schools they taught in? Did the overseas teaching experience benefit their careers?

Travelling abroad was certainly an act of courage. For example, the decision made by Elizabeth Hewett in 1882 to take on a six-week voyage to the other side of the world, in order to take up the position of acting principal at Otago Girls' High School, was at the very least adventurous. What must she have thought as she disembarked at Port Chalmers? Could she feel at home in the austere surroundings of Otago Girls'? She could not have helped but compare where she was with her former Queen's College and English boarding school surroundings. By the time she reached the Port of Napier the following year,

connected through religious and family networks. The board chairman, Sir John Ormond, and board secretary, the Reverend Dr Sidey, were particularly impressed that Elizabeth Hewett was one of three daughters of the Rev John William Hewett, a Clerk in Holy Orders in the Parish of Whitwick, Leicester. Further, the Rev Hewett, with an MA from Oxford, had at one time taught Admiral Lord Jellicoe, later to be Governor-General of New Zealand.[447]

The provincial Napier board of governors was not alone in seeking to secure English school mistresses as senior staff in newly established colonial girls' secondary schools. By the early 1880s, women graduates of the University of New Zealand had already been appointed to New Zealand schools in the main towns. However, the Napier board meeting reports give the impression that even if New Zealand women graduates had applied, they were not quite what was wanted. What was important, it seemed, were English credentials, public boarding school training, religious values, and the ways of 'home'. The daughters of the region's pastoralists, doctors, clergy, merchants, and bankers were sent with confidence to Miss Hewett, and she did not let them down. Glowing reports of her stewardship were forthcoming, including her being 'a good disciplinarian, calm and dignified … with great charm and personality'.[448]

she may have been better prepared, but coming to a frontier rural town must surely have represented a refreshed kind of culture shock.

On the other hand, the New Zealand women graduates who sailed to England to work and study were perhaps better prepared. In the main, their parents had been born in Great Britain, and most of their New Zealand schooling and university education curricula and literature originated from there. All their lives, they had possibly imagined this 'home' of which they had heard and read much.

Those who were admitted to study or appointed to teach had been permitted to do so because of their ability to contribute in some way. New Zealand and English boards of governors, for example, controlled the gates to leadership of girls' secondary education and, in the case of New Zealand women, to specialist postgraduate study as well. In accepting or appointing those from the other side of the world, those in power imagined the effects of their decisions. At some point, the girls who were to be taught by these women would benefit from the contact.

For the women graduate teachers, this meant an opportunity to intervene *actively* through the introduction of a range of new ways of knowing, extracted from both 'home' and the current location. It made possible a contesting of tradition and custom and, rather than *passively* accepting these, using the new space to create new possibilities for girls' schooling. In this diaspora space, at the intersection of the borders, in the 'in-between' of home and away, they were well placed to mingle among themselves and to try out new ideas.

A number of state girls' schools in New Zealand sought founding principals around the time when the first women graduated from the University of New Zealand. In New Zealand, as in Australia, educated women preceded suffrage, and New Zealand women were amongst the first in the British Empire to be awarded degrees proper. Some boards of governors opted for 'genteel and Christian women' from 'home' to serve as the principals of the first girls' secondary schools. For example, Mrs Margaret Burn from Edinburgh was recruited to Otago Girls' High School in 1870,[449] and Mrs Georgiana Ingle from England, via Tasmania, to Christchurch Girls' High School in 1877.[450] The case of Georgiana Ingle is worthy of comment because it highlights both the strengths of Australasian male educational networks, and emerging thinking on appropriate models of secondary schooling within new geographical locations, away from 'home'.

Georgiana Ingle had little practical experience as a teacher, but she was selected on other grounds (including the fact that she was well connected) from fifty-seven applicants for the much-sought-after position, with a salary of £450. Her father had been the rector at the Boys' High School in Hobart, and her late husband had been the rector of Kew Boys' High School in Melbourne. Mr Ingle had died suddenly at the age of thirty-two, leaving Georgiana a widow with three children under five years of age. It is not clear whether her personal circumstances influenced the decision to appoint her as Christchurch's first woman principal, but in announcing her appointment, the board emphasised her working knowledge of the structures and organisation of Australian *boys'* schools.[451]

Other founding principals of state schools had no higher education; for example, Miss Martha Hamilton was appointed to Wellington Girls' High School in 1883,[452] while Southland Girls' High School appointed in turn Miss E. Hood (from Victoria, Australia), Miss Spence (Scotland), Miss Purnell (England), and Miss Jessie Christie (Scotland).[453] These were the first and last of the nongraduate women principals in New Zealand public girls' secondary schools. However, a pattern was to emerge in some schools which produced a legacy of English and Scottish graduate leadership, such as at Napier Girls' High School (1884–1900) and at the Anglican girls' schools, Auckland Diocesan School (1903–1950), and Nga Tawa Diocesan School (1891–1951).

Anne Whitelaw: a global educator

As Chapter 5 showed, Anne Whitelaw was the first New Zealand woman holding a British degree to be appointed principal of a New Zealand girls' secondary school; but her subsequent career took her back to Britain and further afield, before she finally retired to New Zealand.

Her first move abroad had been to Girton College, Cambridge, in 1894. The wealth of primary- and secondary-source biographical and career material about her contains nothing to suggest how she would have considered such a move, which was previously unheard of for a New Zealand woman. Her brother and sister treated it very much as an aside in their memories of their sister.

Girton College, Cambridge—originally a women's college—produced many outstanding educationalists who would work in New Zealand, such as Anne Whitelaw, Jessie Hetherington, Winifred Boys-Smith, Eliza Edwards, and Ethel Sandford. GIRTON COLLEGE, CAMBRIDGE

However, it is clear that she must have been influenced by someone in New Zealand who had perhaps themselves attended an English university. Moreover, her mother had agreed not only to the move itself, but probably also to making a financial contribution to what was a substantial undertaking. As well as the travel, distance, and financial cost, it also meant adjustment to new academic requirements and to leaving a very large colonial family for life in a residential English college. Anne Whitelaw did not have the advantages of a private boarding school background or the networks that went with that. She was very much on her own.

Yet she did much better than mere survival: she achieved a First Class in mathematics in the Girton College entrance examinations; in the following year she passed mathematics, classics, and mechanics; and by 1896 she had completed a Mathematical Tripos with second class honours, first division.[454] This was a titular degree, often listed beside a woman's name as AA (Associate of Arts). Although the women students at Cambridge University passed exactly the same courses as their male counterparts, they could not have full degrees conferred upon them until 1948. Like many of her peers, Anne Whitelaw later took up the offer of converting her Tripos to a Master of Arts degree, in her case at Trinity College, Dublin. Back in New Zealand, her former headmaster at Auckland Grammar School, Mr J. Tibbs, an Oxford graduate and mathematician, singled out her overall achievements in his annual prizegiving report of 1897.[455]

As she was completing her qualifications, it is likely that she was looking for a suitable first teaching position. Frances Dove, founder principal of the prestigious English school Wycombe Abbey School for girls, appointed her as a mathematics teaching assistant in 1898.[456] She left to become foundation principal of Auckland Girls' Grammar in 1906 (see Chapter 5), but in 1910 she

196

was appointed principal of Wycombe Abbey, a position she held for fifteen years.

The career of Anne Whitelaw in both England and New Zealand can be traced in some depth because of the archives, manuscripts, photographs, and records preserved for safekeeping in both locations. In the main, this was because Anne Whitelaw kept such good records herself; but credit must also go to the Old Girls' Associations of the schools with which she was associated. Former pupils and teachers kept up to date with what 'AW' (the nickname often used by both pupils and colleagues) was thinking and doing; but this information also prompted

Wycombe Abbey School for girls, England, where Anne Whitelaw was principal (1910–1925). Whitelaw was the first New Zealand woman to lead an English girls' school.
AUCKLAND GIRLS' GRAMMAR SCHOOL

correspondence, invitations, and newspaper reports that in turn generated further details of her career and life as a school principal.[457] At both Wycombe Abbey and Auckland Girls', these associations engendered the maintenance of strong networks, ongoing newsletters, and regular reunions. In these ways, women kept in contact with one another, shared information, and in their later years, recorded their schoolday memories, including the years they spent as pupils of 'AW'. Both Old Girls' Associations on either side of the world thought

Auckland Girls' Grammar School, Howe Street, Auckland, 1926. Anne Whitelaw (MA TCD) was principal from 1906 to 1910, the first New Zealand woman with English university qualifications to lead a New Zealand girls' school.
SPECIAL COLLECTIONS, AUCKLAND CITY LIBRARIES (NZ) 1-W601

Anne Whitelaw at her desk, Auckland Girls' Grammar School.
AUCKLAND GIRLS' GRAMMAR SCHOOL

so highly of Anne Whitelaw that shortly after her death they collaborated and published a forty-page booklet, *A Tribute to the Memory of Anne Watt Whitelaw 1875–1966—A Great Headmistress*.

Upon her resignation from Wycombe Abbey in 1925, Anne Whitelaw devoted the rest of her working life to social and religious work. She was appointed a member of the British Missionary Society Advisory Committee on Education in the Colonies in 1925. Her particular role was to visit and report on the education and welfare of women and girls in Africa, and she travelled to Uganda, Tanganyika, and Kenya with Dr J. H. Oldham and his wife from late 1925 to the end of April 1926. Correspondence between Anne Whitelaw and Dr Oldham indicates that for her part she 'enjoyed it all so very much—a great opportunity',[458] while he clearly believed that she had 'rendered valuable service in this visit to Africa'.[459] Her knowledge of girls' education, combined with a personal mission to bring about change, was no doubt partly responsible for her appointment in 1927 as a member of the Colonial Office Advisory Committee on the education of women and girls.[460]

Anne Whitelaw's official files record for posterity her ideas for improving the welfare and education of girls and women in Africa.[461] The central arguments that she advanced included the introduction of a three-tiered education system, based on her observations that most African women married by the time they were sixteen; that there was little provision for girls' schooling, although some was provided for boys; that the women were the growers of the food crops and needed to be released from the fields in order to attend school; and that native women needed to be trained to be teachers and nurses. Between 1925 and 1927 she refined this plan, recommending to the Advisory Committees that a general school curriculum could be developed for use in mission and state schools:

Group One   Those subjects which are closely connected with the work a woman must do in life and the part she must play. Those are infant welfare, hygiene, cooking, gardening, housewifery, first aid, nursing, and mothercraft.

Group Two   Recreative subjects—singing, drawing, games, and drill.

Group Three Some formal school subjects as are needed to help create an intelligent mind.[462]

What Anne Whitelaw increasingly came to realise was that while a basic educational training should be available in the villages, there should also be more girls' boarding schools. Realising just how few European women missionaries and African women teachers were available, Whitelaw recommended that English-trained teachers could be recruited to teach in African schools with the co-operation of the government. It was not a new idea to co-opt trained women teachers to colonial church boarding schools. The Godolphin Society had already done so in other parts of Africa. However, what Whitelaw was suggesting was that the schools themselves:

> … begin a type of education of women and girls on new lines suitable for the African woman rather than an old fashioned stereotypical English education … that the curriculum should be thought out boldly in the light of modern educational ideas and not merely be our English High School syllabus adapted to African needs.[463]

From 1928 to 1932, Anne Whitelaw was lecturer and director of women's education at the Selly Oak Missionary College in Birmingham, followed by five years as voluntary warden of Talbot Settlement, an Anglican women's residential house. She returned to New Zealand in 1938, living in Auckland with her sister Edith at 57 Arney Road, Remuera. She was active in the Federation of University Women, kept in regular contact with her former pupils from both schools, and made return trips to England in 1948 and 1954. After she died at home in 1967, memorial services were held at both her schools. In Auckland, the staff and 1100 girls of Auckland Girls' Grammar School gathered in a city church to remember their founding headmistress.[464] At Wycombe Abbey, the service was held in the school chapel that Anne Whitelaw had worked so hard to build. A memorial plaque was placed in the chapel, and 'Miss Whitelaw's seniors' raised sufficient funds to present to the school 'The Whitelaw Library'. It was a gesture that summarised what Anne Whitelaw had often said to them so many years earlier: 'Something abides, something goes on.'[465]

Venturing further afield—spaces and connections

A comparative analysis was undertaken of those New Zealand and British graduates who, having attained their first qualification, then travelled to the other side of the world. In the case of the New Zealand graduates, they undertook postgraduate study and/or took up teaching positions. In the case of the British graduate teachers, all came to New Zealand to take up teaching appointments, having been recruited by New Zealand school authorities. The term 'graduate' is used to refer to British women who attended British universities and gained academic credentials which, if they had been men, would have earnt them graduate status, for example, Tripos or Associate of Arts.

New Zealand women graduates abroad (1880–1930)

Between 1880 and 1930, at least thirty-three New Zealand women travelled to undertake undergraduate or postgraduate study, mainly in England or France (see Appendix). Of those who returned to New Zealand with postgraduate qualifications, seven would become senior mistresses or principals of girls' secondary schools, while two others were to be educational pioneers. One was Jessie Hetherington, the first New Zealand woman graduate to teach at an English secondary school and secondary training college (1913–1914) and to become a secondary school inspector (1926–1942) (see Chapter 6). The other was Helen Richmond (m.Simpson), the first New Zealand woman to be awarded a doctorate in an overseas university, and to teach at a New Zealand university (see Chapter 3). Other graduates who taught abroad included at least four who took up principal positions in Australia. Seven spent some of their careers teaching in girls' secondary schools in the Pacific, while others taught in mission schools in India, South Africa, Argentina, and China.

An outstanding feature of nearly all the girls' schools surveyed in the period reviewed is the number of New Zealand women graduate teachers who applied for, and were granted, leave of absence in order to observe teaching methods and classroom management in English schools. Most young teachers ventured abroad for six months to a year. This may have been because those who held permanent positions were reluctant to relinquish hard-won appointments. However, it seems clear that many boards of governors were favourably disposed to the idea of returning 'home' for the purposes of professional development. Broadening one's experience and expertise through keeping up with new ideas and methods abroad, and especially in England, was generally regarded as very beneficial to all concerned. For example, the Auckland Girls' Grammar School Board was particularly generous, for both educational and health reasons. 'Mistresses were often granted temporary leave of absence to travel overseas—usually to Britain—and sometimes there were requests for leave, often for several months, on the grounds of ill health. The prescribed cure for undue stress from teaching adolescent girls was plenty of rest and a relaxing sea voyage.'[466]

Not all spent their entire time visiting English schools. In 1923, the principal of Nelson Girls' College, Margaret Lorimer, was granted a year's leave of absence. While she did visit English schools (including Cheltenham Ladies' College), she also fitted in climbing Mont Blanc and the Matterhorn. For these pursuits she was accepted for membership of the prestigious Ladies' Alpine Club, a rare honour for a New Zealander.[467]

The Wellington College Board of Governors often granted overseas leave to its teachers. For example, during her fourteen years as principal of Wellington Girls' College (1900–1926), Mary McLean was granted leave on full pay for the whole of 1907, and again in 1918. 'During both periods of leave she visited many eminent schools and colleges in the British Isles, on the

Form captains wearing the dreaded gymslips with sashes, Timaru Girls' High School, 1928. TIMARU GIRLS' HIGH SCHOOL

Continent, and in North America, being determined to keep in touch with educational progress there.'[468] Generations of New Zealand schoolgirls have her to thank for the introduction of the 'gym tunic', which, with modifications, was based on the garments she had seen at Madame Osterberg's College for Drill and Games in Sweden.

Overseas graduates to New Zealand (1878–1930)

Between 1878 and 1930, at least thirty-nine women graduates from other parts of the world travelled to New Zealand to teach (see Appendix).

Trinity College, University of Dublin

Between 1904 and 1907, Trinity College, Dublin (TCD) opened its doors to women. That is, Oxford and Cambridge women who had gained the Tripos examination, but not a degree, could apply for Dublin degrees. Over 700 women did so, including 250 from Girton, and various numbers from Newnham and the Oxford women's colleges. Known as 'steamboat ladies', because of their overnight trips from England to Dublin, many were seeking the right to use BA or MA after their names in order to secure teaching positions or promotion. They were, after all, in competition with women graduates from London, Durham, or Aberdeen, and of course, New Zealand graduates too. Trinity

Frances McCall (MA Oxford)

Frances McCall was a history graduate from St Hugh's, Oxford, who came to New Zealand in 1921 to head Nga Tawa Diocesan School near Marton. She had formerly been a teacher at the Diocesan School for Girls in Grahamstown, South Africa, headmistress of the Co-education Church School, Mbabme, Swaziland, and headmistress of Queenwood School, Eastbourne, England. After twelve years at Nga Tawa, she informed the school board that although she did not want to leave the school or New Zealand, she had to return to Britain to teach. As she explained, 'there were no superannuation schemes for English women in New Zealand, and this posed a concern for her future security'.[469] During her stewardship at Nga Tawa, however, Frances McCall did much

Frances McCall was principal of Diocesan schools in four different countries during her career. Between 1921 and 1933 she led Nga Tawa Diocesan School for Girls, Marton.

NGA TAWA DIOCESAN SCHOOL FOR GIRLS

College charged fees for the graduation, raising more than £10,000. This was used to build a hall of residence for women students in Dublin.[470]

Some of these TCD graduates gained their New Zealand positions through answering advertisements in newspapers or through personal networks. Others applied through organisations for the overseas settlement of British women. Successful applicants were offered second-class passage money, usually in exchange for three years' teaching. The career profiles of these women have been pieced together from a range of primary and secondary sources in both the United Kingdom and New Zealand. In the main, those who held senior positions in New Zealand schools feature in jubilee and centennial histories of the schools with which they were associated. Others have been traced using school archives, official lists of secondary school teachers, and college registers. Even so, there are some gaps, and there are several women whose destination upon leaving New Zealand remains unknown.

Of the overseas graduates, six returned to England to take up principalships or senior teaching positions there. Anne Whitelaw was one of these; Frances McCall was another.

The Diocesan networks worked effectively in securing experienced teachers. For example, Ethel Sandford, a Girtonian who converted her Classics Tripos to a Trinity College Bachelor of Arts, also held an MA from Cambridge. With

to champion closer relations between the New Zealand Diocesan schools and English public schools. She was instrumental, for example, in linking the Association of Headmistresses of Independent Schools in New Zealand with its English counterpart. She did this because, she said, New Zealand schools should be 'in touch with all educational developments at "home"'.[471] During her twelve-year reign, almost all her staff were from England, many coming as part of the British women's settlement scheme. This may also have had something to do with the generous employment conditions offered. Nga Tawa could afford to pay English teachers from the time they left England (including their passage by ship), and provided accommodation in the grounds of the school. Miss McCall's policy of emulating the English girls' boarding school went down well with Nga Tawa parents. The school roll doubled in two years, with girls being sent from all parts of New Zealand. Later, pupils of the time would suggest that one of the main reasons for the school's popularity was because 'Miss McCall came from "home", while others said that they were sent there to lose their New Zealand "twang"'.[472]

nineteen years' teaching experience, she came to New Zealand in 1926 as principal of Auckland Diocesan School for Girls. She stayed for five years, before returning to teach at Beverly High School (East Yorks), Malvern Girls, and Roedean.[473]

Others from Girton College who spent short periods of time in New Zealand before returning to Britain included Janet Vernon Harcourt, who taught with Anne Whitelaw at Wycombe Abbey, and then spent two years at Auckland Girls' Grammar while Anne was principal. Janet Vernon Harcourt returned to England in 1911, where she spent the rest of her career at Runton Hill School in Norfolk.[474]

In the 1920s there were several English graduates who were associated with higher education either before or after they came to New Zealand. For example, Margaret Dyer (Tripos 1908, MA 1923), former head of household arts at Kings College London (1911–1923), was appointed New Zealand's first Inspector of Domestic Subjects, a position she held from 1924 to 1931, when she retired to Blackheath in England.[475] Someone with less teaching experience was Florence Cadell (Languages Tripos 1918, MA London 1934), who came to New Zealand to teach at Nga Tawa Diocesan School for Girls between 1921 and 1924. She then took up poultry farming in New Zealand for four years before returning to England, where she was university extension lecturer in the history of art at Nottingham.[476]

Another who stayed about the same length of time was Ida Haward. She had studied history at Girton, gaining an MA in 1925 and a PhD from London in 1929. She may well have been the first exchange lecturer in a New Zealand university, coming in 1921 from her position as lecturer in history at Bedford College, London, to Canterbury College, Christchurch. Ida Haward certainly took advantage of new possibilities in New Zealand. From a one-year exchange post, she ended up staying nine years before becoming a radio journalist in New Zealand. Significantly, this experience was good enough to secure her a prestigious position at 'home' when she returned to England to work for the BBC.[477]

Others stayed away from 'home' and in New Zealand for much longer. Beatrice Ward was one of these. A London graduate who had taught at Cheltenham Ladies' College, Beatrice Ward was senior mistress at Auckland Diocesan School from 1903 to 1915. Her successor, London graduate Eva

DIOCESAN SCHOOL FOR GIRLS AUCKLAND

*Auckland schools for girls employed
a series of English women graduates
including above, Mary Pulling (BA
(Hons)), principal of Auckland Diocesan
(1903–1929) and left, Blanche Butler
(BSc), Auckland Girls' Grammar School
(1911–1920). Both were graduates of the
University of London.*

Necker, stayed for ten years. After a trip to England in 1926 she returned to New Zealand as acting principal of Nga Tawa, which led in turn to her appointment as foundation principal of Waikato Diocesan School for Girls.[478]

There were others who did not return to England. Elizabeth Hewett was forced by ill health to retire after eight years as principal of Napier Girls' High School, and died a year later in 1893, aged thirty-four.[479] Mary Pulling, a graduate of the University of London and a student of Dorothea Beale's at Cheltenham Ladies' College, was appointed founding principal of Auckland Diocesan School for Girls (1903–1926). She came to New Zealand, she said, 'mainly from missionary motives',[480] yet remained for the rest of her life.[481] Blanche Butler (BSc London), principal of Auckland Girls' Grammar School, stayed for nine years from 1911 to 1920, leaving to marry and live in Australia.[482] Winifred Boys-Smith, a Girtonian, was the first woman professor of the University of New Zealand, taking up her appointment in 1910. This had much to do with her subject expertise: she was the foundation professor of home science at Otago, having been a lecturer in science at Cheltenham Ladies' College from 1896 (see Chapter 3).[483] Annie Young (Classics Tripos 1913, LLB London 1929) took some time out to come and teach in Anglican girls' schools in New Zealand. She taught classics and history at Nga Tawa from 1932 to 1936. From there she was appointed lecturer at the Hugenot University College in South Africa, where she lived for the rest of her life.[484]

Roughly equal numbers of women travelled in both directions; in the case of New Zealanders, this usually involved postgraduate study in England, and about the same proportions of each group who travelled and taught eventually returned to their country of origin. Many used the experience gained abroad to enhance their career profiles, and it is clear that this experience was valued by employing authorities on both sides of the world. Many of the women graduates who had travelled at a younger age secured principal positions at girls' schools. More often than not, they also surrounded themselves with staff who had similar overseas experience. In this way, the Wycombe Abbey, Cheltenham Ladies' College, and Girton College networks worked to the advantage of New Zealand schoolgirls, while Auckland Girls' Grammar and Auckland Diocesan School for Girls provided respectable employment histories for the English women who taught there.

Far from being a one-directional professional benefit being gained by New Zealanders travelling to 'home' and back, the English women graduates also enjoyed the advantages that antipodean work experience could provide. In many cases, it opened up a range of totally new possibilities, facilitating a release from 'home' with all the concomitant freedoms—personal, professional, and political.

'An International Parliament of Women': the New Zealand Federation of University Women

It was because of the value placed upon such educational experiences abroad that many of the women who had travelled, studied, and taught in other countries became members of the New Zealand Federation of University Women (NZFUW). New Zealand was early to be affiliated to the International Federation of University Women (IFUW), which was established in 1920. At the second conference of the IFUW, held in Paris in 1922, New Zealand was represented by Catherine Hogg (MA), who was studying at the Sorbonne at the time. Remarkably, given the time and cost of travel, New Zealand was represented by at least one delegate at every international conference to 1939 (there were no conferences between 1940 and 1947). Even in 1939, the year war was declared, no fewer than fifteen delegates travelled to Stockholm.[485]

Many of the key players in the founding of the NZFUW, and of the branches within regional centres, have been canvassed in earlier chapters. In the main, they were single women who were senior teachers, academics, or medical specialists. For example, Professor Helen Rawson (m.Benson) had travelled to Canada and the United States in 1919 and met with founders of the organisation. Both she and her University of Otago colleague Gladys Cameron, who was the first New Zealand woman to win a Rockefeller International Scholarship and who had studied soil analysis in Chicago, realised just how isolated they were in New Zealand, especially from new theories and ideas within their respective subjects. Further, both had first-hand experience of the benefits of associating with other women graduates in North America. They were instrumental in gathering together a group of women graduates in Christchurch in 1921, to draft the NZFUW constitution, which was presented in Paris by Catherine Hogg.[486] Helen Rawson was the founding president of the Otago branch of the NZFUW, a position she held from 1920–1924, although, as Mrs Benson, she returned to take the helm in 1929 and 1930, and between 1936 and 1939 was the Dominion President.[487] At the Easter conference in 1924, she made clear the aims of the New Zealand Federation, saying that it 'was the linking together of nations by ties of individual friendship founded in mutual sympathy and understanding; such relations would bring respect for the opinions of others, and the desire to seek together common truths'.[488]

The first New Zealand conference was held in Dunedin in 1923. For many of the twenty delegates, 'there was no quick alternative to the fourteen-hour train journey from Auckland to Wellington, the overnight trip on the steamer to Christchurch, and the day on the train to Dunedin'.[489]

The appeal of the FUW to women graduates of the 1920s was having contact with leading thinkers in Europe and North America, attached to universities with greater facilities than those in New Zealand. As was highlighted earlier, numbers of women graduates travelled to England or the Continent for holidays or postgraduate study, and an association with the IFUW afforded new opportunities such as 'hospitality, exchange positions, fellowships for further study, clubhouses in several countries, and the pooling of ideas for the betterment of education'.[490]

Four branches of the FUW were established in New Zealand: Dunedin and Auckland (1920), Canterbury (1922), and Wellington (1923). It was decided to rotate the New Zealand Executive among the branches of the university centres every three or four years, so it was usually the president, or her nominee, who led the New Zealand delegation to the international conference. The delegation was comprised of a designated number of voting members, according to the total number of a nation's membership. Others could attend, but without voting rights. Until 1929, all national federations were expected to present a report of their activities, with the reports being published in the conference proceedings. In this way, it is known that Dunedin Executive member Gladys Cameron represented the New Zealand Federation as delegate to the 1924 international conference held in Oslo, Norway. There she reported that the New Zealand membership was 200, and that the immediate goal was to increase the membership further and raise funds for the establishment of Crosby Hall, the London-based clubhouse.[491]

Meantime, international president Professor Bonnevie canvassed in her address the topic of a Language of International Intercourse (later to be introduced as Esperanto). The setting of international standards for degree equivalence and the establishment of the Committee on Intellectual Co-operation under the auspices of the League of Nations was undertaken by Madame Marie Curie, Professor Gilbert Murray, and Professor Albert Einstein.[492] Other topics under discussion by delegates included School Preparation for the Universities, the Interchange of Teachers, and one that might have certainly interested Gladys Cameron—Science and Internationalism.[493]

It is likely that Gladys Cameron was able to combine university research and subject conferences with her trip to Norway. It is also likely that she partially funded the travel herself. In any case, she was in a position to be able to represent New Zealand again at the 1925 conference in Brussels, where she reported that the membership had now reached 250 and that in Auckland,

Dominion Secretary Jean Rudall (BSc Otago 1917) of Epsom Girls' Grammar (1919–1948) had organised some 'very good occasions for publicity' around international women visitors, and had arranged receptions 'to which many people who should be interested in the Federation are asked'.[494] Gladys Cameron was the Dunedin FUW President in 1926, at a time when the local membership alone had reached nearly 100. Her many contributions to the federation were recalled at the time of her death in 1928, at the age of thirty-nine.

Gladys Cameron (BSc, BHSc Otago), first New Zealand woman Rockefeller Scholar. Cameron was lecturer at the University of Otago and First National Secretary of the NZFUW. HOCKEN COLLECTIONS, UARE TAOKA O HAKENA, UNIVERSITY OF OTAGO S08-006C

Dominion President Dr Hilda Northcroft (1925–1929), who was based in Auckland, ran a tight ship as far as procedures and organisation of the federation were concerned, ensuring that IFUW committee requirements were met. The older and experienced Cecil Hull (MA Auckland 1905) of Auckland Girls' Grammar (1915–1936) was appointed Corresponding Secretary for Intellectual Co-operation, while the younger Valeria Johnson (MSc Auckland 1920), newly appointed to Epsom Girls' Grammar, was in charge of the International Fellowship Funds. Every opportunity was taken to arrange scholarship and other fundraising occasions for the 100 members, usually around a visiting speaker. Nearly everyone turned out in 1928 to such an occasion, hosted by the Auckland President (1925–1929) and Dominion Vice-President Marguerita Pickmere (m.Mulgan). For many present, the speaker was their former school principal, namely Anne Whitelaw, 'who spoke eloquently on the subject of her travels in Africa when she had accompanied a British Commissioner who was investigating native education'.[495]

Dr Hilda Northcroft (MB ChB 1908 LM 1911) gained her medical qualifications from the University of Edinburgh and was a well-known Auckland doctor from 1919. She was politically active including being National President of the NZFUW (1925–1929) and represented New Zealand on the International Council of Women (1932–1942). She lobbied for women to become Justices of the Peace and was one of the first to be appointed in 1926. ALEXANDER TURNBULL LIBRARY, WELLINGTON, NZ. JULIA LESLIE STUDIOS PHOTOGRAPH C-025095-1/2

The spirit of fostering national and international links between university-educated women was a cornerstone of the FUW. Those attending international conferences, for example, reported back on the growing number of clubhouses by 1925, such as those in Paris, Washington, New York, Baltimore, Philadelphia, Rome, Athens, and London. The London clubhouse, Crosby Hall, had special significance for New Zealand members. Each of the four branches had raised £100 for its refurbishment, not an insignificant amount for the time. It was understood that for the many New Zealand members who travelled to England and Europe, there were real advantages in having ready access to full residential meeting facilities, plus a library, in central Chelsea. Not only did it fulfil the practical requirements of women travellers, but it also gave them the opportunity to attend public lectures and meet with other international members staying at Crosby Hall. In this way, New Zealand members kept up to date with issues, such as in July 1927, when the Auckland branch revisited the key elements of a debate a member had witnessed at Crosby Hall, when Professor Salvemini spoke on 'National Prejudice and School Teaching'.[496]

Three New Zealand members had attended the opening of Crosby Hall in 1927, and later, the parquet floor in the Minstrels' Gallery was donated by New Zealand as a memorial to Kate Edger.[497] Crosby Hall was also the home of the English Federation of University Women, and its archives and records were housed as part of the Sybil Campbell Collection. However, the original Hall, built in 1466, was expensive to maintain, and increasingly occupied a most valuable site. In 2005, the English Federation reluctantly sold the property and the Sybil Campbell Collection was offered space at the University of Winchester Library, where the research for this section was completed.

In Canterbury, the founding branch president in 1922–1923 was Christchurch Girls' High School principal Mary Gibson (MA Canterbury 1888). She was succeeded in turn by her Christchurch Girls' senior mistress colleague, Kathleen Gresson (MA Canterbury 1898); Canterbury University College history lecturer Alice Candy (MA Canterbury 1911); and Christchurch Girls' High School senior mistress Mary Sims (MA Otago 1920). In 1927, Canterbury had only half as many members as the other branches, and they met five times a year. Annual events were the hosting of a morning tea for women graduates of the year, and the staging of a dramatic production.[498]

While local activities such as these provided important social and networking occasions, those wanting to engage with international issues also had opportunities for doing so. By 1929, when the Canterbury branch served as the Dominion Executive, it was already receiving the League of Nations quarterly *Bulletin of University Information.* This was an initiative of the International Committee on Intellectual Co-operation, a standing committee of the IFUW. While many outside the federation might have considered women working across national boundaries to promote international peace and understanding to be merely a lofty ideal, those within the organisation did not. Right from the start, Professor Winifred Cullis, cofounder of the IFUW, and Sophia Jex-Blake, Chair of Physiology in the London School of Medicine, spoke about the interchange of international scholars; Dr Jex-Blake said this 'was really the key to the whole problem of international understanding ... . She herself had two opportunities that enriched her life not only with great experiences but with a wonderful amount of friendship.'[499] The *Bulletin* became a mechanism for arranging exchanges between universities and was compiled from Geneva. The League of Empire was also involved in arranging exchanges, and by 1937 it was reported that these had already occurred.

The first of the NZFUW travelling scholarships for research was modest. In 1939, a special Postgraduate Scholarship of £135 was awarded 'to a candidate now doing research in English at the University of London'.[500] Having completed her research, on her sea journey home this same scholar later recounted an event that highlighted other benefits of FUW membership:

> A black-out collision in the Atlantic left us shipless in Capetown for nearly three months ... It was not until I was landed with very little money in a strange land that I realised what membership of the federation could mean. I was adopted immediately into the life of Capetown, invited to the homes of graduates, taken to concerts and plays, guided up Table Mountain, and driven out to visit gardens, vineyards and the big old Dutch farmhouses.[501]

The first International Fellowships occurred much later in New Zealand. In 1946, Miss E. J. Batham (MSc), a graduate of the University of Otago, was awarded a British-sponsored International Senior Science Fellowship worth £300. This enabled her to further her research in zoology at Cambridge

University.[502] New Zealand sponsored its own fellowships only after £1000 had been raised locally, and a further £1000 given by the Fraser Government. The first was awarded in 1949 to British FUW member Dr Eila Campbell of London, to enable her to come to New Zealand to undertake research in geography. The first New Zealand-funded Fellow was botanist Brenda Slade (later Dr Shore) of the Otago branch, who took up her scholarship at Cambridge University in 1951.[503]

International FUW stalwart Professor Cullis was particularly influential in promoting travelling fellowships. She believed that such experiences could help break down prejudices between nations, as scholars became acquainted and spent time in other countries. In 1929 she said:

> It was indeed the duty of all women, but in the university women of the world, who had had the great experience and special privilege of a university education, it was

Dr Agnes Bennett (MB, ChM 1899)

According to Dr Bennett's biographers, the federation 'was something after her own heart, a core round which women of higher education all over the world could unite to help others receive the same benefits. She saw hope in it for the future peace of the world.'[504] Agnes Bennett also believed in the value of a sabbatical year when one could study and visit, in her case, obstetric hospitals, which she did in 1925, spending time at the Mayo Clinic and maternity hospitals in San Francisco, Chicago, and New York. She combined this trip with the British Obstetrics Conference in London, and meeting the political activist, Lady Astor, and Mary Allen, the founder of the Women Police. In 1931, she was, with Dr Easterfield, selected as the first woman to represent the New Zealand Medical Association at the British Conference in Eastbourne. The research she presented on her training of midwives at St Helen's Hospital was very well received and later mentioned at the League of Nations in Geneva. On that trip she also attended the centenary of the Cheltenham Ladies' College, where she had been a pupil under the famous Dorothea Beale. Crosby Hall was her residence for a period of time during this sojourn.[505]

Seated centre Dr Agnes Bennett, stalwart of the NZFUW and Superintendent of St Helen's Hospital, Wellington. Agnes gained her BSc in geology and biology from the University of Sydney in 1884 before completing medical qualifications at the University of Edinburgh. ALEXANDER TURNBULL LIBRARY, WELLINGTON, NZ. PA COLL-0040-17

felt that there might be a group that could meet on a common plane and moreover meet with less difficulty, since knowledge is not limited to nationalities, that education should already have been to them something of an international experience.[506]

Others, such as Mary Jenkins of the Headmistresses' Association of the Eastern States of America, believed that teacher exchanges could have long-reaching effects on promoting human understanding. Having raised funds for this purpose, she asked school principals to forward names of teachers for selection for the teacher exchange programme.[507]

Meantime, Dean Virginia Gildersleve of Barnard Women's College, Columbia University, and Dean Ada Comstock of Smith College, early presidents of the American Association of University Women, furthered the idea of having representation on international peacekeeping bodies, such as the League of Nations,[508] and later on UNESCO, and at sessions of the United Nations, as reported in 1947.[509] In 1924, Professor Cullis illustrated just why some educated women were likely to make more impact on high-level decision making than some educated men when she relayed the tale of a leading academic who had been offered a new position in another university. When a friend enquired of a daughter of the family, 'Well, what has your father decided?' she replied that 'Father is upstairs praying for guidance. Mother is downstairs packing.'[510]

In Wellington, the indefatigable Dr Agnes Bennett was the founding branch president in 1923 and served again in 1939 and 1940.

The Wellington branch had 120 members by 1927, and held at least five meetings per year. An annual event was a home-hosted celebration for the women graduates, and in 1927, fifty women gathered for that purpose at Dr Bennett's home, 'Inverleigh'.[511] Other Wellington branch presidents to 1945 included medical practitioners Dr Ada Paterson, Dr Sylvia Chapman, and Dr E. Bryson, and Wellington Girls' or Wellington East Girls' teachers Edith Hind (MA Victoria 1909), Alithea Batham (BA Canterbury 1901), Irene Wilson (MA Canterbury 1910), Violet Greig (MA 1900, BSc 1905), Clara Heine (BA Victoria 1913), Margaret Smith (MA Otago 1917), Esma North (BA Victoria 1915), and Beryl Jackson (MA Victoria 1926).

By 1936, when Dr Agnes Bennett led the New Zealand delegation of seven to Cracow in Poland, she had been Medical Superintendent of St Helen's Hospital for nearly thirty years. She brought back to Wellington the discussion points from the conference, especially those related to the restrictions placed upon married women's participation in the paid workforce. No doubt recalling her own rebuttals of Truby King's attitude to higher education for women, Agnes Bennett might well have agreed with President Professor Johanna Westerdike's argument that: 'the present drastic laws against the employment of married women seem to be violent emotional explosions, indicative of a psychological attitude on the part of Adams which should be stubbornly resisted'.[512]

A range of issues came to the fore in the 1930s. One was the encouragement of federation women to stand for election to local bodies and authorities. In 1939, at the NZFUW conference held in Dunedin, there was much to celebrate. Four members had been elected to university-associated boards: Helen Rawson (m. Benson) (BSc TCD 1919) and Dr Sylvia Chapman (MD Otago 1934) to the University of New Zealand Senate; Helen Young (m.Leversedge) (MA Canterbury 1911) to the Canterbury University College Council; and Muriel May (MA Otago 1923) to the University of Otago Council. Otago and Auckland Hospital Board positions had also been won respectively by Ethel McMillan (m.Black) (MA Otago 1926) and Dr Hilda Northcroft. Further, Dr Alice Woodward (m.Horsley) (MB ChB Otago 1900) had received the OBE for her work at the Auckland City Mission; and for the first time, two New Zealanders, Helen Benson and Mrs Hall-Kenny, had been elected to the IFUW International Committee for Exchange.[513] All this occurred at the outbreak of World War Two. When the IFUW next reconvened in 1947, internationalism and world peace would be firmly on the agenda.

Notes

445 *Daily Telegraph,* 2 July 1883, p. 3; Garnham & Cowlrick, 1984, pp. 3–4.
446 *Otago Daily Times,* 4 November 1883.
447 *Ibid*; Revell, 1993, pp. 211–212.
448 *Ibid.*
449 Wallis, 1972, 1993.
450 Peddie, 1977.
451 Peddie, 1977.
452 *Ibid.*
453 Deaker, 1979.
454 *Girton College Admission Register, 1897.*
455 *Auckland Girls' Grammar School Archives,* Headmaster's report, 1897.

456 Flint, 1989; O'Connor, 1967.
457 I am very grateful to Robin Fraser, Archivist at the Auckland Girls' Grammar School, for her advice, assistance, and research notes on Anne Whitelaw's years at Auckland Girls' Grammar School. Similarly, to Professor Joyce Goodman, University of Winchester, for the material relating to Wycombe Abbey School.
458 *The Joint International Missionary Council of British Missionary Societies Africa and India Archives.* Correspondence, Anne Whitelaw to Dr Oldham, 30 April 1926; and Dr Oldham to Anne Whitelaw, 23 June 1926.
459 *Ibid.*
460 *The Joint International Missionary Council of British Missionary Societies Africa and India Archives.* Correspondence, Dr Oldham to Rev Stevenson, 21 January 1927.
461 *The Joint International Missionary Council of British Missionary Societies Africa and India Archives.* Report of Miss Whitelaw to the African Education Group 1925–1927. The Education of Women and Girls—Uganda, Box 207, mf 79; Proposals for Education of Women and Girls in Tanganyika Territory, Box 207, mf 79–80; Memorandum on the Training of Native Teachers, Box 207, mf 233–234.
462 *Ibid.*
463 *The Joint International Missionary Council of British Missionary Societies Africa and India Archives.* Notes on meeting on the Education of Women and Girls in Africa, Edinburgh House, London, 1 June 1927.
464 Flint, 1989; Northey, 1988; O'Connor, 1967.
465 A. Whitelaw, cited in Flint, 1989, p. 55.
466 Northey, 1988, p. 89.
467 Voller, 1982, p. 79.
468 Harding, 1982, p. 59.
469 Whitmore, 1991, p. 78.
470 Hunt & Barker, 1998.
471 Whitmore, 1991, p. 67.
472 Whitmore, 1991, pp. 42, 71.
473 Butler & McMorran, 1948, p. 145; Johnson & Jensen, 1953.
474 Johnson & Jensen, 1953, p. 124.
475 Johnson & Jensen, 1953, p. 168.
476 Johnson & Jensen, 1953, p. 261.
477 Johnson & Jensen, 1953, p. 283.
478 *Ibid*; Whitmore, 1991.
479 Garnham & Cowlrick, 1984.
480 Hercock, 1996.
481 *Ibid.*
482 Northey, 1988.
483 Butler & McMorran, 1948, p. 48.
484 Butler & McMorran, 1948, p. 219; Whitmore, 1991.
485 IFUW, 1921–1945; Macdonald, 1982.
486 Macdonald, 1982, p. 35.
487 Angus, 1982; Macdonald, 1982, pp. 147, 170.
488 Angus, 1982, p. 22.
489 Angus, 1982, p. 36.
490 Angus, 1982, p. 37.

491 IFUW, 1921–1925, Vol. 1, 1924, p. 54.

492 IFUW, 1921–1925, Vol. 1, 1924, p. 76.

493 IFUW, 1921–1925, Vol. 1, 1924, pp. 83–85, 92.

494 IFUW, 1925, Report of the Council Meeting, Brussels.

495 Report of the NZFUW, presented to the 12th Council meeting, IFUW, Madrid, September 1928, p. 75.

496 *Ibid.*

497 Macdonald, 1982, pp. 40, 47.

498 IFUW, Report of the 12th Council meeting, Madrid, 1928, p. 75.

499 IFUW, Report of the 2nd Conference, July 1922, Paris, p. 58.

500 IFUW, Report of the 8th Conference, Stockholm, 1939, p. 71.

501 IFUW, Bulletin 24, Report 1941–1943, p. 6.

502 IFUW, Report of the 9th Conference, Bulletin 26, Toronto, 1947, p. 34.

503 Macdonald, 1982, p. 154.

504 Hughes, 1996a; Manson & Manson, 1960, p. 126.

505 *Ibid.*

506 IFUW, Report of the 5th Conference, Geneva, 1922, p. 49.

507 IFUW, Report of the 5th Conference, Geneva, 1922, p. 85.

508 IFUW, Report of the 5th Conference, Geneva, 1922, p. 82.

509 IFUW, Bulletin 26, Report of the 9th Conference, Toronto, 1947, p. 160.

510 IFUW, Bulletin 26, Report of the 9th Conference, Toronto, 1947, p. 92.

511 IFUW, Report of the NZFUW, 1927, presented at the 12th Council meeting, IFUW, Madrid, 1928, p. 75.

512 IFUW, Bulletin No.18, Report of the 7th Conference, Cracow, 1936, p. 23.

513 Macdonald, 1982, p. 47.

Afterword

This history of the higher education of New Zealand girls and women before 1945 is not a compensatory history, a story to be set alongside that of men, nor is it intended as a purely celebratory history, a story of struggle and eventual triumph. While elements of both can certainly be found within this book, what has emerged is that women received and benefited from higher education, yet any advantages it bestowed upon them were determined by social, cultural, economic, and political forces. Early pathways to higher education were governed initially by parental influence, executed with a steely determination to succeed and made possible through various branches of funding. What women graduates then chose to do with their advanced learning was limited to a range of professions to which their entry was not opposed. In the main this was teaching in the girls' secondary schools located in larger towns and in the district high

Flora McLean Allan on the occasion of her MA graduation at the University of Otago, 1888. After a period teaching at Braemar House, a Dunedin private girls' school, Flora Allan returned to teach at Otago Girls' High School where she had been a pupil. She was principal of Otago Girls' (1912–1922) and an active member of the Otago branch of the New Zealand Federation of University Women.
HOCKEN COLLECTIONS, UARE TAOKA O HAKENA, UNIVERSITY OF OTAGO S08-006

schools of provincial centres. Many chose to marry and in most cases gave up a career at that point. Others pursued a full career, retiring only when reaching the then compulsory age limit. All influenced other young people with whom they came in contact, especially the teachers and the doctors. Just knowing that it was possible to extend learning beyond secondary school opened up possibilities, particularly for young women.

Of course, those who were enabled to take up higher education before 1945 were but a small proportion of the total population. Those who received little schooling because they were needed to help at home or on the farm often did not even gain the required pass to advance through the 'standards' in primary school, let alone reach the final year to sit the Proficiency Examination. There were those who completed primary schooling and even a few years of secondary schooling and chose to enter trades and vocations not requiring higher education. There were those who achieved well throughout their schooling but for a variety of reasons did not continue their education, even though it was their dream to do so. It is the theme of 'opportunity lost' that has surfaced time and again throughout this research and public presentations of it. Women who are now our more senior citizens state openly that far from 'being happy with their lot', they have regrets about their levels of education. In many cases, persuading parents to allow them to take up teaching or nursing rather than a secretarial course was a battle won only with the support of a significant teacher. It is important to remember that entering teaching or nursing was viewed as a pinnacle as well as a pragmatic educational and career goal for young women. That is, neither required a degree, especially for kindergarten or primary teaching, and being paid to train made both teaching and nursing more accessible to women from a wide range of socioeconomic backgrounds.

It would be reasonable to assume that those few highly educated women and men before 1945 encouraged the next generation to go further with their education. However, from the data collected on 'father's occupation' within the first cohort of New Zealand women graduates, there were clearly some who encouraged their daughters to go further with their education than they themselves had done.

When I began this project I did so in the knowledge that in the period to 1945, women graduates comprised between 30 and 40 percent of the total graduates from the University of New Zealand. Newspaper commentators and contributors to *The New Zealand Schoolmaster*, a journal for all teachers, for example, greeted women's academic success with a mixture of accolade and bemusement. In this book, I argue that because New Zealand had early to produce its own women graduates in order to be able to produce teachers for secondary schools and district high schools, women graduate teachers were welcomed. This was not always the case for those few women who qualified in law and medicine. However, attitudes towards women doctors in particular appeared to soften after their outstanding work with the armed services during World War One and the 1918 influenza epidemic.

Numbers of women graduates compared with those of men declined from 1940 and did not regain at least equal numbers until the late 1980s. In the main this was because of a combination of factors associated with post-World War Two promotion of women as 'mothers-of-the nation': a bid to increase the child population and ensure a future fighting force should it be once more required. It was not until the 1990s that unprecedented numbers of women compared with men graduated from New Zealand tertiary institutions, yet this ongoing trend has resulted in accolades for their success being mixed with messages of equality out of control and campaigns to convince boys of the merits of academic pathways. This current debate fuels a long-held and deep-seated suspicion that when girls and women excel in higher education and associated professional careers, it is somehow at the expense of boys and men. New Zealand requires both well-educated young women and men from all ethnic groups and socioeconomic backgrounds to remain or return to contribute to our increasingly diverse New Zealand society. For this reason, trends in higher education from 1945 to the present day will provide the focus for the sequel to this book.

There remains one other matter of unfinished business. As part of the research enterprise, I designed and created four major databases: educational profiles of the women graduates of the University of New Zealand 1877–1920; career profiles of New Zealand women graduate teachers 1877–1950; career profiles of the first women graduates from outside New Zealand who taught in New Zealand girls' schools 1880–1930; and a listing of New Zealand girls' secondary schools 1855–2008. After ten years, these databases are relatively comprehensive and not easily reproduced alongside this text. Therefore, the intention is to make each available online in the near future through Eastern Institute of Technology-Hawke's Bay. The aim is two-fold: to make accessible much first-time data on individual women, and to create an opportunity for those interested to make contributions in order to continue to update the information. As I survey the contents of the databases I am reminded that researching women's lives and the roles they have played in our historical past is akin to working on a never-ending jigsaw puzzle. Putting online the profiles of New Zealand's first women in higher education to place alongside this book will go some way towards acknowledging all of them, but *in their own right*.

Bibliography

ABBREVIATIONS
AJHR—Appendices to the Journals of the House of Representatives
DHS—District High School
GHS—Girls' High School
IFUW—International Federation of University Women
NZFUW—New Zealand Federation of University Women
NZG—New Zealand Gazette
NZPD—New Zealand Parliamentary Debates
TCD—Trinity College, Dublin
UNZ—University of New Zealand

i. Manuscripts and unpublished sources

Auckland Girls' Grammar School admissions registers, school rolls, school lists, list of prizes, staff lists, headmaster/headmistress reports (1888–1893). Auckland Girls' Grammar School Archives, Howe Street, Auckland.

Auckland Girls' Grammar School scrapbook (1963). Auckland Girls' Grammar School Archives, Howe Street, Auckland.

Buck, P. (1899). *The decline of the Maori race.* Paper presented at the third conference of the Association for the Amelioration of the Maori Race, Wellington. Alexander Turnbull Library, Wellington.

Christchurch Girls' High School Registers 1877–1891. MacMillan Brown Library, University of Canterbury. (Accn. 80)

Connor, H. (2006). *Writing ourselves 'home': Biographical texts, a method for contextualising the lives of wahine Māori, locating the story of Betty Wark.* Unpublished PhD thesis, University of Auckland, Auckland.

Girton College Admission Register, 1894. Girton College Archives, Cambridge. (Vol. 1, Accn No. GCAC 2/1/1/12)

Girton College Admission Register, 1897. Girton College Archives, Cambridge. (Vol. 1, Accn No. GCAC 2/2/2/12)

Goodman, J. (c.1939). *Database of Girton College graduates, Cambridge and Newnham College graduates Oxford 1870–1939.* Held by author.

Hetherington, J. (n.d.), *Numbering my days.* Unpublished manuscript, Alexander Turnbull Library, Wellington. (Accn. MS 0644:1)

Hukarere Girls' College MS Collection, Eve Magee MS Collection, annual reports, admission registers, annual reports of principal, newspaper scrapbooks (1875–1945). Hukarere College Archives, Napier.

Hukarere Native School Records, NA BAAA 939a; NA BAAA 1001 938c; NA BAAA 10011 939a; BA BAAA 939a 56g. Department of Education. National Archives, Auckland.

Morris Matthews, K. (2006a). *Database of the educational profiles of the first women graduates of the University of New Zealand 1878–1920.* Held by author.

Morris Matthews, K. (2006b). *Database of the career profiles of women graduate teachers from outside New Zealand 1880–1930.* Held by author.

Morris Matthews, K. (2006c). *Database of the career profiles of the first New Zealand women graduate teachers 1878–1920.* Held by author.

Morris Matthews, K. (2007). *Database listing of New Zealand girls' secondary schools with foundation principals' names and dates of service (public and private schools) 1855–2007.* Held by author.

Morton, M. (1986). *Women named in* The Cyclopedia of New Zealand. Auckland: New Zealand Society of Genealogists. Microfiche. Alexander Turnbull Library, Wellington.

Ngata, A. (1897). *The employment of Maoris after leaving school.* Paper presented at the first conference of the Association for the Amelioration of the Maori Race. Alexander Turnbull Library, Wellington.

Prentice Papers, Down Whakapapa. Hawke's Bay Museum Library, Napier.

Prince Albert College MS Collection, prospectus, admission registers, and roll books (1895–1900). The Kinder Library, St John's Theological College, Meadowbank, Auckland. (Accn MET 067/1/00/1 1896–1904)

Taua, P. (1983). *A history of Queen Victoria School 1844–1975.* Unpublished MA thesis, University of Auckland, Auckland.

The Joint International Missionary Council of British Missionary Societies Africa and India Archives (1910–1945). The University of Western Australia Library, Perth. Microfiche. (Box 207, mf. 79/80; 233; Box 207 mf 79; 233–234)

The University of New Zealand minute books, calendars, meeting papers (1873–1945). National Archives, Wellington. (AAMJ W3119 446–457)

Winkelmann Collection. Special Collections, Auckland City Library. (Accn 7-A11074; 7-A11223; 7-A4483)

ii. Printed primary sources

Arthur, A., & Buttle, N. (1950). *A tale of two colleges: Wesley College and Prince Albert College*. New Zealand: Wesley Historical Society (New Zealand Branch). (Kinder Library, St John's Theological College, Auckland.)

Appendices to the Journals of the House of Representatives (AJHR). (1871–1946). Reports of the University of New Zealand. *G, H, & E.*

Appendices to the Journals of the House of Representatives (AJHR). (1878–1930). Reports of secondary schools, listing of staff of district high schools. *Education (E; E-1; E-2).*

Appendices to the Journals of the House of Representatives (AJHR). (1880–1946). Reports of the native schools. *E; G Reports.*

Appendices to the Journals of the House of Representatives (AJHR). (1880). The Native Schools Code, 1880. *H-1 F*, pp. 1–7.

Auckland Girls' Grammar School. (1967). *EMJ—A tribute to the memory of Elsie Millicient Johnston*. Auckland: Author.

Auckland University College Calendar. (1883–1908). Auckland: Auckland University College. (Registry Office, University of Auckland.)

Blow, E. H. (1933). *The golden jubilee book of Auckland University College, 1883–1933*. Auckland: Auckland University College. (J. C. Beaglehole Room, The Library, Victoria University of Wellington.)

Butler, K. T., & McMorran, J. L. (1948). *Girton College Register 1869–1969*. Cambridge: Girton College. (Girton College Archives, Cambridge.)

Canterbury College Electoral Register. In *Canterbury University College Calendar* (1877–1900). Christchurch: Canterbury University College. (MacMillan Brown Library, University of Canterbury.)

Canterbury University College Calendar. (1877–1900). Christchurch: Canterbury University College. (MacMillan Brown Library, University of Canterbury.)

Daily Telegraph. (1883, 2 July). Girls' High School, Napier.

Dalrymple, L. W. (1872). *A few words on the higher education of women*. Dunedin: University of Otago. (Christchurch Public Library Archives.)

Dixon, G. F. (1934). *Spike*. Silver Jubilee Number, Easter, 39–41. (J. C. Beaglehole Room, The Library, Victoria University of Wellington.)

Gisborne Herald. (1964, 21 August). Obituary, John Hope.

International Federation of University Women. (1921–1945). Conference reports, Council reports. (Sybil Campbell Collection (formerly held at Crosby Hall, London), University of Winchester Library.)

New Zealand Gazette. (1891; 1900). Gazette Supplement: Classified List of Teachers, 1261–1291.

New Zealand Graphic. (1903, 1 March). Auckland: Queen Victoria School. (Auckland City Library.)

New Zealand Graphic. (1904, 23 July). Auckland: Queen Victoria School. (Auckland City Library.)

New Zealand Herald. (1877, 11, 12 July). Article on University of New Zealand graduates ceremony.

New Zealand Herald. (1902, 15 February). Advertisement.

New Zealand Parliamentary Debates. (NZPD) (1877, 37). Sir Charles Bowen.

Newnham College Register 1871–1971. (1979) (Vol. 1). Newnham College, Cambridge.

O'Connor, I. (1967). In grateful remembrance AW Headmistress. *Wycombe Abbey Gazette Supplement.* (Auckland Girls' Grammar School Archives.)

Otago Daily Times. (1883, 4 November). Girls' High School.

Reichel, H., & Tate, F. (1925). Report of the Royal Commission on University Education in New Zealand. *Appendices to the Journal of the House of Representatives* (AJHR). IE-7A.

The cyclopedia of New Zealand. (1908). Vol. 1 Wellington; Vol. 2 Auckland; Vol. 3 Canterbury; Vol. 4 Otago and Southland; Vol. 5 Nelson, Marlborough and Westland; Vol. 6 Taranaki, Hawke's Bay & Wellington. Wellington: Cyclopedia Co. 1897–1908. (National Library, Wellington.)

The Dominion. (1917, 12 December). Letter to the editor.

The Native Trust Ordinance. (1844). Statutes of New Zealand, 1841–1853.

The New Zealand Education Act. (1877).

The New Zealand Schoolmaster. (1892–1904). (New Zealand and Pacific Collection, University of Waikato Library.)

The University of New Zealand. (1897). *The University of New Zealand: Its history and its system.* Wellington: The University of New Zealand. (Alexander Turnbull Library Serials, Wellington.)

The University of New Zealand. (1948). *Alphabetical roll of graduates of the university.* Christchurch: Whitcombe and Tombs.

The University of New Zealand Calendar. (1873–1879; 1881–1883; 1885; 1886; 1888/89–1897/98; 1900–1951). Wellington: The University of New Zealand. (Alexander Turnbull Library Serials, Wellington.)

Trinity College Calendar, University of Dublin. (1904, 1905, 1906, 1907, 1909). (Trinity College Library, Dublin.)

University of Otago Calendar. (1880–1905). Dunedin: University of Otago.

Wairarapa Times-Age. (1965, 18 September). Obituary, Nina Barrer.

iii. Secondary sources

Abbot, G. (Ed.). (1991). *Wanganui Girls' College 1891–1991.* Wanganui: Wanganui Girls' College Centennial Committee.

Adams, P. (1996). *Somerville for women: An Oxford college, 1879–1993.* Oxford: Oxford University Press.

Airey, M. (1991). Helen Connon 1860–1903. In M. Penfold, C. Macdonald, & B. Williams (Eds.), *The book of New Zealand women* (pp. 150–154). Wellington: Bridget Williams Books.

Angus, J. (1982). *By degrees: The Otago branch of the NZFUW 1921–1983.* Dunedin: NZFUW Otago Branch.

Arnold, R. (1987). Women in the New Zealand teaching profession 1877–1920. A comparative perspective. In R. Openshaw & D. McKenzie (Eds.), *Reinterpreting the educational past* (pp. 39–53). Wellington: New Zealand Council for Educational Research.

Arnold, R. (1996). McLean, Mary Jane 1866–1949. *Dictionary of New Zealand biography.* Wellington: Ministry for Culture and Heritage. Retrieved 24 January 2008, from http://www.dnzb.govt.nz/

Ashburton High School. (1956). *75th anniversary celebrations.* Ashburton: Ashburton High School Old Pupils' Association.

Ashburton High School. (1981). *Ashburton High School Centenary 1881–1981.* Ashburton: Ashburton High School Old Pupils' Association.

Avery, G. (1991). *The best type of girl: A history of girls' independent schools.* London: Andre Deutsch.

Barr, J. (1953). *Within the sound of the bell.* Christchurch: Whitcombe & Tombs.

Barrer, N. A. R. (1966). *The misty isle.* Christchurch: Whitcombe & Tombs.

Barrowman, R. (1999). *Victoria University of Wellington 1899–1999.* Wellington: Victoria University Press.

Beaglehole, J. C. (1937). *The University of New Zealand: An historical study.* Wellington: New Zealand Council for Educational Research.

Beaglehole, T. (1996). Zedlitz, George William Edward Ernest von 1871–1949. *Dictionary of New Zealand biography.* Wellington: Ministry for Culture and Heritage. Retrieved 24 January 2008, from http://www.dnzb.govt.nz/

Belcher, M. (1964). *A history of Rangi Ruru School*. Christchurch: Rangi Ruru.

Berman, S. R. (1996). Myers, Phoebe 1866–1947. *Dictionary of New Zealand biography*. Wellington: Ministry for Culture and Heritage. Retrieved 24 January 2008, from http://www.dnzb.govt.nz/

Bird, W. (1930). A review of the Native Schools systems. *Te Wananga, 2*.

Bremner, C. S. (1897). *Education of girls and women in Great Britain*. London: Sonnenschein.

Bremner, J. (1998). Irvine-Smith, Fanny Louise 1878–1948. *Dictionary of New Zealand biography*. Wellington: Ministry for Culture and Heritage. Retrieved 24 January 2008, from http://www.dnzb.govt.nz/

Brittain, V. (1960). *The women at Oxford: A fragment of history*. London: George Harrap.

Britten, R. (1988). *Rangi Ruru*. Christchurch: Rangi Ruru.

Brown, J. M. (1974). *The memoirs of John Macmillan Brown*. Christchurch: Whitcombe & Tombs.

Butchers, A. G. (1930). *Education in New Zealand*. Dunedin: Coulls, Somerville, Wilkie.

Butler, K. T., & McMorran, J. L. (1948). *Girton College register 1869–1946*. Cambridge: Girton College.

Campbell, A. (1941). *Educating New Zealand*. Wellington: Department of Internal Affairs.

Campbell, J. D. (2007). Benson, Gertrude Helen 1886–1964. *Dictionary of New Zealand biography*. Wellington: Ministry for Culture and Heritage. Retrieved 23 April 2008, from http://www.dnzb.govt.nz/

Campbell, V. (1930). *George Street School jubilee souvenir 1880–1930*. Dunedin: Jubilee Committee.

Canterbury College. (1927). *Girls' High School Christchurch, jubilee record 1877–1927*. Christchurch: Christchurch Press.

Canterbury New Zealand Federation of University Women. (1972). *A history of the Canterbury branch of the New Zealand Federation of University Women*. Christchurch: Author.

Carpenter, K. (2003). *Marsden women and their world 1878–2003*. Wellington: Samuel Marsden Collegiate School.

Caversham School 125th jubilee 1861–1986. (1986). Dunedin: Caversham Reunion Committee.

Chapple, L. (1968). *Southbridge District High School 1868–1968*. Southbridge, Canterbury: Southbridge District High School.

Cheekland, O. (1980). *Queen Margaret Union, 1890–1980: Women in the University of Glasgow*. Glasgow: University of Glasgow.

Christchurch Girls' High School. (1928). *Jubilee record 1877–1927*. Christchurch: Canterbury College.

Cole Catley, C. (1985). *Springboard for women: New Plymouth Girls' High School, 1885–1985*. Whatamongo Bay: Cape Catley for the Centennial Committee of New Plymouth Girls' High School.

Coney, S. (1986). *Every girl: A social history of women and the YWCA in Auckland*. Auckland: YWCA.

Coney, S. (1991). Elsie Griffin 1884–1968. In M. Penfold, C. Macdonald, & B. Williams (Eds.), *The book of New Zealand women* (pp. 260–263). Wellington: Bridget Williams Books.

Coney, S. (Ed.). (1993). *Standing in the sunshine: A history of New Zealand women since they won the vote*. Auckland: Penguin.

Craig, F. (1964). *The history of Mt Eden College*. Auckland: F. L. Craig.

Cumming, I., & Cumming, A. (1978). *History of state education in New Zealand, 1840–1975*. Wellington: Pitman.

Dakin, J. (1973). *Education in New Zealand*. Newton Abbott: David Charles.

Dalziel, R. (1990). Müller, Mary Ann 1819/1820?–1901. *Dictionary of New Zealand biography*. Wellington: Ministry for Culture and Heritage. Retrieved 24 January 2008, from http://www.dnzb.govt.nz/

Dannevirke High School. (1978). *Dannevirke High School 75th jubilee 1903–1978*. Dannevirke: Dannevirke High School Board of Trustees.

Dannevirke High School. (1993). *Dannevirke High School 90th jubilee, 1903–1993*. Dannevirke: Dannevirke High School Board of Trustees.

Dashfield, H. (1989). *To the stars: St. Matthew's Collegiate School for Girls*. Masterton: Trinity Schools Trust Board.

Davey, I. (1928). *Fifty years of national education in New Zealand, 1878–1928*. Auckland: Whitcombe & Tombs.

Day, B. (1992). Women in technical education: An historical account. In S. Middleton & A. Jones (Eds.), *Women and education in Aotearoa* (Vol. 2, pp. 68–82). Wellington: Bridget Williams Books.

de Porres, S. M. (2000). *Mercy comes to Wellington: A history of St Mary's College*. Wellington: St Mary's College.

Deaker, O. (1979). *Not for school but for life: Southland Girls' High School: 1879–1979*. Invercargill: Southland Girls' High School.

Delany, V. (1990). Maher, Mary Cecelia 1799–1878. *Dictionary of New Zealand biography*. Wellington: Ministry for Culture and Heritage. Retrieved 24 January 2008, from http://www.dnzb.govt.nz/

Dennan, R., & Annabel, R. (1968). *Guide Rangi of Rotorua*. Christchurch: Whitcombe & Tombs.

Diamond, P. (2007). *Makereti: Taking Māori to the world*. Auckland: Random House.

Dunedin Teachers' College. (1975). *Dunedin Teachers' College centennial register for students 1876–1975*. Dunedin: Author.

Dyhouse, C. (1981). *Girls growing up in late Victorian and Edwardian England*. London: Routledge & Kegan Paul.

Dyhouse, C. (1995). *No distinction of sex? Women in British universities 1870–1939*. London: UCL Press.

Else, A. (Ed.). (1993). *Women together: A history of women's organisations in New Zealand Nga ropu wahine o te motu*. Wellington: Department of Internal Affairs/Daphne Brasell Associates Press.

Epsom Girls' Grammar. (1967). *Epsom Girls' Grammar golden jubilee 1917–1967*. Auckland: Author.

Epsom Girls' Grammar. (1992). *Book of memories: Epsom Girls' Grammar 1917–1992*. Auckland: Author.

Fitzgerald, T. (2001). Fences, boundaries and imagined communities: Re-thinking the construction of early mission schools and communities in New Zealand 1823–1830. *History of Education Review*, 30(2), 14–25.

Fitzgerald, T. (2003). Creating a disciplined society: CMS women and the remaking of Nga Puhi women 1823–1835. *History of Education Review*, 30(1), 84–98.

Flannagan, M. D. P. (2004). *No half measures*. Wellington: Sisters of Mercy.

Flashoff, R. (1993). Williams, Anna Maria 1839–1929. *Dictionary of New Zealand biography*. Wellington: Ministry for Culture and Heritage. Retrieved 24 January 2008, from http://www.dnzb.govt.nz/

Flint, L. (1989). *Wycombe Abbey School 1896–1986*. Wycombe Abbey School.

Fouhy, H. (1993). *One love, many faces: Brigidines in New Zealand 1898–1998*. Masterton: Congregation of St Brigid.

Fry, R. (1985). *It's different for daughters: A history of the curriculum for girls in New Zealand schools 1900–1975*. Wellington: New Zealand Council for Educational Research.

Fry, R. (1993). *The Community of the Sacred Name—A centennial history 1893–1993*. Christchurch: The Community of the Sacred Name.

Gambrill, M. D. (1969). *A history of Queen Margaret's College*. Wellington: Queen Margaret's College.

Gardner, W. J. (1979). *Colonial cap and gown*. Christchurch: University of Canterbury.

Gardner, W. J. B. (2007). Candy, Alice Muriel Flora 1888–1977. *Dictionary of New Zealand biography*. Wellington: Ministry for Culture and Heritage. Retrieved 24 January 2008, from http://www.dbnz.govt.nz/

Gardner, W. J. B., Beardsley, E., & Carter, T. E. (1973). *A history of the University of Canterbury 1873–1973*. Christchurch: University of Canterbury.

Garnham, J., & Cowlrick, G. (1984). *Ad lucem: Napier Girls' High School 1884–1964*. Napier: Napier Girls' High School.

Gillespie, F. D. (1958). *The Akaroa schools' centennial: Official programme and history of the schools*. Akaroa: Mail Print.

Goldberg, D. (1993). *Racist culture: Philosophy and the politics of meaning*. Oxford: Blackwell.

Goodman, J. (2002). Their market value must be greater for the experience they had gained: Secondary school headmistresses and Empire, 1897–1914. In J. Goodman & M. Martin (Eds.), *Gender, colonialism and education: The politics of experience* (pp. 175–176). London: Woburn.

Gore School Committee. (1928). *Gore School jubilee 1878–1928*. Gore: Author.

Gosset, R. (1985). *From boaters to back-packs: The school history and list of St Margaret's College, 1910–1985*. Christchurch: St Margaret's Old Girls' Association.

Green Island School souvenir: 73rd anniversary, 1853–1926. (1926). Dunedin: C.S.W.

Greymouth State School golden jubilee, 1876–1926. (1926). Greymouth.

Grimshaw, P. (1987). *Women's suffrage in New Zealand*. Auckland: Auckland University Press.

Grossmann, E. S. (1905). *The life of Helen MacMillan Brown: The first woman to graduate with honours in a British university*. Christchurch: Whitcombe & Tombs.

Gunby, D. (1984). *Rangiora High School 1884–1984—A centennial history*. Rangiora: Rangiora High School.

Gunson, N. (1878). *Messengers of grace: Evangelical missions in the South Seas 1797–1860*. Melbourne: Oxford University Press.

Haggard, N. (Ed.). (1941). *Who's who in New Zealand*. Wellington: Watkins.

Hall, D., & Leibowitz, S. L. (1998). Hall, Mere Haana 1880/1881?–1966. *Dictionary of New Zealand biography*. Wellington: Ministry for Culture and Heritage. Retrieved 24 January 2008, from http://www.dnzb.govt.nz/

Hamilton High School. (1971). *Hamilton High School's diamond jubilee 1911–1971*. Hamilton: Author.

Hamilton, S. (1987). *Women and the Scottish universities c.1869–1939: A social history*. Edinburgh: University of Edinburgh.

Hankin, C. (1993). Connon, Helen 1859/1860?–1903. *Dictionary of New Zealand biography*. Wellington: Ministry for Culture and Heritage. Retrieved 24 January 2008, from http://www.dnzb.govt.nz/

Harding, O. (1982). *Wellington Girls' College: One hundred years*. Wellington: Wellington Girls' College Centennial Committee.

Harrison, N. (1961). *The school that Riley built: The story of the Wellington Technical College from 1886 to the present day*. Wellington: Wellington Technical College.

Hercock, F. (1996). Pulling, Mary Etheldred 1871–1951. *Dictionary of New Zealand biography*. Wellington: Ministry for Culture and Heritage. Retrieved 24 January 2008, from http://www.dnzb.govt.nz/

Herstory. (1989). Auckland: New Women's Press.

Hight, J., & Candy, A. (1927). *A short history of the Canterbury University College: With a register of graduates and academics of the college*. Christchurch: University of Canterbury.

Hill, J. (1991). *We built a school: Solway College, a pictorial history, 1916–1991*. Wellington: Millwood Press, Solway Old Girls' Association.

Hughes, B. (1993). Edger, Kate Milligan 1857–1935. *Dictionary of New Zealand biography*. Wellington: Ministry for Culture and Heritage. Retrieved 24 January 2008, from http://www.dnzb.govt.nz/

Hughes, B. (1994). Hetherington, Jessie Isabel 1882–1971. *Dictionary of New Zealand biography*. Wellington: Ministry for Culture and Heritage. Retrieved 24 January 2008, from http://www.dnzb.govt.nz/

Hughes, B. (1996a). Bennett, Agnes Elizabeth Lloyd 1872–1960. *Dictionary of New Zealand biography*. Wellington: Ministry for Culture and Heritage. Retrieved 24 January 2008, from http://www.dnzb.govt.nz/

Hughes, B. (1996b). Coad, Nellie Euphemia 1883–1974. *Dictionary of New Zealand biography*. Wellington: Ministry for Culture and Heritage. Retrieved 24 January 2008, from http://www.dnzb.govt.nz/

Hughes, B., & Ahern, S. (1993). *Redbrick and bluestockings: Women at Victoria 1899–1993*. Wellington: Victoria University Press.

Hunt, F., & Barker, C. (1998). *Women at Cambridge: A brief history*. Cambridge: Cambridge University Press.

Irvine-Smith, F. (1948). *The streets of my city*. Wellington: A. H. & A. W. Reed.

Jenkins, K., & Morris Matthews, K. (1994). *Te Maranga o te Ihu o Hukarere: A photographic history*. Napier: Te Whanau o Hukarere.

Jenkins, K., & Morris Matthews, K. (1995). *Hukarere and the politics of Māori Girls' schooling 1875–1995*. Palmerston North: Hukarere Board of Trustees with Te Whānau o Hukarere.

Jenkins, K., & Morris Matthews, K. (1998). Knowing their place: The political socialisation of Māori women in New Zealand through schooling policy and practice, 1867–1969. *Women's History Review*, 7(1), 85–105.

Jenkins, K., & Morris Matthews, K. (2005). Mana wahine: Māori women and leadership of Māori schools in Aotearoa/New Zealand. *New Zealand Journal of Educational Studies*, 40(1), 45–59.

Jillett, J. (2007). Batham, Elizabeth Joan 1917–1975. *Dictionary of New Zealand biography*. Wellington: Ministry for Culture and Heritage. Retrieved 23 April 2008, from http://www.dnzb.govt.nz/

Jobson, N. (1916, November). The education of girls. *White Ribbon*, 22, 1–4.

Johnson, S. (2000). Stevens, Joan 1908–1990. *Dictionary of New Zealand biography*. Wellington: Ministry for Culture and Heritage. Retrieved 24 January 2008, from http://www.dnzb.govt.nz/

Johnson, V., & Jensen, H. (1953). *A history of Diocesan High School for Girls, Auckland, 1903–1953*. Auckland: Diocesan School.

Jolly, M. (1991). To save the girls for better lives: Presbyterian missions and women in the south of Vanuatu 1848–1870. *Journal of Pacific History*, 26(1).

Kandel, I. L. (1937). *Impressions of education in New Zealand and inverted snobbery and the problem of secondary education*. Wellington: New Zealand Council for Educational Research.

Keen, D. (2001). *In a class of its own: A Dunedin College of Education anniversary history*. Dunedin: Dunedin College of Education.

Kelly, R. (1985). *Degrees of liberation: A short history of women in the University of Melbourne*. Parkville, Vic: Women Graduates Centenary Committee, University of Melbourne.

Kerslake, J. (1998). *Chilton St James 1918–1998—A celebration of 75 years*. Lower Hutt: Chilton Historical Trust.

King, F. (Ed.). (1925). *The feeding and care of baby*. London: MacMillan.

King, T. (Ed.). (1906). *The evils of cram*. Dunedin: Whitcombe & Tombs.

Kirk, M. R. (1998). *Remembering your mercy: Mother Mary Cecelia Maher and the first Sisters of Mercy in New Zealand 1850–1880*. Auckland: Sisters of Mercy.

Labrum, B. (1991). Ethel Benjamin. In M. Penfold, C. MacDonald, & B. Williams (Eds.), *The book of New Zealand women* (pp. 75–77). Wellington: Bridget Williams Books.

Labrum, B. (2000). Simpson, Helen Macdonald 1890–1960. *Dictionary of New Zealand biography*. Wellington: Ministry for Culture and Heritage. Retrieved 24 January 2008, from http://www.dnzb.govt.nz/

Lawrence, A. (1980). *Lively retrospect: Timaru Girls' High School 1880–1980*. Timaru: Centennial Committee.

Lee, H. (1996). Marchant, Maria Elise Allman 1869–1919. *Dictionary of New Zealand biography*. Wellington: Ministry for Culture and Heritage. Retrieved 24 January 2008, from http://www.dnzb.govt.nz/

Lints, M. (2006). *Fideliter 125: Whangarei High Schools 125 years*. Whangarei: Whangarei Boys' High School and Whangarei Girls' High School.

Logan, C. (1986). *Women at Glasgow University: Determination or predetermination*. Glasgow: University of Glasgow.

Lovell-Smith, M. (2004). *Easily the best: The life of Helen Connon 1857–1905*. Christchurch: Canterbury University Press.

Low, E. (1993). Dohrmann, Elsie 1875–1909. *Dictionary of New Zealand biography*. Wellington: Ministry for Culture and Heritage. Retrieved 24 January 2008, from http://www.dnzb.govt.nz/

Macaskill, P. (Ed.). (1980). *Ako Pai 1880–1980*. Wellington: Price Milburn.

Macdonald, W. (1982). *Footprints of Kate Edger: History of the New Zealand Federation of University Women 1921–1981*. Auckland: New Zealand Federation of University Women.

Mackey, J. (1967). *The making of a state education system*. London: Geoffrey Chapman.

Mackinnon, A. (1986). *The new women: Adelaide's early women graduates*. Adelaide: Wakefield Press.

Mackinnon, A. (1990). Male heads on female shoulders? New questions for the history of women's higher education. *History of Education Review, 19*(2), 36–47.

Mackinnon, A. (1997). *Love and freedom: Professional women and the reshaping of personal life*. Cambridge: Cambridge University Press.

Maguire, B. (1994). *Gisborne Catholic education 1894–1994*. Gisborne: Logan Print.

Main, G. (Ed.). (1989). *Iona College: A chronicle of 75 years*. Havelock North: Iona College.

Maloney, D. (1982). *One hundred years of Catholic education in the Buller 1882–1982*. Westport: Catholic Schools.

Mangan, J. A. (Ed.). (1990). *Making imperial mentalities: Socialisation and British imperialism*. Manchester: Manchester University Press.

Manson, C., & Manson, C. (1960). *Doctor Agnes Bennett*. London: Michael Joseph.

Marlborough High School. (1950). *Marlborough High School Register*. Blenheim: Author.

Marsh, N. (1986). *The history of Queen Elizabeth College.* London: King's College.

Martin, J. (1999). *Women and the politics of schooling in Victorian England.* London: Leicester University Press.

Maxwell, M. D. (1990). *Women doctors in New Zealand.* Auckland: IMS (NZ).

May, M. (1966). *St Hilda's Collegiate School: The first seventy years 1896–1966.* Dunedin: St Hilda's Collegiate School.

May, M. W. (1973). *Freshly remembered: Half a century of school.* Christchurch: Whitcombe & Tombs.

McCarthy, S. M. A. (1970). *Star in the south: The centennial history of the New Zealand Dominican Sisters 1870–1970.* Dunedin: St Dominic's Priory.

McClean, R. (1993). Bews, Mary Ellen 1856–1945. *Dictionary of New Zealand biography.* Wellington: Ministry for Culture and Heritage. Retrieved 24 January 2008, from http://www.dnzb.govt.nz/

McCulloch, G. (1988). Imperial and colonial designs: The case of Auckland Grammar School. *History of Education, 17*(4), 257–267.

McDonald, H. (2007). Boys-Smith, Winifred 1865–1939. *Dictionary of New Zealand biography.* Wellington: Ministry for Culture and Heritage. Retrieved 23 April 2008, from http://www.dnzb.govt.nz/

McDonald, H. S. (1984). *'This educational monstrosity ...' A study of the foundation and early development of the school of home science.* Unpublished long essay, University of Otago, Dunedin.

McEwan, M. (1975). *The making of a school: Wyndham District High School 1875–1975.* Wyndham: Wyndham DHS Board.

McGeorge, C., & Snook, I. (1981). *Church, state and New Zealand education.* Wellington: Price Milburn.

McKenzie, J. D. S. (1985). The Proficiency Examination 1930–1935, a political controversy. In J. Codd, R. Harker, & R. Nash (Eds.), *Political issues in New Zealand education* (pp. 253–266). Palmerston North: Dunmore Press.

McKenzie, J. D. S. (1987). The growth of school credentialling in New Zealand: 1878–1900. In R. Openshaw & D. McKenzie (Eds.), *Reinterpreting the educational past: Essays in the history of New Zealand education* (pp. 82–106). Wellington: New Zealand Council for Educational Research.

McKenzie, P. (1986). *Craighead 1911–1986.* Timaru: Craighead Board.

McLaren, I. (1970). Education and politics: Background to the Secondary Schools Act, 1903, Part 1: Secondary education for the privileged. *New Zealand Journal of Educational Studies, 5*(2), 94–114.

McLaren, I. (1971). Education and politics: Background to the Secondary Schools Act, 1903, Part 2: Secondary education for the deserving. *New Zealand Journal of Educational Studies, 6*(1), 1–23.

McLaren, I. (1987). The politics of secondary education. In R. Openshaw & D. McKenzie (Eds.), *Reinterpreting the educational past* (pp. 64–81). Wellington: New Zealand Council for Educational Research.

McLaren, I. A. (1974). *Education in a small democracy: New Zealand.* London: Routledge & Kegan Paul.

McLeod, A. (1991a). Edith Searle Grossmann 1863–1931. In M. Penfold., C. Macdonald, & B. Williams (Eds.), *The book of New Zealand women* (pp. 263–267). Wellington: Bridget Williams Books.

McLeod, A. (1991b). Müller, Mary Ann 1819/1820–1901. In M. Penfold, C. Macdonald, & B. Williams (Eds.), *The book of New Zealand women.* Wellington: Bridget Williams Books.

McWilliams-Tullberg, R. (1975). *Women at Cambridge: A men's university—though of a mixed type.* London: Victor Gollancz.

Memmi, A. (1965). *The colonizer and the colonized.* New York: Orion Press.

Middleton, S., & Jones, A. (Eds.). (1992). *Women and education in Aotearoa* (Vol. 2). Wellington: Bridget Williams Books.

Middleton, S., & May, H. (1997). *Teachers talk teaching 1915–1995.* Palmerston North: Dunmore Press.

Mills, C. (1933). *Nelson College for Girls—fifty years.* Nelson: Nelson College Old Girls' Association.

Minogue, W. J. D. (1977). *The first fifty years: Takapuna Grammar School 1927–1977.* Auckland: Takapuna Grammar School.

Moore, L. (1991). *Bajanellas and semilinas: Aberdeen University and the education of women 1860–1920.* Aberdeen: Aberdeen University Press.

Moore, L. (2003). Young ladies' institutions: The development of secondary schools for girls in Scotland 1833–c.1870. *History of Education, 32*(3), 249–272.

Morrell, W. P. (1969). *The University of Otago: A centennial history.* Dunedin: University of Otago.

Morris Matthews, K. (1988). *Behind every school: A history of the Hawke's Bay Education Board.* Napier: Hawke's Bay Education Board.

Morris Matthews, K. (2001). Simply madness? Historical perspectives on teachers and university study. *History of Education Review, 30*(2), 1–13.

Morris Matthews, K. (2003). Imagining home—women graduate teachers abroad 1880–1930. *History of Education*, 32(5), 529–545. Also available at http://www.informaworld.com/openurl?genre=article&issn=0046-760X&volume=32&issue=5&spage=529

Morris Matthews, K. (2005). Boundary crosser: Anne Whitelaw and her leadership role in girls' secondary schooling in England, New Zealand and East Africa. *Journal of Educational Administration and History*, 37(1), 39–54.

Morris Matthews, K., & Jenkins, K. (1999). Whose country is it anyway? The construction of a new identity through schooling for Māori in Aotearoa/New Zealand. *History of Education*, 28(3), 339–350.

Morrison, E. (1923). *Dr Margaret Cruickshank, MD: First woman doctor in New Zealand*. Christchurch: Whitcombe & Tombs.

Morrison, E. (c.1928). *New Zealand's first lady doctor*. Christchurch: Whitcombe & Tombs.

Mosgiel District High School. (1931). *Mosgiel District High School 1871–1931*. Mosgiel: Mosgiel DHS Board.

Mt Eden College. (1914). *History of the college: Principals—the Misses Bews 1895–1914*. Auckland: Mt Eden College Old Girls' Association.

Murdoch, J. H. (1943). *The high schools of New Zealand: A critical survey*. Wellington: New Zealand Council for Educational Research.

Murray, J. (1951). *Palmerston North High School historical survey 1902–1951*. Palmerston North: H. Young.

Murray, T. (1967). *Marsden: A history of a New Zealand school for girls*. Wellington: Marsden School Old Girls' Association.

Musgrove, F. (1978). Curriculum, culture and ideology. *Journal of Curriculum Studies*, 10(2), 99–111.

Nash, R. (1981). The New Zealand District High School: A case study in the selective function of rural education. *New Zealand Journal of Educational Studies*, 16(1), 150–160.

Neville, R. J. W., & O'Neill, C. J. (Eds.). (1979). *The population of New Zealand: Interdisciplinary perspectives*. Auckland: Longman Paul.

New Plymouth Girls' High School. (1935). *New Plymouth Girls' High School jubilee 1885–1935*. New Plymouth: New Plymouth Girls' High School Jubilee Committee.

New Zealand Council for Educational Research. (1943). *Higher education and its future*. Wellington: Author.

Nicol, J. (1940). *The technical schools of New Zealand: An historical survey*. Wellington: New Zealand Council for Educational Research.

Nolan, M. (2000). *Breadwinning: New Zealand women and the state.* Christchurch: Canterbury University Press.

Nolan, M. (2001). Putting the state in its place: The domestic education debate in New Zealand. *History of Education, 30*(1), 13–34.

Norris, B. (1975). *Blackboards and shipmasts: A history of the Lyttelton Main School's first century.* Lyttelton: Lyttelton Main School Centennial Committee.

Northey, H. (1988). *Auckland Girls' Grammar—The first one hundred years.* Auckland: Auckland Girls' Grammar School Old Girls' Association.

Oakley, H. D. (1929). King's College for Women. In F. J. C. Hearnshaw (Ed.), *The centenary history of King's College London, 1828–1928.* London: King's College.

Olssen, E. (1979). Breeding for the Empire. *List,* 18–19.

Olssen, E. (1980). Women, work and family: 1860–1926. In P. Bunkle & B. Hughes (Eds.), *Women in New Zealand society* (pp. 159–183). Wellington: Allen & Unwin.

Olssen, E. (1981). Truby King and the Plunket Society: An analysis of a prescriptive ideology. *New Zealand Journal of History, 15*(1), 3–5.

Openshaw, R. (1995). *Unresolved struggle: Consensus and conflict in state post-primary education.* Palmerston North: Dunmore Press.

Openshaw, R., Lee, G., & Lee, H. (1993a). *Challenging the myths: Rethinking New Zealand's educational history.* Palmerston North: Dunmore Press.

Openshaw, R., Lee, G., & Lee, H. (1993b). Educational equality or educational differentiation? Gender, class and the post-primary curriculum, 1915–1935. In R. Openshaw, G. Lee, & H. Lee (Eds.), *Challenging the myths: Rethinking New Zealand's educational history* (pp. 132–161). Palmerston North: Dunmore Press.

Otago Daily Times. (1921). *Otago Girls' High School jubilee magazine 1871–1921.* Dunedin: Author.

Oxford University Press. (1961). *Somerville College register, 1879–1909.* Oxford: Author.

Page, D. (1991). Caroline Freeman 1856–1914. In M. Penfold, C. Macdonald, & B. Williams (Eds.), *The book of New Zealand women* (pp. 223–225). Wellington: Bridget Williams Books.

Page, D. (1992). The first lady graduates: Women with degrees from the University of Otago, 1885–1900. In B. Brookes, C. Macdonald, & M. Tennant (Eds.), *Women in history* (Vol. 2, pp. 98–128). Wellington: Bridget Williams Books.

Palmerston North Girls' High School. (1962). *Palmerston North Girls' High School jubilee, 1902–1962.* Palmerston North: Author.

Parry, G. (1982). *A fence at the top: The first 75 years of the Plunket Society.* Dunedin: Royal New Zealand Plunket Society.

Parton, H. (1979). *The University of New Zealand*. Auckland: Auckland University Press.

Payne, J. (1993). Fraser, Mary Isabel 1863–1942. *Dictionary of New Zealand biography*. Wellington: Ministry for Culture and Heritage. Retrieved 24 January 2008, from http://www.dnzb.govt.nz/

Peddie, B. (1977). *Christchurch Girls' High School 1877–1977*. Christchurch: Christchurch Girls' High School Old Girls' Association.

Penfold, M., Macdonald, C., & Williams, B. (Eds.). (1991). *The book of New Zealand women*. Wellington: Bridget Williams Books.

Perkins, G. (1985). *Pieces of chalk: A history of the Riverton District Schools*. Invercargill: Riverton and District Schools 125th Celebration Committee.

Pool, I., Dharmalingham, A., & Sceats, J. (2007). *The New Zealand family from 1840: A demographic history*. Auckland: Auckland University Press.

Pope, R. D., & Verbeke, M. G. (1976). Ladies' educational organisations in England, 1865–1885. *Paedagogica Historica, 16*(2), 336–361.

Prentice, A., & Theobald, M. (1991). *Women who taught: Perspectives on the history of women teaching*. Toronto: University of Toronto Press.

Ramsay, A., Stead, H., & Ludemann, E. (1987). *The honour of her name: The story of Waitaki Girls' High School 1887–1987*. New Zealand: Waitaki Girls' High School Centennial Committee.

Revell, D. (1993). Hewett, Mary Elizabeth Grenside 1857–1892. *Dictionary of New Zealand biography*. Wellington: Ministry for Culture and Heritage. Retrieved 24 January 2008, from http://www.dnzb.govt.nz/

Rhodes, L. (2007). Curtis, Kathleen Maisey 1892–1994. *Dictionary of New Zealand biography*. Wellington: Ministry for Culture and Heritage. Retrieved 23 April 2008, from http://www.dnzb.govt.nz/

Roberts, H. (1993). Grossmann, Edith Searle 1863–1931. *Dictionary of New Zealand biography*. Wellington: Ministry for Culture and Heritage. Retrieved 24 January 2008, from http://www.dnzb.govt.nz/

Ross, A. (1996). Ross, Frances Jane 1869–1950. *Dictionary of New Zealand biography*. Wellington: Ministry for Culture and Heritage. Retrieved 24 January 2008, from http://www.dnzb.govt.nz/

Roth, H. (1952). *George Hogben: A biography*. Wellington: New Zealand Council for Educational Research.

Sanderson, K. (1991). Mary Barkas 1889–1961. In M. Penfold., C. Macdonald, & B. Williams (Eds.), *The book of New Zealand women* (pp. 45–47). Wellington: Bridget Williams Books.

Sargison, P. (1993). *Notable women in New Zealand health*. Auckland: Longman Paul.

Sargison, P. (2007). Henderson, Christina Kirk 1861–1953. *Dictionary of New Zealand biography*. Wellington: Ministry for Culture and Heritage. Retrieved 24 January 2008, from http://www.dnzb.govt.nz/

Scobie, K. (1986). *Women at Glasgow University in the 1920s and 1930s*. Glasgow: University of Glasgow.

Shaw, L. (2006). *Making a difference: A history of the Auckland College of Education 1881–2004*. Auckland: Auckland University Press.

Shedden, V. (1965). *Columba College: The first fifty years*. Dunedin: Columba College.

Simmonds, E. J. (1983). *NZEI: An account of the New Zealand Educational Institute 1883–1983*. Wellington: New Zealand Educational Institute.

Simon, J. (1993). Secondary schooling for Māori: The control of access to knowledge. In G. H. Smith & M. Hohepa (Eds.), *Creating space in institutional settings for Māori*. Auckland: Research Unit for Māori Education, University of Auckland.

Simon, J. (1998). *Ngā kura Māori: The native schools system 1867–1969*. Auckland: Auckland University Press.

Sinclair, K. (1983). *A history of the University of Auckland 1883–1983*. Auckland: Auckland University Press.

Sisters of Mercy. (1952). *Gracious is the time: 1850–1950 centenary of the Sisters of Mercy Auckland*. Auckland: Whitcombe & Tombs.

Sisters of Our Lady of the Missions. (1968). *Sacred Heart College: St Joseph's School: Centenary, 1868–1968*. Christchurch: Centennial Committee.

Sisters of Our Lady of the Missions. (1984). *For the glory of God in New Plymouth—Taranaki —New Zealand*. New Plymouth: Centennial Committee.

Smart, R. N. (1968). Literate ladies—a fifty year experiment. *St Andrews University Alumnus Chronicle, 59*, 21–31.

Smith, L. T. (1999). *Decolonising methodologies, research and indigenous peoples*. London: Zed Books.

Smith, S. (2000). Retaking the register: Women's higher education in Glasgow and beyond, c.1796–1845. *Gender and History, 12*(2), 310–335.

Smyth, M. (1919). *St Andrew's Collegiate School, 1903–1919, reunion souvenir: A history of the school*. Dunedin: Coulls Somerville Wilkie Ltd.

Snook, I. A., & McGeorge, C. M. (1981). *Church, state and New Zealand education*. Wellington: Price Milburn.

St Cuthbert's College. (1994). *St Cuthbert's College register, 1915–1994*. Auckland: Author.

Stenson, M. (1996). Morrison, Annie Christina 1870–1953. *Dictionary of New Zealand biography*. Wellington: Ministry for Culture and Heritage. Retrieved 24 January 2008, from http://www.dnzb.govt.nz/

Stephens, S. R. (1965). *To celebrate a century: Alexandra and consolidated schools 1864–1964*. Alexandra: Centennial Committee.

Strong, T. B. (1931). The education of South Sea Island natives. In P. Jackson (Ed.), *Maori and education/the education of Natives in New Zealand and its dependencies* (pp. 188–194). Wellington: Ferguson & Osborn.

Strong, T. B. (1934). New Zealand—The University. In *The year book of education* (pp. 278–284). London: Institute of Education, University of London and Brown Brothers.

Stuart Mill, J. (1869/1964). *The subjection of women*. London: Dent.

Sutherland, G. (1973). *Wairarapa High School; Masterton Technical School; Wairarapa College: Golden jubilee*. Masterton: Wairarapa College.

Sutherland, G. (1990). The plainest principles of justice: The University of London and the higher education of women. In P. M. L. Thompson (Ed.), *The University of London and the world of learning, 1836–1986* (pp. 35–56). London: Hambledon Press.

Taumarunui High School Jubilee Committee. (1984). *Taumarunui District High School and High School 1918–1984*. Taumarunui: Author.

Taylor, K. (1998). Weitzel, Hedwig 1900–1971. *Dictionary of New Zealand biography*. Wellington: Ministry for Culture and Heritage. Retrieved 24 January 2008, from http://www.dnzb.govt.nz/

Taylor, L. (1998). King, Mary Harriet McGowan 1884–1967. *Dictionary of New Zealand biography*. Wellington: Ministry for Culture and Heritage. Retrieved 24 January 2008, from http://www.dnzb.govt.nz/

Taylor, L. (2007a). Gregory, Elizabeth 1901–1983. *Dictionary of New Zealand biography*. Wellington: Ministry for Culture and Heritage. Retrieved 23 April 2008, from http://www.dnzb.govt.nz/

Taylor, L. (2007b). Strong, Ann Monroe Gilchrist 1875–1957. *Dictionary of New Zealand biography*. Wellington: Ministry for Culture and Heritage. Retrieved 23 April 2008, from http://www.dnzb.govt.nz/

Tennant, M. (1977). Natural directions: The New Zealand movement for sexual differentiation in education during the early twentieth century. *New Zealand Journal of Educational Studies, 12*(2), 142–153.

Thames High School Board. (1980). *Thames High School 1880–1980*. Thames: Author.

Theobald, M. (1996). *Knowing women: Origins of women's education in nineteenth century Australia*. Cambridge: Cambridge University Press.

Thom, A. H. (1950). *The District High Schools of New Zealand*. Wellington: New Zealand Council for Educational Research.

Thompson, G. (Ed.). (1920). *A history of the University of Otago 1869–1919*. Dunedin: Wilkie.

Thompson, J. (1987). *Madras College 1833–1983*. Kirkcaldy: Madras College.

Thompson, M. B. (1957). *We built a school*. Masterton: Author.

Thomson, H., & Thomson, S. (1963). *Ann Gilchrist Strong: Scientist in the home*. Christchurch: Pegasus Press.

Timaru Catholic Secondary Schools golden jubilee 1937–1987. (1987). Timaru.

Trembath, K. A. (1969). *Ad Augusta: A centennial history of Auckland Grammar School 1869–1969*. Auckland: Auckland Grammar School Old Boys' Association.

Tritenbach, P. (1981). *Auckland's historic schools*. Auckland: Auckland Historic Schools Trust.

Tuke, M. (1939). *A history of Bedford College for Women, 1849–1937*. London: Oxford University Press.

Upton, S. (1998). Spencer, Anna Elizabeth Jerome 1872–1955. *Dictionary of New Zealand biography*. Wellington: Ministry for Culture and Heritage. Retrieved 24 January 2008, from http://www.dnzb.govt.nz/

Van der Kroght, C. (1998). Barrer, Nina Agatha Rosamond 1879–1965. *Dictionary of New Zealand biography*. Wellington: Ministry for Culture and Heritage. Retrieved 24 January 2008, from http://www.dnzb.govt.nz/

van der Linden, M. (1990). *St Joseph's Māori Girls' College 1867–1990*. Palmerston North: Dunmore Press.

Varnham, M. (1994). *Beyond blue hills: One hundred years of Woodford House*. Havelock North: Woodford House.

Villa Maria College. (1993). *Villa Maria College 75th jubilee 1918–1993*. Christchurch: Author.

Voller, L. (1982). *Sentinel at the gates: Nelson College for Girls 1883–1983*. Nelson: Nelson Girls' College.

Voller, L. (1996). Lorimer, Margaret 1866–1954. *Dictionary of New Zealand biography*. Wellington: Ministry for Culture and Heritage. Retrieved 24 January 2008, from http://www.dnzb.govt.nz/

Waimate High School. (1979). *Jubilee history of Waimate High School*. Waimate: Waimate High School Board.

Waipukurau District High School Jubilee Committee. (1956). *Waipukurau District High School jubilee souvenir 1866–1956*. Waipukurau: Author.

Walker, R. (1991). *Liberating Māori from educational subjugation*. Auckland: Research Unit for Māori Education, University of Auckland.

Wallis, E. (1972). *A most rare vision: Otago Girls' High School: The first one hundred years*. Dunedin: Otago Girls' High School Board of Governors.

Wallis, E. (1993). Burn, Margaret Gordon 1825–1918. *Dictionary of New Zealand biography*. Wellington: Ministry for Culture and Heritage. Retrieved 24 January 2008, from http://www.dnzb.govt.nz/

Wanganui Girls' College. (1991). *Wanganui Girls' College 1891–1991 Centenary in retrospect*. Wanganui: Wanganui Girls' High School.

Wanganui Technical College. (1961). *Wanganui Technical College jubilee celebration 1892–1911; 1911–1961*. Wanganui: Author.

Wart, T. (1935). *Roll of graduates of the University of Aberdeen, 1901–25*. Aberdeen: University of Aberdeen Press.

Webb, L. (1937). *The control of education in New Zealand*. Auckland: New Zealand Council for Educational Research.

West Christchurch School. (1924). *West Christchurch School jubilee history 1874–1924*. Christchurch: Christchurch Press.

Whakatane High School. (1982). *Diamond jubilee reunion of the eighties 1920–1980 Whakatane High School*. Whakatane: Author.

Whitmore, M. (1991). *Nga Tawa: A centennial history*. Marton: Nga Tawa.

Wilkie, R. (1993). Gibson, Helena Francis 1868–1938 & Gibson, Mary Victoria 1864–1929. *Dictionary of New Zealand biography*. Wellington: Ministry for Culture and Heritage. Retrieved 24 January 2008, from http://www.dnzb.govt.nz/

Wilson, M., & Bronwyn, L. (1991). Christina Henderson. In M. Penfold, C. Macdonald, & B. Williams (Eds.), *The book of New Zealand women* (pp. 285–288). Wellington: Bridget Williams Books.

Wollstonecraft, M. (1792/1964). *The rights of woman*. London: Dent.

Woods, S. (1981). *Samuel Williams of Te Aute*. Christchurch: Pegasus Press.

Wright, M. G. (1996). Hickey, Mary St Domitille 1882–1958. *Dictionary of New Zealand biography*. Wellington: Ministry for Culture and Heritage. Retrieved 24 January 2008, from http://www.dnzb.govt.nz/

Yuval Davis, N. (1997). *Gender and nation state*. London: Sage Publications.

Zainu'ddin, A. (1973). The admission of women to the University of Melbourne. *Melbourne Studies in Education*, 51–104.

Appendix

New Zealand women who gained first university qualifications abroad

University of Sydney	Rosa Lichtscheindl (m.Innes)	BA 1893	Wellington Girls' High School
	Helen Millicent Brown (m.Baxter)	BA 1909	Rangi Ruru
	Dora Glasgow (m.Eipper)	BA 1915	Nelson Girls' College
	Mayah Perkins	BA 1928 DipEd 1929	Epsom Girls' Grammar
University of London	Elspeth Smellie	MB ChB	St Margaret's School
Newnham College, Cambridge	Frances Parker	History Tripos 1899	Private tuition
Girton College, Cambridge	Anne Whitelaw	Maths Tripos 1897 MA 1905 Trinity	Auckland Grammar
University of Edinburgh	Grace Russell (m.de Courcy)	LRCP, LRCS	Auckland Grammar
	A. Balfour	MB ChB 1903	Timaru Girls' High School
	Hilda Northcroft	MB ChB 1908 LM 1911	Auckland Grammar
	Jessie Scott	MB ChB 1910	Christchurch Girls' High School
	S. A. Robertson (m.Buckingham)	MB ChB 1917	Auckland Girls' Grammar
University of Glasgow	Alice Moorhouse	MB CM 1901	Christchurch Girls' High School
University of Queensland	Frances Black (m.Savage)	MB ChB	Timaru Girls' High School
Oxford University	Joan Carrington (m.Hulley)	BA	St Margaret's
	Maureen Raymond	MA	St Margaret's
University of Brussels	Grace Russell (m.de Courcy)	MD 1899	Auckland Grammar

New Zealand women graduates (UNZ) who gained postgraduate qualifications abroad

University of London	Mary Blair	MD BS
	Jessie Hetherington	DipEd 1907
	Esma North	Dip Pedagogy 1913
	Mary Barkas	MRCS LRCP 1918
	Helen Richmond (m.Simpson)	PhD 1923
Girton College, Cambridge	Jessie Hetherington	Law Tripos 1905 History Tripos 1906
	Eileen Fairbairn	Dip Geography 1920
Newnham College, Cambridge/ Trinity College, Dublin	Clara Taylor	MA 1907 (won a government research grant in organic chemistry to Cambridge. She remained in England to teach.)
	Eliza Edwards	MA 1914
	Mina Holderness	MA 1922 (taught in England)
University of Edinburgh	Emily Siedeberg	1912
	Margaret Cruickshank	1913
University of Glasgow/ Queen Margaret College	Helen Baird (m.Cowie)	MB ChB 1903
	Agnes Baird	MB ChB 1905
Trinity College, Dublin	Emily Siedeberg	Obstetrics & gynaecology 1897
	Margaret Cruickshank	1913
	Jessie Hetherington	MA 1907
	Jenny Stewart	MA 1924
University of Sorbonne, Paris Conferred language diplomas	Eleanor Crosby	1900
	Kathleen Gresson	1900
	Patricia Clark	Cert D'Et.Sup 1925
	Catherine Hogg	1926
	Jenny Stewart	1923
University of Berlin	Emily Siedeberg	1897

New Zealand women with university qualifications from abroad who returned to teach in New Zealand

Helen Macdonald Richmond	MA 1920 PhD London 1923	Teacher, Rangi Ruru School for Girls Teacher, Rangi Ruru School for Girls Christchurch Training College Canterbury College	1916–1920 1924
Catherine Hogg	Sorbonne 1926	Senior Mistress, Hamilton High School	1927–1947
Patricia Clark	Cert D'Et. Sup 1925 Sorbonne	Principal, Christchurch Girls' High School	1928–1940
Kathleen Gresson	Sorbonne 1900	Principal, Avonside Girls' High School	1928–1942
Eliza Edwards	MA 1914 TDC	Principal, Waikato Diocesan School for Girls Principal, Auckland Diocesan School for Girls	1929–1932 1932–1952
Esma North	Dip Pedagogy 1913	Principal, Wellington Girls' College	1938–1950
Jenny Stewart	Sorbonne 1923	Principal, Christchurch Girls' High School	1948–1954

New Zealand women graduates who took up overseas teaching positions

Lilian Edger	MA 1882	General Secretary, Theosophical League, India 1909–1913 Principal, Hindu Girls' School, Benares 1913–1919
Janette Grace Grossmann	MA 1884	Methodist Ladies' College, Melbourne 1889 Principal, West Maitland High School Principal, North Sydney Girls' High School
Althea Tendall	MA 1893	In Melbourne to teach
Rose Davey	MA 1895	To teach in India
Mabel Lilian Crump	MA 1897	To teach at Clarendon College, Ballarat
Isabella McKellar	BA 1899	To teach in Argentina
Anne Forsyth Ironside	MA 1907	To Girton Grammar, Bendigo 1921
Elsie Johnston	MA 1910	To teach at Durban Girls' High School 1914–1919
Agnes (Kitty) Merton	BA 1910	To be principal of a Presbyterian girls' school, Berwick, Victoria
Hilda Hoodless (m.Adlington)	MA 1914	To be principal of Suva Grammar School, Fiji
Esma North	BA 1915	To teach in Australia 1927

New Zealand women graduates who served in overseas missions/schools

Marion Ferguson (m.Wallis)	BA Otago 1888	Methodist mission in Fiji
Lilian Williams (m.Blyth)	MA Canterbury 1890	Melanesian mission 1896–1899
Mary Moore	BA Otago 1893	Missionary in China 1896–1950
Mildred Davey (m.Matthews)	MA Otago 1895	As Sister Mildred, missionary teacher at Madras High School, India
Isabella McKellar (m.Hercus)	BA Otago 1899	With husband as Presbyterian missionaries to Peru and Argentina 1904–1911
Anna Smyth	BA Victoria 1905	Missionary worker for the Salvation Army in Japan for over thirty years
Mina Holderness	MA Canterbury 1919	Principal of Queen Phillipa College
Beryl Jackson	BA Auckland 1921	Teacher at Suva Girls' Grammar School 1923–1924

Women graduates from Australia and the USA

University of Melbourne	Nancy Jobson	MA	To Queen Margaret's as headmistress
	Amacie Haydon (Ulrich)	MA	To Queen Margaret's as headmistress 1921–1924
Columbia University	Lilian Storms	PhD	To University of Otago as lecturer in chemistry and nutrition 1925–1928
	Gladys McGill	BSc	To University of Otago as lecturer in clothing and textiles 1925–1928
University of California	Rosetta Baum	BPhil 1891	First woman appointed to Auckland Education Board and Auckland Grammar School Board

Women graduates from the UK who taught in New Zealand 1880–1930

Girton College, Cambridge	Katherine Browning	Moral Science Tripos 1886	Napier Girls' High School 1888–1895 Otago Girls' High School 1895–1905 Braemar 1905–1907
	Anne Whitelaw	Mathematical Tripos 1897	Auckland Girls' Grammar 1907–1910
	Janet Vernon Harcourt	Natural Science Tripos 1902	Auckland Girls' Grammar 1909–1910
	Winifred Boys-Smith	Natural Science Tripos	University of Otago as Professor of Home Science 1911–1920
	Florence Dorothy Cadell	Medieval and Modern Language Tripos 1918	Nga Tawa School for Girls 1921–1924
	Winifred Ida Haward	History Tripos 1919 MA, PhD London	Canterbury College 1921–1930
	Dora Hinton	MA TCD	Nga Tawa School for Girls 1923–1929
	Margaret Harvey	Language Tripos	Marsden Collegiate School for Girls 1924–1926
	Margaret Dyer	Natural Science Tripos 1908	Inspector of domestic subjects for Department of Education 1924–1931
	Ethel Helen Sandford	Classics Tripos 1906 MA 1926	Auckland Diocesan School for Girls 1927–1932
	Annie Mary Young	Classics Tripos 1913	Nga Tawa School for Girls 1933–1936
	Mary Leake	Maths Tripos	One year teaching in New Zealand
Newnham College, Cambridge	Ingegard Palme	AA MA TCD	Woodford House 1902–1904
	Frances Parker	AA	Auckland Diocesan and Auckland Girls' Grammar 1902–1910
	Miss B. Ayton	AA	Southland Girls' High School 1905
	Helen Rawson (m.Benson)	BSc TCD	University of Otago as lecturer in home science 1910 Appointed professor in 1920–1924
	Marguerite Hartley	AA MA 1930	Marsden Collegiate School for Girls 1923–1925

	Frances Stevens (Vickers)		One year teaching in New Zealand
	Hedwig Streigg (Segal)	MA TCD	Five years teaching in New Zealand
	Helen Wilson (Mathers)	Natural Science Tripos	Auckland Diocesan School for Girls 1927–1929
University of London	Mary Etheldred Pulling	BA (Hons)	Auckland Diocesan School for Girls 1903–1926
	Beatrice Anna Ward	BSc	Auckland Diocesan School for Girls 1903–1915
	Blanche Butler	BSc	Auckland Girls' Grammar 1911–1920
	Eva Necker	BSc	Auckland Diocesan School for Girls 1916–1926
	Marguerite Turner	MA (Hons)	Wellington Girls' College 1920–1921
	Lesley Hussey	BA	St Hilda's College 1924
Oxford University	Elizabeth Hewett	AA	Otago Girls', then Napier Girls' High School as principal 1883–1892
	Muriel Winter	AA	St Margaret's 1914–1920, then Nga Tawa as principal 1920
	Frances McCall	AA	Nga Tawa as principal 1921–1933
Somerville College	Grace Desmond	AA	Auckland Diocesan School for Girls 1927–1930
St Andrew's	Minnie Matthews	LLA	Tapier Girls' High School as principal 1893–1900
University of Edinburgh	B A MacDiarmid	MA	Auckland Girls' Grammar 1917–1925
University of Glasgow	Helen Hodge	MA	Palmerston North Girls' High School 1922–1923

Index

Gibson, Lucy Margaret (m.Rutherford) 110, **110**
Gibson, Mary (Mrs) 108, 111
Gibson, Mary Victoria 100, 109, **109**, 167, 210
Gibson, Ruth Constance Manning 111
Gibson, Winifred Graeme 110, 111
Gildersleve, Virginia 213
Gilray, Professor 71
girls
    education linked to domestic role 11, 12, 23–8, **26**
    working class 16–17
    see also Māori girls
Girls' College, Devonport 133
Girton College for Girls, Christchurch 64, 70, 92
Girton College for Girls, Dunedin 63, 64, 70
Glasgow, Dora (m.Eipper) 244
Godley, E. J. 152
Godolphin School for Girls 185
Godolphin Society 199
Government Service Equal Pay Act 1960 31
graduates, women
    career profiles database 219–20
    career profiles, graduates from outside New Zealand 219–20
    educational profiles database 219–20
    expectations held by family and society 13
    finding 28–30
    from Australia and the USA 247
    from the UK who taught in New Zealand 248–9
    impact of World War One 72–3, 141–3
    New Zealand, to overseas missions/ schools 247
    New Zealand, to overseas teaching positions 246
    New Zealand women who gained first qualifications abroad 244
    New Zealand women who gained postgraduate qualifications abroad 245
    patterns of connection 30–3
    percentage of total University of New

Zealand graduates 218–19
    travel abroad, New Zealand graduates 183, 193–202, 206, 211–12, 245, 246
    travel to New Zealand by overseas graduates 202–6, 212
Grant, Catherine Donaldson 140, 141, **141**
Gray, Christina 138–9
Greenfield, Mary (m.Rose) 161, 162
Greensill, Nina (m.Barrer) 46–7, **46**, 100
Gregory, Elizabeth 82
Greig, Violet 70, 83, 213
Gresson, Kathleen 100, **110**, 210, 245, 246
Grey, George 14
Gribben, Ellen (m.Dunne) 112–13
Griffin, Annie 104
Griffin, Elsie 135, 136–7
Griffin, Isabella 104
Griffin, T. N. 104
Grossmann, J. P. 116
Grossmann, Janette **191**, 246
Guide Maggie, *see* Papakura, Makereti
Guide Rangi, *see* Ratema, Rangitiaria (m.Dennan)
'gym tunic' **201**, 202

Habens, W. J. 19
Hall, John 52–3
Hall, Mere 51–4, **52**
Hall-Kenny, Mrs 214
Hamilton High School 134, 136, 145, 151, 246
Hamilton, Martha 158–9, 195
Hamilton West District High School 134, 151
Hampden District High School 73
Hampton, Lena 70
Hanan, J. A. 22
Hanna, Mrs 133
Harriet Vine Kindergarten, Wanganui 164
Harrison, Clementine 100, 112
Hartley, Marguerite 248
Harvey, Margaret 248
Haslam, Professor 95–6
Hastings District High School 182
Haward, Ida 204, 248
Haydon, Amacie (Ulrich) 247
Headmistresses' Association of the Eastern

official encouragement to return to local
districts after formal education 43, 48,
52
socioeconomic conditions following
land wars 49
urbanisation 57
Māori denominational schools 11, 13–14,
36, 38
academic subjects taught at 41, 46, 47
fees beyond the reach of majority of
Māori 55
higher school examination success 48
Hogben's views on 19, 41
scholarships to 38, 47
technical education at 20–1, 41, 46, 48
Māori denominational schools for girls
13–14, 38–55, 131, 133
academic subjects taught at 46–7, 48–9
first Māori woman principal, Agnes
Down 43, 44, **44**
higher school examination success 49,
51–2
Tauranga **37**
technical education at **22**, 41–3, **45**, 46–7,
48–9, 51
see also names of specific schools
Māori district high schools 38, 56–7
Māori girls
churches' concern for education 11, 13,
36, 38
Continuation Scholarships for teacher
training 52, 54
education for domestic role 39–40, 41–3,
46, 48–9, 51, 56–7
education for leadership 46–7
political socialisation of 39–40
Māori language 37, 51, 53, 57
Māori women
as mechanism for transformation of
Māori society 13, 36, 38–40, 49
Catholic Church religious 54
in service 42, 43, 47
professional careers 47, 48, 49, 50, 51,
52, 54–5
Māori Women's Institutes 57
Māori Women's Welfare League 57
Marchant, Maria 68, 100, 106–7, **106,**

119–20
Marchant, Mona Elise Allman 100
Marist College 131
Mariu, Theresa 54
Marlborough High School 162
marriage
and pupil-teacher apprenticeship
system 15
married women doctors 76
married women teachers 72–3, 105, 136,
140
restrictions on participation of married
women in paid workforce 214
university-educated women 13, 71–3,
218
University of Otago women graduates
71–3
Victoria University women graduates
160
Marsden Collegiate School for Girls 172,
248; *see also* earlier name, Fitzherbert
Terrace School for Girls
Marsh, Ngaio 119, **119**
Marton District High School 182
Master of Arts degree
Canterbury University College 88, 93,
101
first woman MA with honours, Helen
Connon 93
Masterton District High School 161, 162
mathematics 26, 60, 149
Anne Whitelaw excels in 129, 196
Auckland Girls' Grammar School 130
Kate Edger excels in 126
University of Otago women graduates
81
Matriculation Examination 17, 18, 23, 54,
90, 91, 186
Matthews, Minnie 249
May, Muriel 214
medicine
attitudes towards women graduates 219
Otago women graduates 74–6
Melmerely Collegiate School 133
Melrose College, Invercargill 63, 70
Melville, Ellen 138
Merton, Agnes (Kitty) 111, 246

Images are reproduced with the permission of:

Alexander Turnbull Library, pages 27, 42, 45, 76, 82, 112, 125, 140, 142, 174, 175, 177, 183, 209, 212; Auckland City Libraries (NZ), pages 40, 46, 130, 132, 147, 148, 195; Auckland Girls' Grammar School, pages 128, 130, 166, 197, 198, 205; Auckland War Memorial Museum, pages 37, 47, 132; Canterbury Museum, pages 75, 98, 109, 114; Christchurch City Libraries, pages 75, 91, 96, 101; Christine Cole Catley, pages 141, 181; College of Education, Victoria University of Wellington, page 176; Diocesan School for Girls Auckland, pages 168, 205; Honor McKellar, page 79; Hukarere Girls' College, pages 18, 22, 35, 39, 44, 50, 52, 54, 55, 56; J. C. Beaglehole Room, The Library, Victoria University of Wellington, pages 157, 163; Napier Girls' High School, pages 9, 12, 25, 26, 120, 192; Nelson Girls' College, pages 24, 91, 113, 117; New Plymouth Girls' High School, pages 141, 181, 182; Nga Tawa Diocesan School for Girls, page 202; Otago Girls' High School, pages 17, 63, 70; Otago Settlers Museum, pages 60, 64, 65; Samuel Marsden Collegiate School, page 27; Southland Girls' High School, page 75; Special Collections, The Hocken Collections, Uare Taoka o Hakena, University of Otago, pages 59, 67, 73, 80, 106, 209, 217; Special Collections, MacMillan Brown Library, University of Canterbury, pages 87, 88, 89, 93, 94, 110, 115, 118, 127, 191; Special Collections, University of Auckland Library, pages 137, 138, 139, 183, 197; St Margaret's College (image supplied by Christchurch City Libraries), page 119; Timaru Girls' High School, page 201; Waitaki Girls' High School, pages 15, 66; Wellington Girls' College, pages 32, 102, 159, 170, 181, 191; Woodford House, page 21.

Every effort has been made to contact copyright holders. If you can provide further information please contact the publisher.

Front cover

TOP: Nelson Girl's College staff, 1904. Back: Marie McEachen (MA Canterbury 1899), Millicent Kirton (MA Canterbury 1899), Marguerita Pickmere (m.Mulgan) (MA Auckland 1902), Ellen Gribben (m.Dunne) (BA Canterbury 1888). Front: Henriette Jenkin (MA Victoria 1911), Florence Livesy (BA Auckland 1899), Althea Tendall (MA Canterbury 1893) (Principal), Mrs Satchell, E. Chisholm. Reproduced with permission of Nelson Girls' College.
BOTTOM: Napier Girls' High School science class, 1903, Napier Girls' High School. Reproduced with the permission of Napier Girls' High School.

Back cover

Gymnasium, Otago Girls' High School, 1908. Reproduced with permission of Otago Girls' High School.

Acknowledgements

The author and publisher would like to thank the following institutions for permission to publish images from their collections: Napier Girls' High School; Nelson Girls' College; Otago Girls' High School, Dunedin; Hukarere Girls' College, Napier; Hocken Collections, Uare Taoka o Hakena, University of Otago; Wellington Girls' College; Special Collections, Auckland City Libraries (NZ); Auckland Girls' Grammar School; Diocesan School for Girls, Auckland; Auckland War Memorial Museum; Alexander Turnbull Library, Wellington; MacMillan Brown Library, University of Canterbury, Christchurch; J.C. Beaglehole Room, The Library, Victoria University of Wellington; Special Collections, University of Auckland Library; Canterbury Museum; Christchurch City Libraries; Otago Settlers Museum, Dunedin; St Margaret's College, Christchurch; Timaru Girls' High School; Nga Tawa Diocesan School for Girls; New Plymouth Girls' High School; Waitaki Girls' High School, Oamaru; Woodford House, Havelock North; Samuel Marsden Collegiate School, Wellington; Southland Girls' High School; College of Education, Victoria University of Wellington. Thanks are also due to Taylor and Francis/Routledge for permission to publish the extract from *History of Education*; permission has been requested to publish the extract from *Journal of Educational Administration and History*.